D1570753

PHOENIX 13

Americal Division Artillery Air Section Helicopters in Vietnam

'Vietnam Helicopter "TINS"* From Americal Division Artillery Air Section'
Chu Lai, Vietnam 1968 and 1969

*TINS, an acronym for war stories that are more or less supposed to be true: 'This is no shit.'

Driving a Scout Helicopter in Vietnam can be Dangerous to your Health!

PHOENIX 13

Americal Division Artillery Air Section Helicopters in Vietnam

DARRYL JAMES

Pen & Sword
MILITARY

AN IMPRINT OF PEN & SWORD BOOKS LTD.
YORKSHIRE – PHILADELPHIA

First published in Great Britain in 2020 by
PEN & SWORD MILITARY
An imprint of
Pen & Sword Books Ltd
Yorkshire - Philadelphia

ISBN 978 1 52675 942 9

A CIP catalogue record for this book is available from the British Library

Typeset in Ehrhardt MT & 11/13
by SJmagic DESIGN SERVICES, India.

Printed and bound in the UK by TJ Books Limited

Pen & Sword Books Ltd incorporates the imprints of Pen & Sword Archaeology,
Atlas, Aviation, Battleground, Discovery, Family History, History, Maritime,
Military, Naval, Politics, Social History, Transport, True Crime, Claymore Press,
Frontline Books, Praetorian Press, Seaforth Publishing and White Owl

For a complete list of Pen & Sword titles please contact

PEN & SWORD BOOKS LTD
47 Church Street, Barnsley, South Yorkshire, S70 2AS, England
E-mail: enquiries@pen-and-sword.co.uk
Website: www.pen-and-sword.co.uk

Or

PEN & SWORD BOOKS
1950 Lawrence Rd, Havertown, PA 19083, USA
E-mail: Uspen-and-sword@casematepublishers.com
Website: www.penandswordbooks.com

Contents

About the Author

Excerpts from an article in the *Permian Basin Oil and Gas Magazine*, September 2010, pp.24-25.

Surviving the odds
By Lana Cunningham, Special Correspondent

Darryl James can say he survived the odds. An officer and a helicopter pilot, he served a one-year tour of duty in Vietnam from September 1968–69. 'I was one of 10,000 helicopter pilots in Vietnam,' he said one afternoon in his office at H.L. Brown, where he worked as a geoscience manager. One-fourth of all casualties in Vietnam were officers, and of that number one-fourth were helicopter pilots. Half of all the helicopter pilots crashed or were shot down. Add one more statistic to that: James was one of the few pilots to have a Master's. He grew up in Sayreville, NJ, and at Rutgers University, he joined the ROTC 'because it interested me'. After obtaining a Bachelor's Degree in geology, he was given a two-year deferment to stay in college and work on a Master's Degree. During college, he volunteered for the Army flight program and earned a private pilot license. After graduating in 1967 with his Master's Degree, James entered the Army and eventually Darryl James was one of the 10,000 helicopter pilots assigned to Vietnam. 'I wanted to go into fixed-wing but the Army needed helicopter pilots,' he explained.

The basic helicopter training school was located in Mineral Wells, and the assignment gave James his first taste of Texas and Mexican food. Advanced helicopter training was at Fort Rucker, in Alabama. Orders came to head to Chu Lai, Vietnam, with American Division Artillery Air. 'I had three days of orientation flying a scout helicopter, which is a single-pilot aircraft,' he said. 'Most helicopter pilots went over there and flew as co–pilot in a Huey for four months before being allowed to become aircraft commander. On my fourth day, I went solo on a combat mission in the small scout helicopter…'

James saw his share of combat missions. By the time he returned to the States, he had received sixteen Air Medals, which equated to twenty-five combat missions for each medal.

'Serving in the Army gave me leadership qualities and made me confident in myself,' James said in looking back on those experiences. 'My year in Vietnam was memorable. That year, I developed a confidence and trust in myself that steered me successfully through life. There is nothing like the camaraderie and friendships made in the military service,' James said. 'These men in my unit have remained my friends and are like my own brothers.'

Acknowledgements

Robert 'Lee' Leffert, Warren Fuller and Connor Dotson provided details for several of the stories included within this 'TINS' collection. Richard 'Tricky' Cross, First Cav Loach Driver and recipient of the Silver Medal, provided careful proofreading. Robert McNaughton and Warren Fuller provided proofreading services and wordsmithing.

Author's Foreword

This collection of stories is closely based on my and my unit's experiences flying small scout/observation helicopters in Vietnam in '68–'69. We were assigned to fly 'Ravens' (OH-23G) and 'Loaches' (OH-6A) in American Division's Artillery Air Section.[1] The stories are as I remembered. Minor parts portrayed of the enemy are fictionalized. Otherwise, each story is what I experienced or what my fellow pilots told me. Details regarding firebase names, landing sites, etc. may or may not be correct.

Storytelling was a daily evening occurrence in our unit. We called these stories 'TINS', an irreverent pilot acronym for 'This is no shit'. Many of the 'TINS' within this collection reveal the closeness and rapport developed among pilots and crew chiefs, a friendship I remember vividly; a brotherhood and comradeship that is perhaps only found in war.

My year in Vietnam was memorable. Like many, I arrived fresh, right out of flight school, apprehensive both about my abilities to perform and the inherent dangers of being and flying in Vietnam.

Flying alone in a small scout helicopter was frightening for a pilot fresh out of flight school. Most Vietnam helicopter pilots flew larger helicopters and had the luxury of working as co-pilot for an experienced aircraft commander. Flying solo, our unit relied on the counsel of our experienced pilots to survive. With their advice and the Army's training, and perhaps some luck, we learned to fly and live through this experience.

American Division's area of responsibility was located in I Corps within a very large area in the northern part of what was then South Vietnam. It stretched from the large city of Da Nang, south to the small town of Duc Pho and west to the Cambodian border. The area we overflew consisted of rugged mountainous jungle bordering a narrow coastal plain with farmlands and rice paddies. The coastal plain bordered a beautiful coastline of the South China Sea.

American Division's headquarters was in Chu Lai, a small village on Highway One about 60 miles south of Da Nang and near the beach. Our unit was the Division Artillery Air Section. When I first arrived in September 1968, we were flying an obsolete reciprocating engine helicopter designated the OH-23G. After a few months these tired old birds were replaced by the latest scout helicopter, the OH-6A, which was nicknamed the Loach. It was a dream to fly, like getting a Corvette to replace an old Ford. Our missions included aerial observation, carrying critical small cargo and key personnel. We flew convoy cover, provided Mac V support, aerial scouting for the Marines in Da Nang and inserting long-range reconnaissance patrols (LRRPs) and SEALs into small landing zones.

Interesting cargo that we carried included high-ranking officers, Vietnamese civilians, Vietnamese officials, wounded soldiers, POWs, hot chow, small-arms ammunition and Red Cross girls, etc. I once carried a Vietnamese family with a child with one arm and their pet chicken.

A typical day started at 0600 hrs. I would shower, shave, have breakfast at the Officers' Club, and then walk back to my hootch (living quarters) where I would grab my M16, my 38-caliber pistol, tactical map, radio frequency book, camera, book, gloves, flight suit, armored chest protector, which we call a 'chicken plate', and my flight helmet. I would walk down to the operations shed to check with the Operations officer for any last-minute instructions. Next, I would walk down to the heliport and meet my crew chief and assigned aircraft. Together we would pre-flight the aircraft. He would hold a fire extinguisher as I cranked up the chopper and he would be my ground guide as I hovered out of the revetment. The revetments were to isolate each aircraft in case of a rocket attack and if one caught fire, it would not endanger the rest of the helicopters. I would get taxiing instructions from the tower, say a short prayer, hover out to the runway and take off. We had to fly low-level for several miles to be below tactical jet aircraft before we could climb to a safe altitude. Typically, we climbed to 1,500ft above the ground to be out of range of small-arms fire. You were vulnerable to be shot at after about five minutes of flight time.

We typically flew single-pilot aircraft missions unless we flew at night. At night, we used two pilots for safety. When we arrived, we had a couple of orientation flights, were assigned an aircraft, provided a map and given a mission. It was very frightening being new and flying alone in a hostile environment in a strange country. On your first mission, you were very scared. You were flying solo in an aircraft in which you did not have many hours, trying to find your assigned firebase or landing zone in the mountainous jungle and flying over terrain where people could shoot at you. I seriously thought if I could last a month, I would be OK.

When we landed, we would gather at the Officers' Club, play liars' dice, tell each other about our missions, which often took the form of war stories (TINS), have drinks and then eat dinner.

Chapter 1

Four Years Prior to Vietnam

0830 hrs, 22 July 1964
Fort Devens, Massachusetts

A 20-year-old ROTC[1] cadet from Rutgers University climbed onto the bleachers with his friends on a hot August morning at Fort Devens. Fort Devens was the summer camp home for ROTC cadets from colleges and universities throughout the north-east that year. He, like hundreds of other cadets, was completing one of the requirements in the college program to become a second lieutenant in the Army. The young man learned that no one at Fort Devens was lower than an ROTC cadet. His drill instructor told their platoon that they were lower than whale shit dropped into the deepest part of the ocean and that lowly PFCs[2] wouldn't give them so much as the time of day. The young men, though, were not unhappy; they were getting 'short' with most of the drudgery of summer camp behind them. Soon it would be over.

The air was still and heavy on this hot, humid morning in the Massachusetts lowlands. Even at this early hour, most of the cadets had the first of many sweat rings developing on their shirts under their armpits.

They were here to get a close-up demonstration of Army aviation. The young ROTC cadet always wanted to fly. In his pre-teens, his room had been decorated with model airplanes hanging from the ceiling by strings. When he was 12, his Uncle Steve took him for a ride in a small plane in Wilkes Barre, Pennsylvania. He had loved it. His thoughts that magical day were suddenly interrupted by the air show's announcer. The announcer introduced each Army aircraft as it flew by the audience at a low altitude. Several helicopters hovered by. A Bell OH-13[3] hovered in front of the bleachers to give them a close-up look. It blew dust around, making the audience cough. The announcer said, 'Oops, sorry gentlemen, it appears Two-Niner got a wee bit too close.'

'Wow,' the cadet thought to himself, 'the helicopters are pretty neat and graceful. I bet they're a piece of cake to fly.'

A bird dog,[4] which reminded the cadet of that ride in Pennsylvania, swooped down gracefully and flew over. A Caribou[5] passed loudly over at about 500ft and made a steep turn in front of the bleachers. There was a delay and the cadet stared out in front of the bleachers to a meadow below them. A large cleared field provided a few hundred yards of unobstructed view. 'Nice field of fire,' thought the cadet, looking out from the high ground and remembering some of his infantry lessons.

'Gentlemen, prepare yourself for the show's finale,' said the announcer. 'Hold on to your butts.'

The young men giggled at the comment and looked around, expecting some kind of surprise. They saw nothing. Then they heard it: a low rumble that developed in the broad valley. They looked all around because they could not quite tell which direction the sound came from. The rumble increased until it seemed the bleachers were vibrating. The audience looked around, confused, trying to decide in which direction to look. The noise became earsplitting when most got the direction right. Behind them, to their left, first one and then another Mohawk[6] popped over the trees and screamed overhead at 50ft in the air.

The Mohawks were a powerful spectacle at max power with their turboprops biting into the hot, humid air. They dipped down into the lower terrain ahead of the bleachers. When they reached the far end of the meadow, they pitched up sharply into a seemingly impossible climb angle. They climbed, one trailing the other, until they became small dots in the blue sky. The audience followed the dots. They could tell the planes were turning back towards them. The Mohawks dove steeply a mile out in front of their viewers. They dipped lower and disappeared below the audience's line of sight. Out of sight, they charged. Everyone could hear and feel their immense power and waited with building anticipation. Suddenly they appeared, heading straight toward the bleachers. Head on, they looked like bug-eyed, fearsome flying insects from a Godzilla film. They roared directly overhead the students at 50ft and as quickly as that they were gone.

'I HAVE GOT TO GET ME ONE OF THOSE,' shouted Cadet Darryl James.

Army Aviation set the hook in at least one ROTC cadet that morning. The cadet had short brown curly hair and dark hazel eyes. The olive hue of his skin was reflective of his Eastern European heritage. He stood 5ft 9in and weighed 150lb, hardened by the vigor of summer camp.

The young man grew up in Sayreville, New Jersey. Sayreville was a small working-class town along the Raritan Bay within the vast, industrial belt bordering the south side of New York City. The cadet came from a large family raised by hard-working parents. Money was always tight, but the family never really lacked for anything. His folks could not afford to send him to college, but there never was any doubt that he would go. He put himself through college by getting a State scholarship for financial needs and working nights in a rock and roll band. In high school, James played lead guitar in a band called the Hubcaps. He formed a new band in college: the Misfits. The Misfits stayed together through his undergraduate and graduate studies, providing the college student enough money to support himself, buy a new car and save a little for his future.

Returning to Rutgers after summer camp, the cadet joined the ROTC Flight Program. The program gave him forty-five hours of civilian flight training and this earned him a civilian private pilot rating. He thought the airplane rating would be a shoo-in for fixed-wing training in the Army. In this, he was wrong. The Vietnam War was a helicopter war.

James graduated in June 1965 with a commission in the United States Army Reserve as a second lieutenant. He did not immediately get to play soldier; he went on to graduate school at Rutgers with a full research assistantship. Two years later, James graduated with a Master of Science degree in geology. He then received orders from the Army for Armor Officers Basic Course at Fort Knox, Kentucky. He graduated from the armor course seventh in his class of fifty-two. He then became a tank platoon leader with responsibility for forty men and five M60A1 52-ton tanks. The responsibility seemed awesome. Like most new platoon leaders, James made frequent mistakes and gaining the respect of his men proved difficult. Gaining respect was not something that could be taught in books; it had to be earned, little by little. It was an uphill battle, but sometimes a large chunk of respect could be gained in one small step. Such a step happened to James.

One morning, the lieutenant woke to a loud ringing at 0330 hours. He fumbled for the phone and picked it up. 'Hello. Ah, I mean, LIEUTENANT JAMES.'

'Sir, this is Sergeant Arson with the Military Police.'

James became instantly alert and said, 'Right, sergeant, what can I do for you?'

'Sorry for the late hour, Sir, but do you have a PFC Jonathan Merriweather in your unit?'

The platoon leader thought to himself, 'Do I? Hell, I don't know everyone that well yet.' He coughed and struggled to remember the name and then said, 'Ah, yes sergeant, I do.'

'Well, Sir, he's in the custody of the police in the town of English, Indiana. It seems the soldier created a ruckus at a local bar last night. The police called us. Before we took any action on this matter, we decided to call you.'

'Well thanks, I appreciate that. Did you say English, Indiana?'

'Yes, Sir.'

'Thanks again, Sergeant, I'll handle it from here.'

'Good luck, Sir, bye.'

James looked by the nightstand and found his briefcase. He called his commanding officer.

'Captain, this is Lieutenant James.'

'Yes?' the captain replied sleepily.

'I am sorry to disturb you, Sir, but I received a call from the MPs. One of my men, a PFC Merriweather, is in custody in English, Indiana for fighting, I think. I am going to drive over there right now and find out what the problem is.'

'OK, Darryl, call me when you can.' The captain hung up the phone. 'Hmm,' thought the captain, 'English is quite a ways away. He does not have to do that. The MPs and authorities could handle this.'

The lieutenant shaved, then put on his green Class-A uniform. He grabbed his hat and stepped down the stairs of the dingy apartment that was upstairs to a drug store in West Point, Kentucky. The main street was dark and quiet. The morning was cold; he could see his breath. The lieutenant climbed into his red Corvair Convertible, started it and let it idle. He pulled the road map out of his glove box and turned the light on. 'Hmm,' he thought to himself, 'I'll go across the river here in West Point and take the Elizabeth Highway to Albany, and then it's a straight shot west to English.' He laid the map on the right leather bucket seat, pushed in the clutch, shifted the four-speed floor stick into first and accelerated into the night.

Three hours later, James pulled into the town square of English. The sun was just coming up, giving the courthouse, which dominated the square, a warm golden glow. James pulled in in front of a small police station off the square. He parked and got out of the Corvair. He carefully checked his uniform for correctness, put on his service hat and walked into the police station. A sergeant looked up from his desk and said, 'Good morning.'

'Good morning, sergeant, do you have a PFC Merriweather here?'

'Yes we do,' said the police sergeant.

'May I see him?'

'Let me check.' The sergeant made a call and said, 'Have a seat.' Ten minutes later another police officer walked in from a back office and said to the lieutenant, 'Merriweather has to see the judge at 9.00 this morning.'

'Can I talk to him?' asked James.

'Come with me.'

The lieutenant was led into a waiting room. He sat and waited another fifteen minutes. He looked up when the police officer walked in with Merriweather. The young soldier was handcuffed and looked seriously hungover. He had obviously slept in his uniform. It was badly soiled and his right pant knee was torn. He needed a shave.

'Whew,' thought James, 'he smells bad. Probably threw up.'

Merriweather looked up. His eyes brightened as he saw his lieutenant. He said, 'Lieutenant, I am so happy to see you, Sir. You can't believe...'

James ignored him, turned toward the police officer and said, 'Sergeant, is there any way PFC Merriweather can shave and clean up, and can we remove his handcuffs?'

The police officer rubbed his chin and thought back to when he was a soldier in the Korean War. He looked back down the hallway, then turned to James and said, 'I'll tell you what, Lieutenant. I am not supposed to do this, but you and I can take him down to the bathroom and watch while he shaves and cleans up. After that, he has to have the cuffs back on.'

Thirty minutes later, the lieutenant sat with the somewhat better groomed PFC. When the police officer walked off, he turned to the handcuffed soldier and said, 'OK, Jon, now what's your story and don't bullshit me. I am here to try to help you. Tell me everything.'

'OK Sir, here's what happened. Friday night I met this neat girl in Louisville. Well I thought she was neat. I drove home with her Saturday morning.'

'In her car?'

'Yes, Sir.'

'How were you planning to get back?'

'I didn't think about that. Anyway, we had something to eat and then we started hitting some Country and Western joints.'

'In the morning?'

'No, Sir, it was afternoon then. We drank all afternoon. That evening at a place called Mojo's, here in English, a dude walks in. She sees him and whispers to me that that's Big Ben, her boyfriend. He sees us and grabs her arm. Then he calls me a piece of Army trash and a freaking Vietnam baby killer. Sir, I haven't even been to Nam. I was the only soldier in the bar. Hell, I probably was the only soldier in the whole town. I stood up and next thing you know, there is one hell of a fight.'

'Hmm, how'd you do?'

'What?'

'How'd you make out? The fight, did you win?'

'Hell no, ah, I mean no, Sir, I didn't. I got what my pappy used to say one hell of an ass-whipping. I think I did get one lick in Sir. Well, next thing I know I am in some jail cell sleeping in puke.'

He put his hands in his head and looked down at the floor.

The lieutenant patted him on the back and said, 'Glad you got in at least one lick, Jon.'

One Hour Later

A police sergeant walked into the courthouse holding the handcuffed PFC. Lieutenant James walked on the prisoner's other side. A white-haired judge with large loose skin on his face looked over reading glasses at the three men. He stared at the prisoner carefully and then at the lieutenant. He said, 'Are you this man's sergeant?'

'Ah, no Your Honor, I am a lieutenant.'

'Whatever! Are you responsible for this man?'

'This soldier is in my unit.'

'You're his boss, right?'

'Ah, I am the man's Platoon Leader.'

The judge put his glasses down and shook his head in frustration, then said in a raised voice, 'WHAT I MEAN, SOLDIER, IS CAN YOU...?' He lowered his voice, 'What I mean, is can you ensure that this boy makes his court appearance on Friday?'

'Yes, Your Honor, I can assure you that he will.'

'Then I'll release him to you. You BE SURE he gets back up here for his appearance.'

'Yes, Sir.'

The judge motioned the three of them over to a clerk who had a legal document for the lieutenant to sign. The sergeant removed Jon's handcuffs. The lieutenant shook hands with the sergeant. The two soldiers walked out of the courtroom and over to the lieutenant's car.

'They feed you, Jon?'

'Tried to, Sir, but I was too sick to eat.'

'I tell you what. Let's get out of this town and I will buy you breakfast in the next town.'

'YES, SIR!'

Four hours later, they arrived at the Company area. Lieutenant James turned the soldier over to his Platoon Sergeant. Sergeant First Class Muldoon glared at Merriweather standing at attention. He then turned to James.

'Sir, I want to thank you for bringing this worthless, sorry ass back here. I will personally guarantee that PFC Merriweather will make his court appearance on Friday. Sir, he will be busy for a while. Actually, he will be busy for a long time. There are a lot of not so nice jobs around here with his name on them.'

Merriweather made his court appearance accompanied by Sergeant Muldoon. Both soldiers looked proper with perfectly-groomed uniforms. Merriweather was fined $75 plus $100 court costs. He borrowed the money from his buddies in the platoon to pay the charges.

James's stock went up considerably in the eyes of his platoon over the incident. From that day on, the enlisted men and non-commissioned officers of his platoon stood solidly behind him. James even noticed a smidgen of respect from the company's first sergeant. The first sergeant, a large Afro-American man named Jeremiah Johnson, mostly ignored new lieutenants. Never spoke to one unless he absolutely had to. James's company commander gave him a high OER[7] when he left the unit with orders for flight school.

The soldier was finally going to fly. Flight school was broken into two segments, Primary and Advanced. The first segment was four and – one half months of primary flight training at Fort Wolters in Mineral Wells, Texas, which the students called 'Miserable Gulch'. At Wolters, James learned to fly the Hiller OH-23D known as the Raven. The Raven, a small, three-place helicopter, was underpowered and used only for training. At least this was what the soldier thought. Later he would learn that this so-called obsolete little helicopter was used in combat and he would spend his first three months in Vietnam flying one.

The days at flight school were hard, sometimes lasting twelve hours. One week they would fly in the mornings and have classroom work in the afternoons. The next week they would switch. After a couple of weeks, the students began to reach their first objective in flight school: to solo. You soloed in three weeks or washed out.

Fort Wolters, Texas
20 November 1967

Two weeks into training, James hovered the small helicopter down the asphalt taxiway at a training stage field in the Texas countryside. Wayne Miller, a tall civilian flight instructor from Southern Aviation, tutored him over the intercom.

'Darryl, settle down,' Miller said. 'You are over-controlling. SET IT DOWN RIGHT HERE.' Darryl put the small helicopter down abruptly.

'Lower the collective,' Miller said, 'all the way.' The student did as he was told. 'OK Darryl, now roll off throttle to flight idle.'

'Oh, Jesus,' thought the student pilot. 'He's shutting me down. We just got started. What did I screw up now?'

Miller opened the door, startling the student pilot. 'He's getting out?'

The instructor got out, stood alongside the door, connected his seatbelt and stowed it neatly on his seat. He said nothing, then he looked up at his student and leaned in close to him and yelled to be heard over the rotor noise, 'DARRYL, WHEN YOU PICK IT UP TO A HOVER, IT WILL BE LIGHT AND COME UP QUICKLY. ADJUST TO THAT AND FLY THE PATTERN THREE TIMES.' He held up three fingers and Darryl nodded.

'LISTEN TO THE CONTROL TOWER. TURN ON YOUR LANDING LIGHT AND DO AS YOU WERE TAUGHT. YOU WILL DO FINE. DON'T BE NERVOUS.'

James nodded his head. 'Right,' he thought. 'I am as nervous as a cat in a room full of rocking chairs.'

'AND DARRYL,' yelled his instructor, 'IF YOUR ENGINE QUITS, LOWER THE COLLECTIVE, ADD RIGHT PEDAL AND TURN INTO THE WIND. REMEMBER IT IS FROM THE NORTH-WEST. GO FOR IT, DARRYL. MAKE ME AND YOUR MOMMA PROUD.'

The student pilot picked up the small helicopter to a hover. It jumped up quickly without the weight of the second pilot, just as Miller had told him. James stabilized the hover and moved carefully down the end of the taxiway. He was the only aircraft on the taxiway. All others had been directed to other taxiways to avoid the solo student. The lieutenant reached the take-off pad, and turned the helicopter to the right in a clearing turn. The student checked his instruments. His altimeter indicated 2,700ft, the ground elevation for the field. He took a deep breath and hovered forward gaining speed. The lieutenant felt the bump when the helicopter entered transitional lift and began climbing. His airspeed steadied at 40 knots as he climbed. He turned right when he reached 3,000ft and climbed to 3,200ft. Then James turned right again and lowered his nose and collective to stabilize at 3,200ft and 60 knots airspeed. The student pilot took a breath, looked right, and aligned his direction to stay parallel with the runway in the downwind direction of the rectangular traffic pattern. James checked his instruments. Something was not normal, something unsettling in his peripheral vision. Alarmed, he glanced left and saw the empty seat. 'What, where's Wayne? ON THE GROUND, DUMBASS,' he answered himself. 'You are soloing!'

The lieutenant turned back and concentrated on his flying. He reached the point perpendicular to his intended landing spot, lowered the collective, raised the nose slightly and descended at 40 knots airspeed. He turned right and entered the crosswind part of his landing pattern. He turned right again and when his altimeter indicated 2,700ft, entered the approach leg of his pattern. James made small corrections on the final approach, culminating in a landing to a 3ft hover. The student hesitated in a stabilized hover for a moment, then moved forward on the taxiway. He made it!

'Aircraft Two-Four, this is tower. That was good. Let's do another just like the last one.'

Suddenly confident, the student pilot hit the trigger on his cyclic stick. 'Roger, tower this is Two-Four going for another.'

James did two more take-offs and landings, but none was better than his first. He finished and was directed to a parking spot and shut the helicopter down. Miller rushed over and slapped him on the back. 'Darryl, that first one was a dandy. The second looked a bit shaky. The third was OK. Congratulations.'

'Thank you, Sir.'

James's 'stick buddy', Lieutenant Stu Moody, ran over and gave him a huge bear hug.

'It's the pool for you today, Shithead.'

'Thanks Stu.'

(Eighteen months later, James would learn that Moody would not return from Vietnam. During a routine test flight in Vietnam, the rotor parted on his Huey. The helpless craft and two maintenance test pilots fell to their death. Seventeen years later, James would make a tracing of his friend's name on The Wall in Washington, D.C.)

The students boarded the Army bus for the ride back to Wolters. The bus stopped at the Holiday Inn and the several students who soloed that day were carried off the bus. James and the others passed under an archway made from OH-23D helicopter rotor blades. A plaque had an inscription that said: 'Through these rotor blades pass the finest helicopter pilots in the world.' One by one, the pilots were tossed into the pool. They climbed out with their flight suits dripping wet. Four months later, James graduated number one in his class at Fort Wolters.

The lieutenant moved to Fort Rucker, Alabama for advanced flight training. James was not a natural helicopter pilot. He had to work hard at it. The next segment was instrument training, which was conducted in a small two–passenger Bell helicopter known as TH-13T. The student pilot struggled learning to fly instruments in the new helicopter. He fell behind and worried he was going to wash out. His instructors encouraged him and gave him a couple of extra hours of instrument time; he passed. After instruments, flight school became fun. His class next transitioned into the much larger helicopter, a jet-turbine helicopter, the UH-1. The UH-1 had been fondly nicknamed 'Huey' by the real Army, the folks who flew them and flew in them. It became an icon of the Vietnam War. The students flew the Huey during the tactical phase of training.

Flight School ended and he received orders for Vietnam.

8 September 1968
United Flight 741 from New York to Seattle

Alone, sitting in window seat 34F, the lieutenant stared at the cloud tops somewhere over the mid-west of the United States. The cumulus build-ups viewed from 34,000ft were white and puffy, sprinkled on their west sides with a bit of orange color from the setting sun. Normally they would seem pretty, a memorable sunset. Not tonight! They seemed cold and foreboding. Sipping his Scotch and water, he looked around. The Boeing 707 was nearly full with mostly business travelers. 'Businessmen would be the only folks traveling to Seattle this time at night,' he thought to himself. 'Well, not the only folks,' he pondered. James felt uncomfortable; his crisp green army uniform seemed a bit out of place. 'Nah,' he told himself, 'they like you.' The flight attendant, he remembered, glanced admiringly at the shiny new aviator's wings on his left pocket flap as he was seated.

'I am proud of those wings, very proud. I worked very hard to get them.' His hand unconsciously touched them on his left breast pocket.

He took a deep breath and sighed. 'I am apprehensive; no, not apprehensive, shit-scared is the term, terrified of what is ahead for me. I may have looked cocky when I had those wings pinned on but I only have 225 hours of helicopter flight hours. That's not much, especially when someone is shooting at you. Odds are I am going to get my ass shot off.' His morbid thoughts were interrupted by a sweet voice,

'Would you like another drink before dinner, Lieutenant?' He looked up at a pretty blonde flight attendant. She smiled pleasantly as the lieutenant answered, 'Sure.'

James noticed, as she left, that the middle-aged businessman sitting in the aisle seat next to him glanced up at him out of the corner of his eye.

The flight attendant returned with his drink and another bag of peanuts and asked, 'Where you headed, Lieutenant?'

'Vietnam,' he replied.

The smile immediately left her face and an awkward moment of silence enveloped them as she fumbled for something to say or do. The silence was broken by the man sitting next to the lieutenant: 'Let me buy the Lieutenant's drink, Miss. Ah, that is, if he allows me.'

The businessman looked over to the lieutenant and smiled. The lieutenant said, 'Sure, thanks, my name is Darryl James.' The men shook hands politely as the flight attendant disappeared.

'Jack Jarson,' replied the man. 'What will you be doing there? Ah, in Vietnam, I mean.'

'Flying helicopters, Sir. I just graduated from flight school.'

'Sounds dangerous. Please call me Jack, Darryl. I am not a SIR. I was a platoon sergeant in the Korean War. I WORKED FOR A LIVING, SON,' he said with emphasis, and chuckled. 'I remember my trip over to Korea. It was different, though. We went by ship as a unit. I wasn't alone like you. Well anyway, I am on my way to Seattle tonight and Fairbanks in the morning, learning just now that you are on your way to Vietnam, I wanted to say hello and buy you a drink.'

'Thanks again, Jack. I really appreciate it. I didn't think many people would want to talk to a soldier. We are, kind of, well not liked. It seems like that anyway.'

'NOT THIS OLD SOLDIER, LIEUTENANT!' he said loudly. He lowered his voice and looked around as he said more softly, 'I guess I belong to President Johnson's so-called Silent Majority; I should speak softly.'

James chuckled politely, and then asked, 'What kind of meeting are you going to?'

'I'm a research geologist with Humble Exploration and Production Research Center in Houston. I attended a meeting with our Exploration management in New York. Now, I'm on my way to see some of our field people in Alaska.'

'NO KIDDING!'

'We are making a big play in Prudhoe Bay with Arco. Have you heard of what's going on in Alaska?'

'No. It sounds exciting, though.'

'It is; it's big. I really can't say much about it.'

'Jack, I really am interested. I have a BS and MS in geology from Rutgers. While finishing up graduate school last year, Humble Oil recruiters came through and talked to me.'

'Great, keep us in mind when you get home. Did you know Vietnam has great potential for oil and gas?'

'No, I didn't.'

'We will be exploring there someday. It may be one of the reasons Kennedy got us in there in the first place. Just come home in one piece, and remember us when you go looking for a job.'

'Thanks, Jack.'

Little did the lieutenant know that three and a half years later he would be working for Humble Oil in New Orleans, Louisiana and beginning an exciting new phase of his life.

Chapter 2

Arrival in Vietnam

1400 hrs, 8 September 1968

The United 707 landed at SEATAC airport in Seattle. First Lieutenant James joined other soldiers and climbed into a military bus for a thirty-minute ride to Fort Lewis. He spent a quiet night at the bachelor officers' quarters. In the morning, he caught a chartered American Airlines Boeing 707 to Tokyo. They climbed an old, weather-beaten aluminum rollaway staircase with United Airlines painted on it and James settled into the middle of the huge aircraft and took a window seat. The long-range, heavily-loaded jet strained into the air and turned west over the Pacific. This was the lieutenant's first trip over an ocean. He looked down at the blue below. From 30,000ft there was nothing to see but the vastness of the Pacific. After eleven hours, the Vietnam-bound soldiers landed in Tokyo for the plane to be refueled. Japanese workers came on to replenish supplies. The tired soldiers on board were not allowed off the plane. The military apparently were concerned some would depart in Tokyo and never return. The plane departed with a new crew for the last leg of the trip: a four-hour flight to Cam Rahn Bay, South Vietnam. As they began their descent to land, the lieutenant felt and then heard the familiar rumble as the flaps and gear came down on the large aircraft. Next, he was startled by the unfamiliar sound of full power applied to the engines. The rattling of flaps and landing gear retreating into their bays made his body tense. 'What the hell? Are we under attack?'

'Gentlemen,' the pilot said calmly over the speaker, 'we are going around yielding to tactical aircraft.'

'Now that's different,' James thought a bit nervously. After landing, an officer came aboard and stood in the middle of the aisle with a mike in his hands. 'Welcome to sunny Vietnam.'

'It's nighttime, you ass,' James thought.

'You will be broken up into groups of officers,' said the officer, 'non-commissioned officers and enlisted men. You will then board the buses outside with the metal mesh over the windows. Don't worry; the mesh is not to keep you in. It is there to keep grenades out,' he chuckled for effect and then started again. 'You will be processed tonight, fed, issued clothing and assigned billets for the short time you will be with us. You will be here about three days, gentlemen.'

2030 hrs, 9 September 1968
Cam Rahn Bay, South Vietnam

James stepped out of the plane kind of expecting to be ducking mortars and rockets. He looked around and saw, surprisingly, only a loud, busy airport. Suddenly, he felt then heard a pair of Phantom F4s[1] lifting off from the runway. The F4s roared by with bombs slung underneath their wings. The rumble from their twin jet engines created a vibration felt deep in the gut of the lieutenant.

The new arrivals were sent one place to pick up their bags, then another place for this and another for that. This drudgery added to the weariness of the already tired soldiers. The lieutenant was beginning to feel tired. He noticed also that he was getting a little tickle in the back of his throat.

They placed all the junior grade officers into barracks. The beds were clean and comfortable. Everyone was tired, but few could sleep. This was it: Vietnam. As James tried to fall asleep, he wondered how many of the young officers in this room would not be coming home in one piece. Would he be one of them? He said a little prayer and thought of his family. He wondered what they were doing at that moment.

The following morning, the lieutenant felt ill and the following morning, he felt worse. He considered seeing a doctor, but decided to tough it out. 'It's just a cold, no big deal.' Aviators were only supposed to go to flight surgeons. He thought that it would be a hassle to find a flight surgeon here. He struggled through breakfast the second day with a sore throat, feeling weak and feverish. After breakfast, he learned that assignments were posted. Reading from a bulletin board, he learned that he was going to the American Division in I Corps. He asked a sergeant behind a desk where that was.

'Way up north,' he answered with the snarky look on his face, 'and it's not good, Lieutenant. It is about the worst place to be sent.' He smiled sarcastically and pointed, 'Look on that map, Lieutenant, for a place called Chu Lai.' He spelled the letters out for him and said, 'It's pronounced "chew lie". It is south of Da Nang. That's real dangerous territory.' James thought, 'Thanks for nothing, Sergeant. Hope you enjoyed those little condescending jibes. I feel rotten enough with this cold and scared, too.... I sure don't need some slimy "REMF"[2] chiding me.'

That evening, James again slept poorly. He had alternating fever and chills, and his throat hurt. He got up during the night to gargle twice with aspirin. In the morning, he dragged himself out of bed and planned to see a flight surgeon as soon as he could. James and others were taken to the airport. Their flight was announced and buses took them to an open back ramp of a Hercules C-130[3] transport airplane. The plane was parked in a large metal and sandbag revetment to provide some protection from mortar or rocket attacks. Some 100 soldiers carrying luggage in their hands walked into the dark, cavern-like bowels of the airplane.

'It's like Jonah walking into the...' His thoughts were interrupted as he looked inside. 'What? No seats? Where in the hell are we going to sit?'

'Gentlemen,' they heard over the speakers, 'this is a tactical insertion. Please be seated on the floor and put your fingers in the cargo tie-down rings on the floor. Hang onto your luggage. A stewardess will be coming down for your beverage orders. Please be polite and don't pinch her cute little ol' ass,' he said in a thick Southern drawl. 'We know you have a choice, thank you for flying Cam Rahn Airlines.'

'You got to be freaking kidding,' someone said.

The lieutenant whined to himself, 'Here I am nervous, sick, and everyone in this shitty place is pulling my chain.'

The Air Force C-130 started up and backed itself out of the revetment. 'I never have seen an airplane back up,' thought the lieutenant. 'I did not know they could do that.' As the plane taxied, he thought there would be a lot more things here that he had not seen before. He was sure of that.

1930 hrs, 11 September 1968
Chu Lai, South Vietnam

An hour later, his uncomfortable plane landed in Chu Lai. The heat was unbearable. He struggled for the strength to carry his luggage and himself off the plane. He boarded a bus, and stood in another line for the seemingly endless array of Army processing and red tape. The lieutenant felt weak standing in the afternoon sun. James dropped his bags and walked up to a Specialist 4th Class[4] behind a desk.

'Specialist, I need to see a doctor. I am sick.'

'Sir, you do look pale.'

The lieutenant stared at the soldier. He seemed fuzzy, like in a dream. 'What? Where am I? Is this a dream?' he thought. 'I feel light-headed,' he said to the clerk. 'I feel...'

The heat, humidity and illness finally got the best of him. James dropped to his knees and passed out. He awoke ten minutes later in a clinic at the airport. He looked up at a man in a white coat. The man said, 'You have a 102-degree fever, Lieutenant. Have you been taking your malaria pills?'

'What? Huh? Holy shit, do I have malaria?'

Two medics transported him and his gear to a field hospital by three-quarter-ton jeep with a red cross painted on the outside canvas canopy. Another doctor examined him, asked an endless array of questions and said, 'You have an acute viral infection. You must have caught the 'flu on the airplane coming over. We will keep you in the hospital until you recover.'

'It's not malaria?' asked James.

'No, it is definitely not. It's impossible to catch malaria this soon.'

He was sent to a ward in the field hospital. The so-called hospital was depressing. He learned it was a battalion MASH unit consisting of several Quonset huts with concrete floors. His building was air-conditioned, a nice plus. He would soon learn that air-conditioning was virtually non-existent in Chu Lai.

Other patients looked the first lieutenant over curiously from their beds. He was the only officer in the drab room with twelve beds. The lieutenant learned that a few patients had been wounded from shrapnel and one large Afro-American Sergeant First Class had jungle rot on his feet.

James thought, 'These people are wounded, and me – the guy who arrived only hours ago – has the 'flu. They probably think this First Lieutenant is a real candy ass.'

The patients had people coming to visit. No one visited James. No one knew him. He was in limbo with no home or local friends. Those who cared about him did not know he was here. Being sick and lonely was depressing.

That evening James called out in his sleep, 'THEY'RE COMING!' A medic rushed over and grabbed his shoulders to calm him.

'We are, ah, where am I?' asked the lieutenant.

'You are in the hospital, Sir. Everything is OK. Relax.'

Then fully awake, he said, 'Sorry, I was having a dream. Sorry if I caused you any trouble. Hope I didn't disturb anyone.'

'No problem, Sir. Go back to sleep.'

Later that night, everyone's sleep was disturbed. The lieutenant experienced his first VC[5] rocket attack. Sirens went off, and the hospital staff led the patients to dark bunkers outside. Fifteen minutes later, it was all over and they were led back to their beds. The ward's lone officer patient lay back, scared and shaken. It took a long time for him or anyone else to fall asleep. He was scared and very lonely.

The next day he felt stronger and his voice was coming back. After lunch, he went for a walk around the grounds. The MASH Unit was located on a U-shaped cliff jutting out 100ft above the ocean below. The cliff overlooked the South China Sea. Deep turquoise water met a horizon of light blue sky and white puffy, scattered clouds. Whitecaps and rolling waves moved toward him, smacking unseen on the cliffs below. White sand beaches spread out beyond the cliff face to his left and right. 'WOW!' he thought, 'this place is beautiful.'

He heard the familiar whup-whup-whup sound of Hueys coming and going. Suddenly, he heard a different but familiar sound. He looked out to see where it was coming from. Low along the beach, at about eye level as he stood on the cliff, he saw an OH-23 Hiller helicopter like those he flew in primary training, months ago in Fort Wolters.

'What...?' he thought, amazed. 'A Hiller, here in Vietnam?'

He could see the pilot clearly as the tiny chopper dashed by at eye level. 'Heck, I thought those damn things were only used in flight school. We were told they are obsolete. Those things are pigs, underpowered. They're certainly not REAL helicopters, and they're not at all fun to fly. What could they possibly use them for here? They look vulnerable; easy as hell, I betcha, to shoot down.'

He remembered a story told at flight school about a similar obsolete helicopter, a Bell OH-13. In this story, an OH-13 was shot down early in the Vietnam War, totaled by nothing more than a well-placed arrow from a tribesman. The arrow was shot into its tail rotor as it was hovering forward to take off.

'I bet an arrow, spear or even a rock thrown into the tail rotor would bring the Hiller down too. I pity the poor, unlucky buggers who have to fly those death-traps here in Nam. With nothing but a little gasoline motor turning a rickety rotor blade, and bad hombres below,' he thought.

One pilot drove the Hiller. At flight school, they were told they would be peter pilots[6] in Vietnam for at least four months. They would sit in the left seat and be under the constant supervision of the aircraft commander in the right seat.

'In a small helicopter,' thought the lieutenant, 'like the Hiller, you are It, the only pilot. No one is there to protect you from screwing up. I would not want to be driving a single-pilot helicopter like that. I want someone experienced nearby when I am learning and ducking bullets.'

1400 hrs, 14 September 1968
Div Arty Air

After lunch, the doctor made his rounds and examined the lieutenant. 'You are doing fine Lieutenant. I am going to send you back to your unit.'

'Thanks, Captain, which unit would that be? Have I been assigned someplace?'

'Oh, that's right, you just arrived.' He looked at his medical file. 'Your paperwork says 123rd Aviation Battalion. I'll call over there.'

The doctor shook the lieutenant's hand and wished him luck. A quarter-ton arrived and took the aviator over a myriad of paved roads past countless buildings.

'It's like a city here. Bigger than the town I grew up in,' he thought.

The jeep pulled up to a wooden building with a sheet metal roof. It had a large white sign that read '123rd Aviation Battalion Operations'. The new pilot got out; the driver helped him with his luggage. James walked in, reported to a clerk and sat down. He waited an hour. 'Hurry up and wait; the Army Way. Where are they going to send me?' he thought, staring at the plywood walls. 'Being an armor officer, I will likely be assigned to gunships or maybe Slicks.[7] I might even get a shot to fly the new Cobra gunship they call the "snake".'[8]

A first lieutenant came out, interrupting his thoughts. James noticed that this lieutenant was not an aviator and secondly, that he was wearing a non-combat branch insignia. 'Paper-pusher,' thought the pilot.

'Lieutenant James, I am Lieutenant Withers, Assistant S1, 123rd Aviation. I have your orders.'

'OK,' replied the pilot.

'How would you like to go to Div Arty Air?'

'As if I have a choice,' the pilot thought. 'I don't know. What's a Div Arty Air?' he answered sarcastically.

'It's the Aviation Section for Division Artillery.'

'I'm Armor, isn't that only for artillery officers?'

'Guess not, Bubba,' answered Withers with a definite condescending tone.

'You little "pencil-pusher",' thought the aviator. 'You think you have power over life and death here.' 'OK, Lieutenant, just what do they fly at this Div Arty Air?' asked the pilot, sarcastically.

'They fly the Hiller OH-23G, an observation helicopter; it's called the Raven.'

'YOU HAVE GOT TO BE SHITTING ME.'

Chapter 3

The Mountains Can Kill You

Ky Ha Heliport, Chu Lai, Vietnam
October 1968

The aircraft's crew chief, Staff Sergeant Jenkins, walked over to help Lieutenant James with the pre-flight. A jeep stopped at the edge of the tarmac and a major carrying an M16 walked up, shook hands with James, and climbed in the helicopter's right front seat. The crew chief picked up the lieutenant's M16 and stowed it around the first-aid kit. He then helped the passenger, Major Burns, get buckled in. He connected the wire on the major's flight helmet to the intercom and gave a 'thumbs up' sign. James climbed in and strapped himself in the center seat. Jenkins picked up his fire extinguisher, and signaled to the pilot that it was clear. The pilot pressed the starter button and the obsolete OH-23G's starter cranked like an old pickup truck. Lots of noise and smoke billowed out of the big reciprocating Lycoming engine as it caught. James checked the magnetos, tuned the UHF radio to Ky Ha tower and received permission to hover out of the revetment.

He became tense when he pulled to a hover in the revetment. The revetments provided little clearance for the tail rotor. They were formidable obstacles made from 55-gallon drums filled with sand and a three-deep layer of sandbags resting on top. 'I know I am new,' thought the pilot, 'but will I ever get used to hovering out of these damn revetments? A little over-controlling and there could be a hell of a mess with me in the middle of it.'

James broke into his first sweat of the day as he fought the controls of the chopper as it hovered out of the revetment. The Raven departed Ky Ha south over the South China Sea, climbed to 200ft and turned left 180 degrees over the harbor. The harbor, as usual, had plenty of villagers fishing in little round reed boats. The Raven soared over the fishermen at 200ft. The pilot remained low to stay below the Chu Lai approach controlled airspace. He turned south over Highway One at the Chu Lai village. Smoke from cooking fires in the village trickled up in many places. It smelled musty to the pilot of the low-flying helicopter. He wrinkled his nose. 'I will never forget this damn Vietnam smell. This smell is, ah, a THIRD WORLD…yeah, that is it, THIRD WORLD, formed from a mixture of things: decay, marijuana, musty wood, mold, cookstoves and smoke.'

Often, kites could be seen sailing in the village during the Vietnamese holidays reaching up to the low-flying helicopters, but not this morning. The pilot looked below at the narrow streets of the village. The houses were small, close together, one- and two-room huts. The larger ones had shiny metal roofs. An occasional house had a lawn, but most had dirt yards filled with junk. The pilot looked back up, glancing at his instrument panel. Then he looked all around to clear the aircraft from other choppers following the highway. He reached forward with his left hand and switched the UHF frequency to Div Arty Operations. He hit the second trigger position on the cyclic switch and said, 'Phoenix One-Three, off Ky Ha heading south on One.'

He recognized the Operations officer's voice reply, 'Roger, Phoenix One-Three, we have you off, report, Quang Ngai, good luck, out.'

James followed Highway One south and stayed below the fast-movers' airspace until well clear of the airport. He eased back on the cyclic, decreasing airspeed from 80 knots to 50 knots, and began climbing. He switched frequency to report in with flight following.

'Salvation, Phoenix One-Three is with you 12 klicks[1] south of Chu Lai heading south along Highway One. We are out of 500 climbing to 1,600.'

'Roger, One-Three, Salvation, out.'

'It is hard work to stay in touch with everyone with one working radio and one pilot,' thought James. 'I heard the new Loaches we will be getting next month have four radios. That will make this job much easier by reducing the chores of us poor ol' solo Div Arty pilots.'

He pressed the intercom trigger of his cyclic and said to his passenger, 'It's a beautiful morning, Sir.'

Major Burns answered, 'Roger that, Lieutenant.'

They made small talk for the next twenty minutes as the chopper flew south. They passed field after field of sugar cane and brown rice paddies with farmers tending their crops on water buffaloes. The countryside looked peaceful south of Chu Lai, but the new pilot remembered that the Operations Officer, Captain Fuller, told him to avoid the peninsula seen off to his left. He glanced out his left door at what was called 'Indian country' by the pilots.

'Indian country' was the Batangan Peninsula,[2] a flat coastal plain with intermixed patches of manicured fields and single-canopy tropical forest. A gorgeous sandy beach to the east bordered the South China Sea.

Fuller had said weeks ago on James's orientation flight, 'It's a bad spot full of VC[3] activity where you are always apt to be shot at. You will want to avoid flying over it.'

The pilot looked ahead and saw a sprawling capital city just ahead. He hit his radio switch and said, 'Operations, One-Three is three klicks north of Quang Ngai, turning south-west toward Eagle Pass along the river.'

'Roger, One-Three.'

They climbed to 4,000ft and the terrain changed from brown, muddy rice paddies to green rolling hills. The foliage on the hills gradually changed from trees and grass to dense jungle that hid the ground. A foreboding north-south trend of large, rugged green mountains loomed dead ahead.

'The terrain reminds me of the movie *King Kong*,' Major Burns said over the intercom.

'Yes, Sir,' replied the pilot. 'It looks like the movie's original version, especially over there to our left with those volcanic spires and columns sticking up. It seems like you might see a pterodactyl fly off from one of those spires.'

'I sure hope we don't see Kong,' he chuckled.

'Yeah, like in VIET CONG,' thought the pilot. 'I get more than a little puckered flying over these mountains. It is always bumpy and there is no place to set down if the "put-put" quits on this whirly-bird.'

They entered the pass and mountains seemed to swallow them. The pilot shivered, suddenly felt naked, exposed to small-arms fire from the slopes on either side as the Raven crept slowly through the pass. James felt his grip tighten on the cyclic. He flexed his fingers to lighten his touch as he rationalized to himself, 'No sane enemy, especially with a 51-caliber machine gun or a 23mm anti-aircraft gun, would want to reveal their position and shoot at a small, puny helicopter like us. Would they? Nah, they would surely wait for a sexier target like an F4 jet-bomber.'

The pilot tuned his radio to the tactical frequency of their destination, LZ Maryann, and transmitted, 'Rebel Gray-One, Phoenix One-Three is 12 klicks out for landing.'

'Good morning, One-Three, this is Rebel Gray-One, all is quiet on the hill.'

'Roger, Rebel Gray-One, glad to hear that, out.'

The LZ, a bald spot on the steep mountain peak surrounded by dense vegetation, was easily visible as they approached from the east. Its flanks were jagged and rocky, a difficult place for the VC to attack. The helicopter spiraled down over the mountain in a tactical corkscrew landing pattern, preparing to land. James knew the final approach to the LZ was tricky because of the landing pad's position on the cliff edge providing only one direction to land, regardless of the wind conditions.

The Raven flared, slowed and then touched down gently on the sandbag landing-pad. The helicopter idled as Major Burns stepped off. A tall, slender, Afro-American first lieutenant and a stout ruddy-faced buck sergeant with red hair walked over. They nodded at the pilot and strapped in four water cans in the right-side seat of the helicopter. The lieutenant got in on the left side and put on a headset. The pilot learned that they were to ferry water and light supplies to the observation post on the top of an adjoining mountain some 1,000ft higher than they were. James looked up at the peak and saw antennae and radar on it. 'Hmm,' he thought, 'I have never been up there; it should be an interesting spot to land.'

He stabilized the helicopter in a hover to ensure he had plenty of power with the load of water cans. It felt good. He checked his engine gauges and saw that everything looked normal. He glanced at his altimeter and read 2,800ft on the instrument. The pilot made a hovering 180-degree turn on the pad and gave one last check of the instruments before accelerating off the cliff face into the thin air.

'What a rush,' thought James. 'One moment you are hovering, the next moment you are 3,000ft in the air.'

James allowed the chopper to dive slightly to gain airspeed. When 40 knots were indicated, he eased back on the cyclic and began climbing. He turned back over the LZ and spiraled up to the OP on the adjoining mountain. He landed on another sandbag landing-pad and was met by soldiers in dirty T-shirts and fatigue pants. They took off the full cans of water and replaced them with empties.

One soldier handed James a handful of mail and said, 'Will you mail these for me, Sir?'

'Sure.'

James placed the precious cargo under his armored plated vest as the men loaded him up. He looked out to enjoy the spectacular view they had on the peak. To the north was a valley and river. The guns below on LZ Maryann provided tactical support to infantry controlling the valley and river.

'This might be a nice, safe place to spend the war,' thought the pilot.

The observation helicopter made four round trips with the passenger obviously only along for the ride. James learned the passenger had been in flight school at Wolters and had some flight time in the OH-23D. He indicated that he quit school for some personal reason. 'Probably washed out,' thought the pilot, cockily.

James lowered the collective to begin his fourth descent to the LZ from the OP when his approach suddenly became dangerous. Quickly, but not quickly enough, he noticed that his descent rate was high and the landing angle too steep; a deadly flight condition in the mountains. The pilot corrected, but to his horror, the helicopter did not respond. In seconds, the approach went from normal to hairy to dangerous, and then to impending disaster. As the passenger sat back, still enjoying the ride, oblivious to what was happening, James pulled the aircraft's nose back sharply and yanked up hard on the collective, fighting to stop their descent. They continued in a high, nose-up attitude down a steep, deadly flight path to impending oblivion. 'WHY ISN'T IT SLOWING?' he screamed to himself. They continued down steep and fast; the terrified pilot realized they were not going to make it. The helicopter, with its nose up and full pitch applied to its rotors, strained to slow as it approached the cliff edge. The pilot could only hold on as the helicopter slid over the cliff edge with the rotor wash kicking dirt high in the air. The helicopter smacked hard on the sandbag pad, and with its tail low and full power applied, it bounced up and back in an uncontrolled hover. Now, with the rotors feeling full ground effect and the cyclic held back in the novice pilot's lap, the OH-23G hovered backwards off the pad and off the cliff face into the thin air. 'HOLY SHIT!' screamed the pilot.

The passenger, who had been enjoying the ride until now, found himself experiencing some of the pilot's abject terror. Hovering at 3,000ft in the thin mountain air, with the helicopter below the cliff-face, James fought for control. After a struggle, he hovered higher, regained control and eased the helicopter forward. The Raven hovered smoothly back on to the mountain and landing pad.

The pilot lowered the collective and the helicopter settled gently on the pad. He sighed, happy to be alive. The passenger quietly got off and James watched him turn his back and walk quickly away. 'I wonder if he is thinking, "And this guy made it through flight school and I didn't".'

The pilot's cockiness, present just moments ago, was gone. James shut down and sat in the helicopter, shaken. 'That was close, you dumb ass, real close.' He let out a deep sigh, trying to drain away the emotion. 'Shit, my IP[4] back at Wolters would have given me a pink-slip[5] on that approach.'

The mountains can kill you. They almost did!

Chapter 4

Flying in Vietnam: 90 Percent Boredom, 10 Percent Stark Terror

0645 hrs, 10 November 1968
Hootch City, Chu Lai

CW2 Tim Booth backed out of the screen door on Div Arty Air Section's wooden gray hootch. He was heavily laden with his flight gear and weapons. As the short, chubby, baby-faced pilot hurried out, he knocked CW2 Lincoln on his butt, who was about to enter the hootch.

'Booth, what the hell?'

'Sorry Steve, didn't see you, I'm late, in a fucking hurry,' he mumbled in his typically irreverent nature as he shuffled quickly down the hill to the Operations hut. He rushed into Operations and mumbled, 'OK, what the hell, Fuller? I was asleep, supposed to have the morning off, when Sergeant Johnson bursts in and wakes me out of a nice dream.'

'It's Captain Fuller, Warrant,' Fuller says, smiling.

'Oh yeah, you're a fucking captain, forgot.'

'Are you always so grouchy?'

'Pretty much, especially when I'm abruptly awoken out of my beauty sleep.'

Lieutenant James, the unit's new safety officer, was laughing at this familiar banter.

Tim Booth was one of the highly-trained pilot warrant officers[1] flying choppers in Vietnam. They had the same training as the officer pilots. They prided themselves on how hard it was to become a warrant officer and make it through Primary Flight School at Fort Wolters, Texas and Advanced Training at Fort Rucker, Alabama or Fort Hunter-Stewart in Savannah, Georgia. Booth had said on numerous occasions that in Vietnam he would not salute anyone below the rank of major who was not a rated aviator. 'What are they going to do?' he said. 'Send me to Vietnam?'

Most of his colorful banter was bullshit, but he liked to throw it around. He was loved by all in Div Arty Air and highly regarded for his piloting skills. He remained one of the unit's colorful characters.

'Booth,' Captain Fuller said, 'You are to take Major Billings from headquarters to Qui Nhon.'

'That red-headed non-rated douche bag?'

'Now come on, Booth, mind your manners. He's an OK guy.'

'OK for a field grade artillery puke living above us on "silk stocking row", a place where we lowly pilots aren't welcome.'

'I was up there once.'

'Aw, they think we are a bunch of grungy cowboys that fraternize with the enlisted men.'

'Go on, get out of here. We have had about enough of your cantankerous bull pucky.'

Booth headed down to the flight line. He greeted his passenger, strapped into his seat and started the old, obsolete OH-23G. He picked it up to a hover and gracefully moved out of the sandbagged revetment. He taxied to the active and departed east over the South China Sea. He turned right and low-leveled south along the beach. It was a gorgeous day and pretty flying along a white sand beach that one day would become a gorgeous resort site. Now, it was a dangerous place.

'It's a great day to fly,' the major said over the intercom.

Booth 'double-clicked' in acknowledgment, obviously not very talkative.

The major looked to the right at the diminutive, chubby warrant officer and depressed the intercom, 'Hear you guys had a big barbeque last night. Moving a little slow, are we?'

Booth, in a pissy mood, stared straight ahead, ignoring the comment.

Once they passed the sprawling Chu Lai Airport, Booth turned inland and flew low-level across the rice paddies. He turned right, roaring off the left side of a farmer riding a water buffalo. The peasant farmer was dressed in black pajamas with a wide-brimmed, pointed straw hat. The Vietnamese farmer shook his fist at the chopper roaring by too close.

'That wasn't nice,' said the major over the intercom.

'I didn't make him bail out. I could have.'

'That would have been worse. We need to make friends here. As General Westmoreland said, "Win the hearts and minds of the people."'

They slowly climbed to 2,000ft to be safely out of small-arms fire as they continued inland. Booth turned south when he reached Highway One.

'Ops, this is Two-Zero, turning south over Highway One.'

'Roger, Two-Zero,' replied Fuller.

As they continued south, they heard over the Div Arty Ops frequency, 'Are you still grouchy, "Mister Alpha Hotel" ("ass hole")?'

Booth acknowledged the non-standard no-call-sign transmission with a double click. He then added, 'Fox-trot uniform ('fuck U').'

The major turned his head to the right with a shit-eating grin, staring at the diminutive chopper driver.

Booth saw him turn out of the corner of his eye, but stared straight ahead, struggling to keep from grinning himself.

They flew south, passing a large black pinnacle with an observation post (OP) on its top.

'Pretty cool structure,' said the major.

'James, our geologist pilot, says it's a volcanic neck of an ancient volcano.'

'Hmm, cool.'

Directly below them was the meandering Song Ha Than River, which emptied to the sea several kilometers to the east.

Off to their left front lay the city of Qui Nhon. Their landing objective, the Admin pad, was off to their front just to the left of Highway One.

Statistically, about half of the chopper pilots were either shot down or crashed in their initial one-year tour in Vietnam. CW2 Tim Booth would end up having one of each experience, and he was about to have his first.

The OH-23G reciprocating engine is loud, especially so with the doors off, which is how they were flown in combat. The OH-23G had relatively low rotor inertia. All helicopters have two rpm needles: one for the engine or transmission RPM and one for the rotor RPM. They are superimposed over one another in the RPM gauge. When practicing autorotation, the pilot rolled off the throttle to flight idle, splitting the needles. The pilot then has to lower the collective and simultaneously put in right pedal. In a low rotor momentum reciprocating engine helicopter like the OH-23G, he had to do both quickly. In flight school, it was said by the instructors: 'Thy rotor RPM is thy staff of life, without it thou shall surely perish.'

Booth was thinking about wind direction to set up a landing to the Admin pad when the engine quit.

The engine quit! Utter silence! The needles split! Time seemed to stand still. Booth reacted almost instantly: he pushed down the collective, shoved in full right pedal, and looked at the rotor RPM. Rotor RPM was in the upper green. 'Good,' he thought, 'now land this thing.'

The major shouted, 'WHAT THE FUCK!'

Booth ignored him. The major grabbed the doorframe with white knuckles.

Booth's mind focused as he thought, 'We took off to the east; wind's to the east. Should I go for the Admin pad, look for a field or turn back to the river? I can make the pad! I can make the pad!' he repeated.

As they descended it looked like he could make it, but suddenly some high wires, invisible earlier, came into focus. 'Oh shit,' he said, as he pulled up on the collective to clear them, bleeding off needed RPM. Rotor RPM dropped to the low green then into the orange. Nearing the ground he flared and pulled up on the collective, now with RPM in the red. They crashed, collapsing the skids, rolling on their side, bending the tail and shattering the plexiglass canopy.

They crawled out, shaken and bruised but otherwise unhurt.

'What the fuck?' said the major. 'That scared the shit out of me.'

'Well, if you can walk away from it, it was a good landing.'

Later That Afternoon

Lieutenants Darryl James and Mark Birmingham flew to Qui Nhon to pick up Booth. James, the new Div Arty Air Safety Officer, took pictures of the crash and discussed it with Booth.

'You sure totaled that puppy,' said Birmingham. 'Sergeant Johnson will be pissed.'

'He'll get another one,' Booth said.

'We are glad you are OK,' James said.

'You know guys, thinking back, I wish I had turned back to the river. I could have turned into the wind and found a sandbank to land.'

'Hindsight is always 20/20,' replied Birmingham. 'Hey, you both walked away. You did well, even for you,' he laughed.

'You know, guys, I didn't let the major know but I was shit scared, terrified coming down.'

James replied, 'They say flying is 90 percent boredom and 10 percent stark terror.'

Chapter 5
A 'Fowl'ed Up Mid-Air Collision

A mid-air collision involving a helicopter is about the worst thing that can happen. In flight school, we had a few such tragedies in Primary School at Fort Wolters and at Fort Rucker that killed several students and instructor pilots. It was said in flight school: 'If this occurs, don't sweat it. There is only one emergency procedure to follow: bend over and kiss your ass goodbye.'

0645 hrs, 20 November 1968
Div Arty Air Operations

Major Fulton, the unit's commanding officer, sat in the Operations hut with Captain Fuller and Captain Bryant. Fulton and Fuller sat at their desks while Bryant manned the Operations radio. Operations keep track of all the Div Arty Air Section pilots in the air, marking their locations, time and position on the large topographic wall map overlaid with plastic.

Warrant Officer Steve Lincoln reported in, 'Phoenix One-Four, landing Duc Pho with two PACs.'

'This is Ops, Roger One-Four,' replied Bryant as he wrote this down on the map with erasable markers.

'Ops, this is Phoenix One-Two, landing Lima Zulu West.'

'Roger One-Two,' replied Bryant.

'What's Birmingham doing out at LZ West?' asked Bryant. 'Heard they took mortar fire and opened up with their Quad 50s[1] last night.'

'Right,' replied Fuller. 'No one was hurt but those 50s knocked down trees and some serious brush. Birm's picking up the chaplain and bringing him back to Division.'

Fuller turned and asked the Operations sergeant a question regarding slick support.

Major Fulton looked up and asked, 'Is it going to rain today?'

'Hell, it rains damn near every day,' replied Fuller.

'The reason I asked, smart ass, is that Colonel Jones is supposed to come over to play cards and drink whiskey tonight. Hate to see the "Old Man" get wet,' he chuckled.

Fulton was highly thought of by the chopper drivers. He was a tall, lean, lanky officer with short brown hair that he wore in a close crew-cut. Unlike the gaggle of pilots, he did not have a mustache. He instead opted for the clean-cut West Point graduate 'strak-look'.

Often aviation commanding officers did not fly combat missions, choosing quietly to fly only non-combat administrative flights under the premise that the boss should not be subjected to hostile fire. Not Major Fulton; he flew combat chopper missions and Admin fixed-wing flights in the unit's Otter and Beaver. This made him greatly respected by the pilots.

Birmingham lifted off from West with Father Flanagan. Captain Flanagan flew frequently with the Div Arty chopper pilots. He was one of the Division Artillery chaplains and spent much time out in the field with the troops conducting Mass, taking confessions, counseling and providing general TLC to the soldiers. He had a terrific sense of humor as well.

Earlier that month

Father Flanagan was flying with Lieutenant James during the monsoon when it rained seemingly all the time. It was foggy with a 100ft ceiling when he and James flew along the road about 10ft off the ground at 80 knots. In Vietnam, you needed to be below 20ft or more than 1,500ft above the ground to be relatively safe from small-arms fire. In between those heights was what the pilots called the 'dead man's zone'. It was difficult to hit a target flying low and fast ducking below the tree line and maneuvering. Above 1,500ft, small-caliber arms could not reach you. The low-level flying was still risky. Div Arty Air suffered a fatality that summer when a pilot low-leveling west of the town of Tam Ky was shot down, crashed and rolled the small helicopter up into a ball.

Low-leveling along Highway One was relatively safe from bad guys, but it had another risk. Other choppers also had to low-level along it in the creepy monsoon weather. You could crash into one and ruin your day. A mid-air collision in a helicopter was fatal. To mitigate this risk, James kept to the right of the narrow macadam two-lane road, had his landing light on and hoped other chopper drivers crazy enough to be flying in this weather would do the same.

They were zipping along just above the mud and slop from the heavy rains. At 80 knots, it was exhilarating going that fast and that low. Rounding a bend in the road, they soared over a bunch of peasant women. One rather large woman had her black pajama pants down with two huge hams exposed. Unashamed to the world, she squatted, pinching off a rather large loaf on the asphalt, safely away from the muck and mud alongside the road. It was a surprising, macabre scene in the foggy air; funny, maybe a bit offensive, but certainly an event worthy of comment.

James thought to himself, 'If you gotta go, you gotta go. Hope that didn't offend our mild-mannered padre.'

No one spoke over the intercom for a few seemingly long minutes. Father Flanagan then quipped, 'Darryl, now I know why the good Lord makes it rain so much over here.'

James burst out laughing, making the chopper wobble. He instinctively relaxed on the stick. They climbed as the cyclic was trimmed back for safety. He regained control and pushed forward on the cyclic to get them down low-leveling again once.

In the poor visibility, he spotted the landing light of another helicopter low-leveling toward them at a high rate of closure. James veered right to avoid a potential collision then continued back along the road, chuckling to himself about Father Flanagan.

0645 hrs, 20 November 1968
Landing Zone West

Birmingham lifted off from LZ West with Father Flanagan, climbed to 3,000ft and headed east toward the coast. He soon found himself in and out of cloud scud. He descended to stay out of the clouds with the weather deteriorating.

'What a crappy day to be flying,' thought Birmingham.

He continued descending and passed through a green, heavily forested valley. He dodged clouds and finally saw Highway One in the distance. It was a welcome sight. He descended to 1,800ft and turned south along the road toward Tam Ky. When he passed the city, he turned to the south-east toward Chu Lai.

Father Flanagan carefully pressed the intercom switch on the cyclic in front of him and said, 'Mark, the Good Lord has us flying today in pretty soupy weather.'

'You have that right, Father; he's making it tough for us to get home.'

'At least it's not raining. It rains so much during the monsoon, it wears these tired bones of mine out. I am looking forward so much for a sunny day. It's been so long since we have seen the sun.'

'We fly in all kinds of weather here, Father. We have to be careful and use our wits to keep from getting in trouble in what we call this, excuse my English, "SHITTY" IFR[2] weather. We have to stay out of the clouds, maintain separation from clouds and keep the aircraft safe.'

'Yes Mark, I'm counting on you and the good Lord to keep us safe.'

They passed over marshland, rice paddies and inland lakes and ponds. They noticed many of the ponds were full of ducks and geese.

'Look at all the waterfowl below. Are we in some kind of a bird migration?'

'Don't know. I see some flying off below to the left of us.'

The visibility was poor and Mark's rotor blades seemed to be in and out of the cloud scud.

Things can happen fast when you're flying. One moment everything is fine and the next moment things can turn to hell in a handbasket.

Out of the corner of Mark's right eye, he saw what seemed to be a shadowy aberration. His eyes turned instantly to the right when what seemed to be an aircraft appeared out of the mist and was on a collision course with their helicopter. He instantly reacted, turning sharply left. Boom, the canopy exploded in front of Father Flanagan.

Back in Operations, Captain Bryant was standing writing on the map wall. Captain Fuller was on the phone and Major Fulton was at his desk doing paperwork.

The radio crackled, 'Operations, this is Phoenix One-Two. We just had mid-air with a B1RD.'

Everyone in Operations jumped up and turned toward the radio as Bryant said, 'WHAT? Say again, One-Two!'

'We just hit a bird, Operations, a big-ass bird. It crashed through our canopy.'

'Are you OK, One-Two?'

'Roger. My passenger's a bit worse for wear. He's full of feathers, guts and blood. Air is rushing in the cockpit blowing crap all around. We are flying OK. Had to slow to 40 knots. We should be at Ky Ha heliport in about 20 mikes.'

'Roger One-Two, is your passenger OK?'

'Yes, he's OK, Ops. He had on a helmet, which took the brunt of the collision.'

'We will alert the tower, and have maintenance and the medics meet you.'

One-Two landed with a crowd of Div Arty Air people gathering. The mid-air with a goose caused quite a stir. Birmingham and Father Flanagan climbed out with a huge crowd watching. Soldiers examined the broken canopy and peered into the trashed-out cockpit.

Major Fulton said, 'Wow, this could have been a disaster. You two are lucky hombres.'

Father Flanagan replied, 'The incident didn't seem to bother Mark, but I was certainly shook up.' He added in his humorous style, 'That, gentlemen, was close to getting my goose cooked.'

Many soldiers laughed.

Birmingham quipped in Flanagan's best style, 'No harm; no fowl.'

Everyone now roared with laughter.

Chapter 6
The Big Splash

Ky Ha heliport
December 1968
1700 hrs

Coming home after seven hours in the mountains, the tired Raven's pilot reached the point near the outskirts of Chu Lai where he had to descend below 200ft. Lieutenant James did a series of S-turns looking for aircraft below them that might be low-leveling along Highway One. As they approached the village, he saw a large CH-47 Chinook[1] helicopter called a Hook passing below and in front of them. He thought about another time he flew near a Hook coming into Ky Ha. That day, he made a serious mistake of turning behind a Hook as they both entered the approach area to Ky Ha heliport. The small OH-23G was instantly pushed down from 200ft of altitude to 50ft. It felt as if a big hand, like the hand from King Kong grabbing the biplane from the Empire State Building, grabbed him and threw him downward. 'You only do that once,' thought the pilot, remembering how badly the incident scared him.

After landing at Ky Ha, he hovered over to the Av gas[2] fuel station. James shut the OH-23G down and thought, 'Cheated death again. You ain't pretty, baby, but you brought me home safely again.'

James filled out the chopper's logbook. Sergeant Jenkins walked over to check out his ship. The pilots just drove them; they belonged to the crew chiefs, who often painted names of their girlfriends or wives on their ship. This one had 'California Dreaming' painted on its side. Jenkins came from Venice, California, and he was proud to let everyone know that with his logo.

'I'm pooped,' thought James as he shut down the idling helicopter. 'I have flown seven hours in this machine, bouncing all over the sky in the mountains until my butt hurts. Soon I'll be up at the club with the guys, relaxing with a Scotch and water.'

Warrant Officer Bill Broderick walked toward the chopper with his gear. James watched him approach. He noticed that the FNG[3] had his chicken-plate[4] and M16. 'What's he doing with that stuff? He should be naked. He's only going over to the practice area.' He noticed that the young warrant officer did have a 45-caliber automatic pistol and a large and obviously brand-new survival knife wrapped around his tall, lean body.

Broderick was tall for a pilot at 6ft 2in. His sandy-colored hair, blue eyes and overall good looks labeled him as someone who would do well with the ladies. The guy was quiet and soft-spoken. Fresh from a month's leave, he hadn't acquired the colorful language pervasive throughout Vietnam. 'Give him time,' thought James. 'Soon, he will be one of the guys, cussing with the best of us.' Like all FNGs, he was nervous. Worried that he would screw something up.

The FNG set his helmet down and began a preflight inspection of California Dreaming. James noticed he did this under the watchful eye of Sergeant Jenkins. The green pilot climbed in, set the start-up card checklist on the dash and carefully went through the start-up procedure. The engine fired with a puff of bluish smoke. James and Jenkins watched him hover to the active.

Broderick tried to concentrate. He was nervous with the controls, paranoid that everyone on the tarmac was watching him. 'I need to settle down and do everything right. James and the crew chiefs are watching ME: the new kid on the block, fresh out of flight school.' He turned on the active runway and faced toward the south. He looked one last time at his instruments. 'Everything looks normal.' He eased the cyclic forward and felt the bump and dip as the helicopter left hovering flight and entered transitional flight, a condition where the helicopter entered forward flight with air coming across as well as down the rotors. At this point, the rotors became more efficient and the helicopter started to climb.

Broderick took off from Ky Ha on his first solo flight in Vietnam. He felt a pilot's moment of joy and excitement as the craft left the hold of Mother Earth and soared into the freedom of the sky. He scanned his instruments as he was taught at flight school as the Raven climbed. 'I have 40 knots airspeed and climbing nicely,' he told himself. 'Everything's cool.'

Then he heard NOTHING; just a deadly quiet!

All at once, things started to happen in Broderick's body. His breathing stopped, adrenaline rushed into his blood supply and his blood pressure went sky-high. Neurons fired off in his brain, and without a conscious awareness of what he was doing, the collective went down, right pedal was applied and the cyclic was pulled back. The aircraft – now devoid of power – flared and settled in the water. It bounced once in the surf and rolled right, flooding the cockpit. All of this happened in tens of seconds.

Moments earlier, James and Jenkins watched Broderick's take-off and heard the abrupt silence as his engine quit over the South China Sea. They watched helplessly as he dropped below their line of sight. They ran across the tarmac to get to a position where they could see.

Broderick undid his seat belt and shoulder harness and climbed out the left side of the chopper as the main rotor flew off in pieces. He jumped, and because of his heavy ceramic and steel chicken-plate went straight to the bottom in 20ft of water.

His feet hit bottom as he struggled with the Velcro release of his chicken-plate. He kicked madly toward the surface.

Off to the left of James and Jenkins, a Cobra gunship[5] hovered slowly toward the active, laboring with a heavy fuel and ammo load. It bounced on the tarmac then dramatically took off from a taxiway between revetments and vehicles laboring with its heavy load. It headed directly toward where they last saw Broderick. The Snake dropped abruptly and hovered at a spot several hundred feet offshore above heavy surf. A helmet surfaced and arms flailed awkwardly for the skids. The Snake struggled to hover with its heavy gross weight and reached for Broderick with the left skid.

Moments earlier Broderick surfaced, getting a mouthful of saltwater under his visor. Water splashed all around his visor. He couldn't see. Then he saw it. It looked like a big, badass dragon. Water, rotor wash and foam blinded him and gave him another gulp of saltwater. A skid nearly poked him and moved off. It came again and he kicked and grabbed it.

The Snake slowly dragged Broderick toward the beach.

The FNG hung on. It seemed forever, but soon he released his grip and dropped 2ft down in shallow water. A wave hit him from behind and knocked him face down in the water. He struggled to his feet and he walked onto the beach.

James and Jenkins stood on the tarmac watching. The Snake departed and a Huey landed on the beach and retrieved Broderick. The Slick circled and returned with a half-drowned FNG to the tarmac.

Broderick got off and stood on the tarmac, pale and shaking like a leaf. He softly repeated to no one in particular, 'The fucking engine quit. The fucking engine quit. It just quit.'

Medics came over, put him in a jeep and drove off. James and Jenkins looked out over the breakers and saw California Dreaming's rotor blade being bounced around in the surf. Jenkins sadly watched his $300,000 ship pounded apart by the surf. 'Lost another; first to Booth, now the FNG.'

Neither man said anything for several minutes.

The pilot shook his head and said, 'Shit, that could have been me.'

'What, Sir?'

'I just drove that chopper around the mountains for seven hours. THAT COULD HAVE BEEN ME, Jenkins. Holy cow!'

'Lieutenant, you definitely need a beer,' said the crew chief. 'Come with me, Sir.'

They walked to the maintenance shed and Jenkins took out a beer from the crew chief's private stash.

'That's nice,' thought the pilot. 'It's very uncommon, I think, for enlisted men to share a beer with me, a piss-ant lieutenant.'

Several crew chiefs came in. No one seemed to mind the intrusion of an RLO[6] into their group. They toasted Broderick's good fortune, and then Jenkins toasted the lieutenant for his luck in bringing California Dreaming home with what appeared to be a bad engine.

Sergeant Thomas said, 'Each engine reaches that certain time when, snap, it just fucking quits. You can't do anything about it.'

'Yeah, Sergeant,' said James, 'but I am sure glad it didn't happen to me over the mountains.'

Later that evening, the Div Arty pilots learned from Broderick that everything happened so fast, he barely remembered anything. The gaggle of pilots told him he did great, and questioned him for any additional morsel he could remember.

The FNG said, 'I remember the silence. You know. Ah, when the engine quit, I don't remember shoving in right pedal and lowering the collective, but I do remember rolling the cyclic all the way over to the right when I hit the water. I sure will never forget struggling with my seat belt with my face underwater. Guys, I can still taste that saltwater; scared the crap out of me. Honestly, I don't remember getting out of the cockpit, but I do remember taking my helmet off.'

'Broderick,' Captain Fuller said softly, 'you didn't take your helmet off. You wore it to the hospital.'

'Oh,' he sighed. 'I was sure I did.' Taking a long pull of his beer, he added, 'I sure had a tough time grabbing on that Snake's skids.'

'I saw you,' said James. 'You held on for dear life.'

'Yeah, and oh, when I surfaced, that gunship was the biggest most beautiful thing in the world. The skids though were about ready to crack me on my bare head, ah, helmet.' Everyone laughed. 'I was scared the Snake was going to take off with me holding on to the skids.'

From that day on, James never strapped his chicken-plate on. Instead, he removed the chicken-plate from its vest and placed the plate over his chest where it would rest in his lap. He would only secure it with his shoulder harness. It wasn't comfortable, but if his engine quit on take-off over the water, he wanted to get out just like Broderick.

The Lord was looking out for the FNG. The five IPs he had at Wolters and Rucker would have approved of his efforts today. Broderick was lucky, but all those weeks of training and his IP's repetitive emergency exercises saved his life that afternoon. Surviving involved learning from all the little mistakes you make and praying that none of them was serious enough to get you. You sure can be gotten in a hundred ways. A bit of luck helped.

Chapter 7

Browning Your Flight Suit

Chu Lai, VN 1968

In 1968, I was flying small one-pilot helicopters for Americal Division Artillery. The twelve months I spent flying OH-23 Ravens and later the OH-6A 'Loach' helicopters was full of harrowing and sometimes frightening experiences. One experience I remember quite fondly now was a different kind of experience. It was an amusing episode of 'poopie pants'.

My problem resulted from the heavy partying our unit had the night before. One of our clever crew chiefs got a case of cheap, tough-as-hide steaks from the Navy CBs (Construction Battalions) in Chu Lai. This crew chief, a sergeant something-or-other, was always good at trading and performing an acceptable kind of military larceny referred to as 'midnight requisitioning'. He found all sorts of useful stuff for us.

The steaks he requisitioned that day were too tough for the usual BBQ. They had to be more carefully cooked. Our Texan chopper driver, Lieutenant Connor Dotson, said, 'Not to worry boys, we will make fajitas out of them tough ol' steaks just like we all do in Texas.' He did, with lots of hot sauce, onions, green peppers and he even made home-made flour tortillas with lard absconded from the Officers' Club.

All the crew chiefs and pilots were eating hot Tex-Mex food, drinking beer and having a damn hot ol' time. We had a real, Katie-bar-the-door, rip-tearing time. One of the majors even came down from their billets up the hill, which we referred to as 'Silk Stocking Row', to partake in our merrymaking.

Later we learned that not all of those inhabitants of Silk Stocking Row appreciated our party. Some of the field grades up on the hill had the audacity to complain to our full bird that the scrubby pilots were at it again, having a good time and worse, carousing with the enlisted men.

I had a memorable time, but I didn't realize then that the next day would be more memorable. In the morning, I felt like a herd of elephants had dropped their biological matter on my tongue. I still had to fly in the mountains over hostile countryside. I crawled out of bed, showered under our makeshift shower formed from a beat-up jet fuel tank, and shaved.

I skipped breakfast, then met some artillery guys I was scheduled to take to Firebase East in the mountains. We took off in the clear, cool morning air and headed to the mountains. Twenty minutes later, we were over the triple-canopy mountainous jungles of I Corps in Vietnam approaching our destination. I began the usual descending circle to set up for a landing on the narrow-edged mountain ridge.

Suddenly, while setting up my approach to land, I got a supreme urge to relieve the pressure in my bubbling lower GI tract. It was urgent – very urgent – and it got worse. It continued to get worse until it became absolutely volcanic.

I squirmed in the pilot's seat, landed, turned off the chopper and with the rotors still turning, ran off at full steam to one of the outhouses on Firebase East. Alas, I was too late.

You know how it is when you have to go REAL BAD and get physically close to the place where you can go and whoops, out it comes. Well it happened just like that: a volcanic eruption.

I fought the many zippers on my one-piece flight suit and sat down on the john to finish my business with real messy skivvies. I did the only thing a refined officer and gentleman would do: I ripped the cotton skivvies off and dropped them down in the hole. I cleaned up and felt like a human being again. I was ready to face the challenges of flying in combat and face death again. I strutted over to the mess tent and made the mistake of having a cup of strong black coffee. Suddenly, it was off to the races again. I ran out from the mess tent to the crapper I christened earlier and nearly made it; honest, I darn near made it.

Now I had a problem: no underwear to sacrifice down the hole. I cleaned up best I could and casually asked the first person I saw where I could find some water.

'To drink?' asked the Spec 4 I saw carrying a wooden box.

'No, I kind of need to clean up a little soldier,' I said sheepishly.

'Try behind the mess tent, Sir.'

I walked quickly but with dignity over to the mess tent and splashed water and soap and tried to clean my gray cotton flight suit the best I could.

I didn't drink any coffee the rest of the day. Perhaps I had some bread or something like that for lunch; I just can't remember. I do remember that I really didn't feel like eating again until it was well past supper time.

I flew back to the Ky Ha heliport, landed and parked in the sand-bagged revetments. My friendly crew chief came out to greet me. I could tell I lit up every sensor in his olfactory panels because he cut me a wide berth.

We had a great time the previous night and although I suffered the following day, I took solace in that those who had to smell me that next day suffered too. Somehow today that makes me smile and think, 'You know, it wasn't always so bad over there.'

Chapter 8
Holes in my Chopper?

1730 hrs, 16 December 1968
Div Arty Air Recreation Room

Just before suppertime, the recreation room was full as usual. The atmosphere was electric, with lots of stories being swapped back and forth. Lieutenant Duffy and two AOs[1] were playing poker. Adult beverages were being consumed and refilled. Warrant Officer Booth returned from his room with his coveted bottle of Galliano and in a remarkable show of generosity offered to share it. James rushed over to him with a fresh glass of ice. Captain Fuller walked into the room, spotted James and came up to him and Booth.

'JAMES, DO I HAVE SOME GOOD NEWS FOR YOU.'

The room suddenly hushed. James became uncomfortable with all eyes on him. 'What have I done now?' he thought.

'Ah, what news is that, Captain Fuller?' James said weakly.

Fuller appeared to be thoroughly enjoying himself. He looked around, smiled and said, 'You know those three holes you put in Jenkins' 5-2-4 chopper?'

'Yes, Captain,' said James, 'I remember those bullet holes.'

'Well James, Jenkins has been checking the records and those holes in her oil pan were put there some two years ago while it was installed on another ship. Sorry, Senor, I guess it wasn't your gig after all.'

'Really?' said James. He let out a sigh, really disappointed by the news. He was proud of those holes. He thought back to the incident at Duc Pho.

Two Weeks Earlier
Duc Pho Air Strip
Lieutenant James returned to Ky Ha heliport in Chu Lai in the obsolete OH-23G, aka 'The Raven'. An AO who was riding in the right seat got out and a captain from division artillery strapped himself into the left seat of the chopper. As they were flying south from Chu Lai, they crossed the westernmost edge of the Batangan Peninsula. This was a place the green pilot was told to avoid. It was a place, his boss Major Fulton said, festooned with VC activity and you were apt to be shot at.

James veered a little to the west to avoid the bad area he was nearing. Suddenly, he heard three loud whacks on the outside of the helicopter. The pilot's blood pressure jumped sky-high as he looked left and right, checked all his instruments and said to himself, 'What the hell was that?'

The passenger looked at him and said over the intercom, 'What were those loud bangs?'

'I don't know,' replied the pilot.

Again, they heard several more loud whacks. James nervously looked left, right and back again to the right. Then he saw it. The seatbelt was hanging loose outside the helicopter. The passenger boarding at Ky Ha had forgotten to fasten it and the pilot forgot to ensure it was fastened. James grabbed the cyclic[2] with his left hand and tried to reach across the right seat with his right hand to grab the seatbelt. He struggled but couldn't reach it. He pressed the button on the cyclic and said to his passenger, 'It's the darn seatbelt banging against the side of the helicopter. I can't reach the darn thing. I'm afraid we will hear it banging all the way to Duc Pho.'

Twenty minutes later, they landed at Duc Pho. James taxied off the runway and shut the chopper down. He and the passenger got out. James fastened the dangling seatbelt and inspected the scratches and small dents caused by the banging seatbelt. James refueled with Av gas and cranked up the old, obsolete, long-in-the-tooth Scout helicopter.

He pressed the button on the cyclic and said, 'Duc Pho tower, this is Phoenix One-Three, requesting permission to taxi and depart to the north.'

'Phoenix One-Three, you are cleared to Runway 16 and cleared for take-off. After take-off you are cleared for a 180-turn right turn to the north.'

'Roger tower.'

James took off to the south and turned right 180° back to the north.

As he departed, the tower called, 'Phoenix One-Three, be advised you have a slight blue exhaust plume coming from the back of your helicopter.'

'Roger tower, Phoenix One-Three.'

James carefully scanned his instruments. They were all in the green. He decided to return to Chu Lai, which was forty minutes north along Highway One. It was a poor decision made by an inexperienced pilot, the pilot's chopper with the word 'Molly' painted on the cowling was leaking oil, and the leak was increasing, making for a potentially lethal condition. His engine could have seized on him on the way back to Chu Lai or he might have been forced to land somewhere not so safe.

Coming back, the pilot noticed a large increase in oil pressure; the gauge stayed in the green, just below the yellow.[3] Everything else seemed fine. On short final, Ky Ha tower said, 'Phoenix One-Three, be advised you have a large, heavy blue smoke trail.'

'Roger,' replied the pilot.

'Yikes,' he thought. He shut down. His crew chief rushed over and pointed to the heavy oil drip under the helicopter.

'Lieutenant, it looks like you had trouble. Molly has a bad oil leak.'

'No kidding?' James asked nonchalantly, but said a silent prayer of thanks to his Heavenly Father for his inattention to the warning from Duc Pho. He should have gone around in the landing pattern to land and check for the cause of the smoke.

Later, when James was up the hill in his hootch, Captain Fuller and Lieutenant Duffy rushed in with Sergeant Johnson and Sergeant Jenkins trailing behind carrying an oily cover plate.

'James, you have three AK-47 holes in your aircraft. One round nicked an oil line. Why in hell didn't you report that in your debrief?'

'Huh? I, I don't remember taking hits. To be honest, though, I had a seatbelt banging on the side of the helicopter and frankly, I am not sure what it feels like to take hits.'

James inspected the plate and put his finger through each hole. He became a little shaky, thinking about what could have happened.

'It feels,' said Fuller, 'like someone hitting your helicopter with a hammer.'

'Well, I sure don't remember anything like that, but I was distracted by the seatbelt banging on the helicopter. Duc Pho did say I was trailing a little smoke when I took off.'

'Sometimes you can't tell when you take hits,' said Fuller. 'The Raven is real loud in the cockpit with no doors or windows, and your helmet keeps out much of the noise.'

Everyone gave James some serious kidding about the incident and his carelessness in not making sure the seatbelt was fastened and not heeding to the tower's warning of blue smoke. Later in the pilot's rec. room, Lieutenant Birmingham said kiddingly, 'You mean James took hits? Shit, we're all dead. He flies so high, he needs oxygen.'

Everyone laughed, but James never said a word. He had been proud of those hits, very proud. It busted his cherry in the unit.

Chapter 9

Christmas in the Philippines

1730 hrs, 16 December 1968
Div Arty Air Recreation Room

Several of Div Arty's chopper drivers were hanging around the recreation room enjoying their favorite adult beverages. The room was very manly-looking, which was not surprising. The only woman to set foot in the recreation room had been Luan, their married hootch maid. Former Div Arty pilots built the comfortable, rustic room two tours before the current crop of pilots. The plywood-paneled walls were adorned with *Playboy* and *Hustler* pin-ups. A sign, which gave an important policy statement for the unit, dominated one wall:

> DIV ARTY AIR SECTION POLICY:
> Div Arty Air pilots cannot under any circumstances have an alcoholic beverage within 12 hours prior to any flight mission. The next flight mission our pilots can make is 4 June 1979.

The comfortable 'wreck room' as the pilots called it, was furnished with two wicker chairs, a wicker couch and a round game table with four wicker chairs. The functional furniture was practically new, acquired by the previous tour's pilots in the Philippines, their gift to the war effort.

The Philippine furniture had a circuitous route getting to the pilots' wreck room. A Div Arty Air pilot bought it on behalf of his buddies while attending the prestigious Air Force Jungle Survival School at Clark Air Base. Adjoining Clark, a wild and woolly town, Angeles City, sold all manner of Philippine goods. The pilot purchased the furniture from a factory on the outskirts of Angeles City for a price of only $250 American dollars. The problem was getting the furniture to Chu Lai. He made a deal with an Air Force friend to ship the furniture to Da Nang via a C-130 transport plane. It arrived a couple of days after the Div Arty pilot returned to Chu Lai. The following Sunday, the Div Arty Air Operations officer sent the Colonel's C & C[1] Huey on a secret mission to Da Nang. Sunday was an especially good day for covert personal missions as the colonel usually took the day off and didn't use his chopper. The Huey brought the coveted furniture home to Chu Lai, much to the cheers of its new owners.

Airfreight for the shipment consisted of a trade for services rendered, in the form of a beat-up but authentic AK-47 rifle and a not-so-authentic North Vietnamese flag sprinkled with chicken blood. 'What the pilgrims didn't know couldn't hurt them,' was the mantra of the traders. The so-called war souvenirs became permanent decorations for the Air Force C-130 unit's Day Room at Clark Air Base. Such trades and swaps were commonplace in Vietnam. This deal was a special one and would be enjoyed by hosts of Div Arty pilots for years to come.

Div Arty Air Recreation Room
1730 hrs, 16 December 1968

Captain Fuller, Div Arty's Operations officer, was kidding around with the gaggle of pilots in the recreation room. He was telling Lieutenant James that the three holes in the oil pan of his OH-23G, an obsolete single-pilot helicopter, were from a previous helicopter and not his bullet holes. He could see the disappointment in James's face. 'Aww, I was just pulling your chain, Magnet Ass. Sergeant Johnson didn't find anything in any records. Your bullet holes are still valid holes. Lighten up a bit, Darryl. Besides, Lieutenant Magnet Ass, I really do have some GOOD NEWS for you.'

Fuller had everyone's undivided attention again. Everyone loved good news.

'How would you like to go to the Philippines for a week?'

'What? Ahhh...sure, what for, Captain?'

'Air Force Jungle Survival School. The 123rd got a slot and passed it on to us. You are one lucky Buck, Senor.'

Everyone in the room dropped their collective jaws. The room filled with green, boot-high envy. 'Wow!' someone said. 'Lucky mother...'

'You leave the day after tomorrow,' said Fuller. 'Here are your orders. You are to travel in khakis, but take your fatigues and field jacket.'

James could hardly breathe. 'Wow,' he thought, 'Christmas in the Philippines. Flushing toilets, no one shooting at you, it will be great. I can call home. Wow!'

21 December 1968
Saigon, South Vietnam

James caught a ride to the Chu Lai terminal and caught a C-130 flight to Saigon. Everyone aboard seemed to be in a happy mood. The flight was full of soldiers sitting in plain web seats going home or to someplace nicer than Chu Lai.

A bus took James to the Officers' BOQ at the airport. At the BOQ, he met several lieutenants and warrant officers who were leaving on various flights in the morning. The group, all newcomers to the city, decided to see something of Saigon. They got advice from the sergeant in charge of housing to take a taxi wherever they decided to go. He recommended the Air Force Officers' Club.

The group went outside and flagged down two three-wheel scooters with a cab on the back. The driver mistakenly thought they wanted to go to the Vietnamese Air Force Officers' Club.

The club's name was really a misnomer as the Vietnamese officers no longer frequented it. Some time ago, it had evolved into a girly place filled with American officers. Downstairs was a wild girly lounge. Upstairs it had a dinner club and another special establishment visited only by senior American officers needing to get their oil changed.

The trip through the city in the back of the three-wheel scooter was frightening for James. As the rig turned in and sped down narrow dark streets, he felt exposed, vulnerable and afraid.

'Where in the hell is he taking us? VC were known to throw bombs and shoot at GIs in the city. Here we are, unarmed, at night, on lonely streets and we do not have any earthly idea where in the hell we are. What if the drivers are VC? We could be dead at any moment.'

They came to a brick, two-story building with a large circular drive. The grounds were meticulously kept. Two large flagpoles stood in front lighted by large spotlights. One flag had the South Vietnamese green and gold national flag and the other held the American red, white and blue. The American flag was a comforting sign to the officers. A South Vietnamese A-4 Skyraider[2] was mounted on a concrete pad, a monument guarding the driveway.

The group entered a corridor that looked like a hotel lobby. They were motioned by uniformed employees into a dimly-lit large room with loud rock music. Scantily-clad Vietnamese girls who wanted the GIs to buy them drinks immediately welcomed them.

The girls said, 'You buy me drink, GI. Luv you too much.'

The group brushed off the pawing girls and grabbed a seat. This was not exactly what they expected, but they settled in the smoky room to enjoy the striptease show on the stage. They had a couple of rounds of drinks and ordered hors d'oeuvres. The food consisted of pork and cheese wrapped in strips of bacon. It was surprisingly good.

Two of the officers from the group finally gave in and allowed girls to sit on their laps. The girls led them to a booth away from the other four officers. James watched as the two giggling officers bought the girls drinks. Although they were being groped and smothered by the bargirls, they seemed to be having fun. James and the other three officers turned away, ignoring their two friends to watch the floorshow.

After another round of drinks, James and three others decided to make it back to their quarters. James's flight to Clark Air Force Base in the Philippines was at 0700 hours and he wanted some sleep.

They walked out to the lobby and inquired about a taxi. As they talked to the maître d'hôtel, an American, full colonel, walked down the stairs. He heard the men talking to the maître d'hôtel, and said, 'How would you gentlemen like a ride to the airport?'

'Sure,' they replied.

The colonel had a car brought around, and he hopped into the driver's seat. It was a '67 Chevrolet Impala painted OD³ green. The colonel made small talk with the lieutenants. He asked how they heard about the club. He indicated that they needed to be careful.

'Gentlemen,' he said, 'it is a real rip-off place. The girls will get you drunk, get you to buy them Saigon tea,⁴ grab your billfold and sometimes grab even more. I suggest next time you go to one of the nice hotels for a drink.' James thought to himself, 'Then why are you here, Colonel? Maybe your oil needs changing.'

The colonel dropped them off at their hotel. The officers thanked him and wished him a good evening.

The next morning, James noticed some heated conversation between the two officers who were with the bargirls the previous night and the desk sergeant. It seemed that both officers had their wallets emptied of money. Their wallets were returned sans cash before they were sent home by taxi. They returned to the hotel quite drunk, oblivious to the theft. The two lieutenants' R&R⁵ would now be delayed. They needed to arrange for new funds.

1400 hrs, 23 December 1968
Clark Air Base, the Philippines

The flight to the Philippines was a Delta Airlines Boeing 707. James stretched out, enjoying the airplane food and the American stewardesses. He almost hated to see the flight end. A bus took them to the Survival School where James and several other aviators from the Army and Air Force signed in and began in-processing. He noticed a tall, slender Army aviator with a First Air Cav patch on his sleeve. The warrant officer had a splendid handlebar mustache with full 270-degree curls to it on each side.

'You here for the Jungle Survival School?' asked James.

'Right, Lieutenant. It's good to see the Army represented. I am Jack Smoot.'

'Darryl James.'

'Nice to meet you, Darryl. I drive Cobras with the Cav.'

'A little bit full of himself,' thought James. The Loach pilot thought about the saying: 'How do you tell a Cobra pilot? You don't need to; he'll tell you within five minutes.'

They learned some really good news. The school would close tomorrow for the holidays. They had ten days off.

'Wow,' thought James. 'This is almost too good to be true. We will be here about two and a half weeks for a four-day school. Pinch me please, I must be dreaming. I cannot believe this good fortune. Oh, thank you Captain Fuller.'

They learned that there was no room at the Air Force BOQ. They were advised to stay in one of the hotels off-post. A sergeant gave them a list of hotels and recommendations to be careful in Angeles City.

'Gentlemen,' said the sergeant, 'it is a cowboy town where anything can happen. You can get into any kind of trouble you want to there. The major also asked me to tell you officers to be careful of diseases that are commonly encountered off-post. Gentlemen, please don't go around dipping your wick in that cesspool of love.'

Everyone broke out in heavy laughter.

'Please use good judgment,' the sergeant continued, 'also, it is not recommended for officers to wear their uniforms.'

'Hell, I don't have any civilian clothes,' thought James.

As if reading James's mind, the Air Force Lieutenant said, 'Gentlemen, you can catch a Base bus here to the PX, where you can purchase civilian clothes if you need to. If you like, Sergeant Howard will make a reservation for you at the Holiday Inn. We can get a special rate for you there.'

James and Smoot decided to let the sergeant make the reservations. They elected to share a double room to save a few bucks. The two Army pilots took the bus to the PX, where they bought clothes and magazines. After getting directions to the Officers' Club, they walked several blocks through a quiet housing neighborhood for majors and lieutenant colonels. They entered the Officers' Club and enjoyed a splendid dinner in the Men's Grill. Each man ordered a thick T-bone steak accompanied by a nice claret wine recommended by his Philippine waiter. Feeling splendid, they asked a clerk at the club to call a taxi to take them to the Holiday Inn. They checked into the hotel and settled into their spacious clean room. They were feeling good with the fine accommodations and the satisfied feeling after having an excellent meal. Each thought how lucky they were to be in such a nice place, away from Vietnam.

Jack noticed there were no towels. He picked up the phone and was having difficulty being understood.

'What?' James heard him say.

Jack covered the mouthpiece, laughed, and said to his roommate: 'You're not going to believe this. I asked him for two towels. He doesn't speak English very well and after a lengthy discourse, he said "What yu wunt, GI, two blow jobs?"'

Now James was laughing, he went back to the phone and said slowly, 'No blow jobs, we want TOW-WELS. Understand, TOW-WELS, NOT GIRL-ELS!'

He hung up, still laughing. The two soldiers had no earthly idea what they were going to get. Ten minutes later, the manager came up to their room with toilet paper, a menu and, of all things, an iron and ironing board. Jack took the toilet paper and said, 'Thanks, but no gals, no towels, no food, no blow jobs, bye, bye.' He shut the door smiling from ear to ear and added, 'What a place.'

They went down to the bar and met three other guys who were also there for the Survival School. Two were Air Force C-130 pilots and one was an Army flight surgeon. The three soldiers were from Vietnam, while the Air Force pilots had orders to Vietnam. The five decided to pal up on their first excursion into town the next day.

24 December, 1968
Angeles City, the Philippines

After breakfast, James and Smoot walked around the hotel. All the Christmas decorations made them homesick. They saw a beautiful pool, which had round-eyed girls[6] sunbathing.

'Probably stewardesses,' thought James.

The two soldiers decided to change and take a swim. Outside they sipped on some kind of blue drink with fruit punch and little umbrellas.

'I hope we don't see anybody we know drinking these things,' said James. 'It wouldn't be so bad for me, but a Snake driver? Are you sure Cobra drivers can drink these things?'

'Give me a break, James; I didn't even know what I was ordering.'

That evening the pilot roommates got together with their new buddies and instead of venturing into town, they decided to spend Christmas Eve at the Officers' Club on the base.

They arrived by taxi. They heard loud music coming from a party going in the main dining room. They went up to the bar and from time to time would peek in the main dining room. Some wives from the party noticed the five stranded, obviously very lonely guys on Christmas Eve. The young officers at the bar were invited to join their party. The fivesome was immediately made to feel welcome. They were introduced to several Air Force officers and their wives and children. The five felt real good to be around families on Christmas Eve.

As the night went on, they learned tomorrow was not apt to be a good day for them. Everything was closed. They learned the club would be closed on Christmas Day and that the Holiday Inn restaurant would be closed in the evening. Hotel guests were expected to go into the hotel kitchen and make their own sandwiches during dinner.

Learning this, a Major John Kelly and his wife Loraine, sitting with the fivesome at their table, invited the men to their house for dinner on Christmas Day. This was unexpected and gracious. That evening at the Holiday Inn, the men bought flowers, a box of chocolates, a white Zinfandel and a Cabernet

Sauvignon. This way they wouldn't come empty-handed to the home of Major and Mrs John Kelly. They tried to buy something for the Kellys' two young children, but nothing suitable could be purchased at the hotel on Christmas Eve.

1800 hrs, 25 December 1968

Clark Air Base, the Philippines
The men arrived at the major's quarters in a colorful Philippine jitney. These colorful jeep trucks were the common taxis used in Angeles City. Each was decorative and brightly-painted but unique. They climbed in one that was a modified jeep truck with a round roof covering the bed. The covered bed had bench seats with cushions. The odd vehicle was painted red, white and blue, and had chrome and horns adorning the hood.

The major and his wife met them at the door and graciously accepted the gifts. Their military quarters were decorated with all the usual Christmas decorations. The guests were served eggnog with bourbon and the major wished everyone a very Merry Christmas. After a special Christmas blessing, they dove into a wonderful dinner of turkey with all the trimmings. Champagne was served, and the meal was topped off with pumpkin pie and whipped cream.

During dinner, they learned that Major Kelly drove B-52s[7] and had been to Vietnam a bunch of times. James noticed that his wife became uncomfortable when the conversation drifted to B-52 arc lights[8] and the dangers of flying in Vietnam. The major had been to Jungle Survival School and told everyone what to expect. He said, 'You will have two days in a classroom and two days in the jungle. The classroom is air-conditioned and nice. The jungle is not. The first day you will be supervised and learn how to find things to eat in the jungle. A sergeant will stay with you both days and the first night. On the second day, you will have one meal of C Rations.[9] The C Rations may seem as good to you, at the time, as Loraine's fine dinner we just had.' He turned to his wife and said, 'No offense, dear. I did say, at the time.'

She smiled back. Major Kelly continued, 'The first night you will sleep all together in whatever you can improvise. The second night you team up with someone and are on your own. You will simulate hiding in the bush. Each student will be given three tokens or chits. Negrito tribesmen will try to find you, and if they do, you must give them one chit. They will receive 5lb of rice for each chit they turn in. You will be evacuated by helicopter in the morning.'

'It doesn't exactly sound like a Boy Scout outing,' said James.

'Well, it's not that bad. It is strenuous, but you all look fit to me. You will all do fine.'

'How about cobras?' asked Jack. 'I may drive Cobras, but I sure as heck don't want to meet eyeball-to-eyeball with one.'

The major laughed and said, 'I wouldn't worry. You will be warned about them, but an encounter is rare. Actually I haven't heard of even one cobra sighting in the school.'

The evening ended on an emotional note as Mrs Kelly gave each man a hug and kiss. She told everyone to be very careful and said, 'God bless each and every one of you, and I pray that He allows you all to return safely to your loved ones.'

The men thanked them both and had watery eyes as they left the home of these fine people.

1800 hrs, December 26-29
Angeles City, the Philippines

The next few days were spent shopping, eating at excellent restaurants and swimming daily in the pool. James bought Army aviator wings carved out of mahogany from a shop in town. He also bought a similarly carved Siamese cat. For the Div Arty Recreation room, he bought a brass spittoon. 'They'll love it,' he thought.

Mau Mau Club
Angeles City, the Philippines

That evening 'The Fab Five', as they now called themselves, were joined by another Army aviator, Joe Thomas. Thomas was a short, trim, fixed-wing pilot that flew generals around Vietnam in a Cessna King Air. 'The-Fab-Five-Plus-One' asked the desk clerk for advice about a good supper club. He called over a jitney driver named Kim who was having coffee and reading the paper. Kim said, 'You must go see the Mau Mau Club. First-class place, all GIs like this place. You must see.'

They loaded up in his jitney and off they went.

The place was hopping; music was blaring all the way outside in the parking lot. The door was guarded by a big guy who greeted them with a nod as they entered. They were directed to a round table and seated. Immediately girls came from all directions, just like at the Saigon Vietnamese Officers' Club, to sit on their laps. They shooed the girls away.

The Mau Mau was full of Americans, mostly single young servicemen, but some, surprisingly, had what appeared to be dates, girlfriends or wives with them. Some of the patrons were dancing. A stand-up comedian told stale, off-color jokes between songs from a rock and roll band. The band was belting out 'Stop, children, what's that sound? Everybody…'

A drum roll brought a new man to the microphone. 'Ladies and gentlemen,' he said, 'welcome to the Mau Mau Club. The floorshow will now begin.'

Suddenly, bright flashing lights appeared on the dance floor. A woman came out and an obvious striptease began. It was a sleazy dance, sensual but not a very artful display of stripping. The Fab-Five-Plus-One was amazed when the striptease continued from the expected G-string or panties to where the young woman was wearing only her high-heeled shoes. What happened next flabbergasted the men.

Unbelievably, without using her hands or feet, she began to pick up fifty-piece centablo coins that were placed by customers on empty San Miguel bottles set up on the floor.

The announcer joked, 'Please do not heat up the coins for the Senorita with your lighter; it is most difficult for her to pick them up. Besides, she is hot enough already, ha, ha...'

As the announcer droned on, she proceeded to pick up the coins and deposit them in a basket. For a finale, she picked up a coin and the beer bottle together and danced around the floor one last time. She was given a standing ovation.

James thought to himself, 'New Jersey was never like this!'

The Fab-Five-Plus-One told each other that that show was unbelievable and sleazy. None of the shows the men saw in Vietnam involved naked women. They believed nothing could top that performance. They were wrong.

Joe Thomas was telling them he had seen a show that outdid this one. He began to describe a show he saw in Juarez, Mexico, when the manager interrupted him. The manager introduced himself and personally invited The-Fab-Five-Plus-One to a special show. The six men walked through two sets of doors into a backroom that looked like an arena. It had wooden bleachers all around a brown leather rectangular piece of furniture about the size of an executive desk.

'What gives?' asked Smoot.

'Haven't the foggiest,' said James.

The Army Flight Surgeon, Tom Swanson, said, 'Maybe we don't want to see this one.'

A large crowd of well-dressed people, mostly Americans, filtered into the arena-like room. When the crowd was seated, the lights dimmed and in walked a woman wrapped in a towel. This person was no beauty. She was chubby and short and certainly not the most attractive girl they had seen in the Philippines. One thing was crystal clear to the audience; she had to be naked underneath that towel. She lay down on the bench, removed her towel and displayed her nakedness. On cue, a Mr Joe Stud walked in, naked, and anatomically standing to attention. Quickly he jumped up onto the bench and, without so much as even a hint of foreplay, began the show. They moved together in a ritual demonstration of twenty-one positions. The movements were obviously practiced, athletic and polished to precision. No position lasted more than thirty seconds. It was a routine worthy of Olympic consideration.

The men watched the surreal spectacle in utter fascination. The graphic nature of the act left the audience wondering was it all real or an illusion?

The surreal scene was offensive but at the same time captivating in a bizarre, macabre sort of way. No matter what sensitivities were tweaked and what emotions were brought forth, for better or worse, it was an event that would be forever etched in the minds of the six men.

Swanson, the flight surgeon, was the most amazed of all. One position he thought was so unbelievable that he brashly went down the bleachers for a closer look in the middle of the performance.

'This is impossible,' the flight surgeon said, 'the man's appendage has to be at a 90-degree angle.'

The show was over in less than fifteen minutes. It ended in thunderous applause. James noticed when the lights came on that there were American women spectators in the audience.

'Who in the world would take their wife or date to a macabre display like this?' he wondered.

'Joe,' said James, 'now what were you saying about a show in Juarez?'

'Forget it,' said the Army fixed-wing pilot, 'I won't even tell my story; it wouldn't come anywhere close to topping that show.'

'Maybe I have led a sheltered life in I Corps,' said James, 'but I never saw anything like this in Vietnam.'

'Nor I,' each of the other Vietnam fliers echoed.

'Mom would never, in a million years, believe a place like this existed,' thought James.

31 December 1968
Angeles City, the Philippines

Kim, the jitney driver, wanted to take The Fab-Five-Plus-One back to the Mau Mau Club for New Year's Eve.

'Special show on New Year's Eve,' he said. 'GIs, you must go see.'

'This guy must have a piece of the action of business he brings to the Mau Mau,' thought James.

'No thanks,' said Crawley. 'We want to go to Old Town.'

Dr. Swanson said, 'A show that tops that one last night would have to involve animals or something.'

'That's more than I want to know,' said James.

They all climbed in Kim's jitney and drove down a busy main street in Old Town. It was full of shops, bars and restaurants. The street was hopping and reminded the men of Bourbon Street on Fat Tuesday. They saw jugglers and street musicians. Street merchants sold clothes, souvenirs and all kinds of things to eat. One of the Air Force pilots spotted a bar with a band playing jazz. The men went inside, drank San Miguel beer and listened to Duke Ellington's *Take the A Train*.

The six walked the streets, taking in the spectacle of New Year's Eve in Angeles City. Suddenly they jumped, startled by nearby fireworks set off by a 10-year-old boy who laughed at them.

'What's a matter, GI?' he said. 'You no like boom?'

'It's a Vietnam thing,' Smoot said somewhat angrily to the Air Force pilots who hadn't been to Vietnam.

The Air Force pukes shrugged their shoulders and the six walked down the strip. They came up to a street vendor selling dolls. She was a plain-looking, matronly-shaped woman with a large pair of breasts. Her outfit was not at all matronly, however. It consisted of hot pants and a sheer halter-top. Her halter-top left little to the imagination, barely containing her huge breasts.

'You GIs want to buy souvenir dolls for your Missy?' she said. 'I sell cheap. Come on now and look. They are nice, see?'

Bill Evans, one of the Air Force pilots, looked closely at the dolls. His inspection brought his face very close to the chest of the real live chubby Barbie with the Godzilla-like cleavage.

She noticed his look and said, 'I tell you what, GI? For only ten American dollar, I show you my tits.'

The men looked with sudden interest.

'Nah,' said Bill.

'All right, GI, five dollars.'

Evans pulled out a five and the men got a ten-second flash of her gargantuan mammary depositories.

'Holy mackerel,' said Smoot. 'She is, for sure, the mother of Godzilla.'

The six bar-hopped most of the night. They celebrated the last minute of the year on the street sharing a bottle of some kind of Philippine champagne they purchased earlier from a street vendor. It was not at all a dry wine, but was nice and cold. 'Happy New Year,' they said to each other.

Some 20 miles north of Clark Air Base

Approximately forty men had been bumped around in the backs of duce-and-a-halves[10] for two hours.

'It looks like the movie set from the movie *King Kong*,' said Thomas.

'I believe I've flown over it before in I Corps,' said James.

'I fly too high in my King Air; I never get to see anything.'

The men spent the day walking through the bush in teams of eight. Each team had two experienced Air Force sergeants showing the men edible plants, discussing how to eat bugs and find water. While they were resting, the men experienced a slight rumbling from the ground.

'Shit, this is an earthquake,' said James.

'Right,' said the instructor. 'Small earthquakes like this happen all the time. The volcano near Clark is active. At least that is what they tell me, and it gives off small quakes frequently.'

They camped in the jungle that night as a group with no shelter. Many of the men, especially James, were worried about snakes, especially cobras. The instructor told them to be sure no food was in their pockets unless it was in an unopened can or sealed in plastic.

'Gentlemen,' he said, 'rats are all around here in the jungle.'

'Who's afraid of rats?' someone said.

'Yeah,' said the instructor, 'it's not the rats so much, but what animal eats rats?' No one said a word.

James made a crude bunk out of tree branches that he placed in a low tree trying to form a platform. If possible, he wanted to be off the ground away from rats and snakes. He slept in the tree but was uncomfortable. Each man had a small tarp, a parachute-half, a jacket and a survival vest. It was a cool, miserable night. They hardly slept a wink.

The next day, the two were assigned to be a buddy team to hide and sleep together in the jungle. The two evaluated hiding places and strategies to move stealthily and hide that night in the jungle.

In the late afternoon, the men were given a meal of C Rations, which tasted delicious just as Major Kelly said it would. Before releasing them, the sergeant warned that the only fatalities in this school had been due to men walking around at night and falling off the steep cliffs. He wanted everyone to find a hiding place before it got dark and not risk walking around at night. The men paired up and went off to hide. The student pairs scattered into the jungle.

James and Joe headed off toward the north with several others. They continued past where many of the other pairs stopped. The two Army pilots reached a meadow of 7ft-high elephant grass. As Joe led and went forward, James pushed the grass back in place behind them to mask their path as they were taught in the school. The grass was so thick that even in the daytime it was difficult to see more than a few feet ahead. They moved through the heavy grass for more than thirty minutes.

'Surely no Negrito tribesman will find us here,' said James, 'and we would be able to hear him coming from a long way off.'

'Hmm, that's right; we should be safe here.'

They trampled down a wide area in the grass to provide ample room to sleep and to make it easier for the helicopters to see them in the morning. It became chilly as night blanketed the jungle. Both men put on their field jackets.

Thomas, at 5ft 6in, managed to get his parachute-half and poncho covering him from head to toe. James was taller than his friend and couldn't wrap up all the way as he did. James elected to have his feet stick out of his bedroll.

'If a snake bites me,' James rationalized to himself, 'I'd rather have him do it in the foot.'

The sounds of the jungle came alive at night. The most disturbing ones were those made by small critters moving through the grass.

'Rats or something worse?' James thought, as he listened to the nighttime jungle sounds. 'I'll opt for rats.'

The pair had only jungle survival knives to protect them. Thomas managed to fall asleep. James could not. He looked up at the starry sky. There was no moon. The dark night sky was breathtaking. It was thick with twinkling stars and bright planets. He saw more stars than he had ever seen before. The Milky Way spread across the sky like a veil.

'It's beautiful; breathtaking,' thought James. 'It was worth the trip just to see this. Is the sky this pretty in Nam?'

He heard a noise, different from before. The sounds seemed to be coming toward them. 'What is that?' James asked himself. He whispered, 'Joe, wake up; someone or something is coming.'

Thomas sat up and listened. He whispered, 'Be real quiet, Darryl and maybe he or it won't find us.'

Both men sat quietly, suddenly frightened. A small shadow revealed itself at the edge of the elephant grass. The shadow moved gracefully toward them. Both men sat frozen as a Negrito boy, no more than 12 years old, walked up to them in the pitch black. He was clad only in shorts and sandals in the chilly night.

'Surely a boy isn't one of the men looking for us,' thought James.

'Hi,' he said politely, in good English.

'Hi,' the men replied.

'What's going on?' Thomas asked him.

'Not much.'

'Do you live around here?'

'Yes,' he said. 'My family lives not too far away in a small village. I heard you walking near me, and I thought I would walk up to see you.'

It became apparent he was not one of the chit hunters, but merely a boy who wanted to see the men spending the night on the land he knew so well.

The men and boy talked for a couple of hours. It was almost light. They gave him everything that was left from the C Rations. Joe gave him a small pocketknife and items from their survival vest that they wouldn't need. James gave him his parachute half. The young boy thanked them and wished them well. The men did the same. The soldiers heard him retreating through the elephant grass the same way he came in.

'He's been around this block once or twice before,' thought James.

As dawn broke, they saw helicopter lights in the distance. Two H-34s were flying in a loose formation toward them. The men spread the remaining parachute half out on the ground so the choppers could see them. As the H-34s got closer, the two Army pilots popped a flare. One of the helicopters saw the flare and parachute-half and turned toward them.

The two had mashed down a large enough grass area for the helicopter to land; otherwise, they would have to be pulled up on a line as the chopper hovered above them. The Air Force H-34 landed and they jumped in.

'Well, what do you know?' James sat in the back of the H-34 and thought, 'Ha, two Army pukes are the first rescued and we have all of our chits. Ha ha, so much for the Air Force.'

They landed at the school and turned in their equipment. They relaxed with their friends and ate the refreshments the school provided for them in the classroom. Soon a bus took them back to their hotel in Angeles City. School was over, but they were too weary to do anything but sleep.

'Tomorrow it's back to Vietnam,' thought James as he drifted off to sleep. 'I am kind of looking forward to it.'

0750 hrs, 4 January 1969
Ky Ha Heliport

James strapped into his assigned OH-23G.

'I've been away only two weeks, but somehow the Hiller feels kind of strange. Somehow, it seems bigger.'

He started the small chopper and pulled up on the collective to bring it to a hover in the confines of the revetment. The hover was jerky and dangerous with its vulnerable tail rotor close to the revetment's 55-gallon drums and sandbags. The combat pilot was over-controlling the aircraft, like a student in flight school. Instantly, James broke out in a nervous sweat. Alarmed, he roughly slipped the helicopter out of the revetment. He was shaken and suddenly unconfident.

'Shit,' he thought, 'have I forgotten how to fly in just two and one half weeks? Have I lost my edge? Get a grip, hotshot; settle down.'

The pilot was spooked, wondering if he had lost his sharpness after the lay-off. He taxied over to the active and took off. In the air, James settled down, thinking he was over his sudden bout of paranoia. He felt his confidence returning.

The pilot's first approach was to a Montanyard mountaintop outpost in the mountains south-west of Chu Lai. The approach was shallow and amateurish. He had to add heavy power during the landing. He took off with a passenger and headed north-west. James relaxed as he cruised at 1,800ft and settled in. Bit by bit his confidence returned. Mid-morning, he shot a fine approach to a narrow ridge on top of a mountaintop called LZ Baldy.

James had a couple of months of solo combat flying, but was still a low-time helicopter pilot with 400 hours, 220 of which were in flight school. Today he learned a valuable lesson; a lesson about himself and his abilities. A combat pilot flying 100 hours a month becomes sharp. The helicopter acts as if it was an extension of his body. Hovering in revetments, approaches to mountaintops, spiraling into tight confined areas were performed without a concern about the mechanics of doing them. This morning James felt cocky; now he felt like a beginner.

To survive, a pilot had to know his limitations and the limitations of the aircraft. Each day, flying was different, filled with perils. There were countless ways to die here. You took each day, one at a time.

Chapter 10

Scouting in Indian Country

Div Arty Operations
0800 hrs, 18 January 1969

Captain Warren Fuller, Div Arty Operations S-3, and Sergeant Jenkins sat at a desk working on the morning's hook[1] schedule. Across the small room at another desk Major Fulton, Div Arty Air Section Head, put a phone in its cradle and stared at the ceiling for a moment. He then looked over at Captain Fuller and said, 'Warren, we have a new mission this morning. It might be a rough one.'

Fuller and Sergeant Jenkins looked up at the major with concern.

'I want you to take two armed 23s[2] up to LZ Baldy and pick up Marine AOs[3] from the 11th Regiment. The Marines need to recon the rocket belt west of Baldy. There has been a flurry of rocket attacks hitting there and around Da Nang. It could be hairy!'

'Yes, Sir,' replied Fuller.

'Ask Captain Bryant to go with you.'

'Bryant? He's too short.[4] He's heading home in a couple of weeks.'

'I know, but you two are my most experienced pilots and this mission could be dangerous. I need both of you, and Bryant, well, he wouldn't miss this mission for anything.'

'Roger that, boss.'

'Sergeant, send a runner up to get Captain Bryant and to meet me at the flight line ready for combat.'

'Yes, Sir.'

Fuller grabbed his Thompson 45-caliber machine gun from behind his desk and stood up. He loved that gun. It was not standard issue here in Vietnam and no one was quite sure how he got it. Rumors had it that he traded some Marine puke an AK-47 and a bloody NVA flag that was manufactured in the village for the gun.

He walked to the next room, got his chicken-plate and helmet, and walked down to the flight line. He was met by Lieutenant John Duffy, Div Arty's Maintenance Officer.

'Duff, I need two ships with crew chief door-gunners. What you got?'

Duffy looked at his notes and said, '423 and 451 are not assigned this morning. Let me get Palmer and Johnson to mount M60s.[5] They will be excited to go with you.'

'It might get hairy; better ask for volunteers.'

'You kidding? The crew chiefs would never let anyone else go with their ships.'

Captain Bryant came running down with his chicken-plate, helmet and carrying his M16. He had a bandolier of ammo draped over his shoulder and a 45-caliber pistol strapped to his waist. He was fully garbed for combat.

'Warren, what's up?' he asked, out of breath.

'We are picking up a couple of Marine pukes at LZ Baldy and going hunting. You game?'

'I'm always game, but never gamey,' he chuckled. 'We leave that to our Mr. Booth.'

Baby-face CW2 Tim Booth was one of Div Arty Air's characters. Liked to cuss and sometimes made his presence known with his body odor.

Twenty minutes later, Fuller and Palmer hovered to the active. Fuller pressed the switch on his cyclic and said, 'Ky Ha Tower, Phoenix Zero–Niner and Zero–Eight are ready for take-off.'

'Zero–Niner, your flight of two is cleared for take-off. Active is to the east.'

'Roger, we will be turning north after take-off.'

The OH-23Gs stayed below 200ft until they cleared the fast-mover's control zone then climbed to 2,000ft and followed Highway One to LZ Baldy, which was located on the highway south of Da Nang. Fuller reported in and landed on a beat-up asphalt tarmac away from the sole east-west runway. He shut the helicopter down. Two Marines carrying M2 carbines came running over. A Marine first lieutenant walked up, ducking below the slowly turning rotor blade to Fuller's chopper.

'Captain, I think we're your rides today.'

Fuller stuck out his hand, 'Roger that, Warren Fuller, and my gunner is Dave Palmer.'

'I'm Bill Jarkowski, nice to meet you guys.'

'Climb in and strap in, Bill.'

The lieutenant climbed in with a folded tactical contour map, an M2 carbine and a bandolier of ammunition. He struggled in finding space to store all his stuff in the small cockpit. He finally got strapped in and put on the spare flight helmet Fuller provided. The other Marine jumped into Bryant's idling chopper.

Lieutenant Jarkowski unfolded the map and showed the planned flight path along the river up into the hills. Fuller nodded in agreement on the track.

He keyed his radio switch on the cyclic, 'Zero–Eight, have you been briefed on the assigned route and are you familiar with the area?'

'Roger, Zero–Nine. Let's go hunting!'

Fuller replied yes from his collective switch with double-squelch clicks.

Jarkowski laid the carbine across his lap with the muzzle pointing out the open door. Fuller cranked up his chopper and the flight of two departed west over the foothills in front of the triple-canopy mountains. Fuller led, with Bryant following behind. When they reached a narrow fast-moving river, they turned north-west following it up into the foothills. The two ships low-leveled along the riverbank at 80 knots, varying their flight paths, weaving back and forth avoiding straight-line flight paths, making it difficult for any enemy elements to get shots at predictable helicopter movements.

They came around a bend in the river near a small village and buzzed across a group of women washing their clothes and bathing nude.

'What a sight,' thought Fuller.

'Zero-Eight, I'm going to come around and get another look. I'm not positive but I thought I saw some Vietnamese "knockers" staring at me as I flew across. Thought I'd better double-check.'

'Roger that, Zero-Niner, it was a sight for sore eyes. A sight I hope to see again when I am back in the world a week from Tuesday.'

They dropped below the trees, turned steeply 180 degrees and skimmed the surface of the water to make another pass on the women. The women waved as they flew by, with some standing proudly bare-chested as they waved.

They turned back along the rocket belt route looking for small clearings, trails, bicycle paths or debris of any sort from the moving of 123mm Soviet-style rockets. They followed the river into the hills and jungle, weaving back and forth over the treetops. Fuller looked ahead with Palmer and Jarkowski staring out their respective doors.

Palmer keyed his intercom switch, 'Captain, I saw a reflection, something shiny out the right door.'

'Zero-Eight, we saw something.'

Fuller turned sharply right and swung back along their path. Jarkowski keyed the intercom switch on his cyclic, 'I thought I saw movement in the trees.'

'Shit, triple-canopy jungle, I can't see the ground.'

They circled the area again, but saw nothing.

'Might have been binoculars or something shiny on a bicycle,' said Jarkowski. 'I'll note the spot on my map.'

They worked both sides of the river for 30 kilometers and saw nothing. They turned to go back to LZ Baldy to refuel. They chatted in anticipation as they approached the horseshoe bend in the river near the village with the bathing women. Low-leveling around the big bend, they stared in amazement. The village and river were now completely empty. No women, kids, water buffalos or any village activity.

'What the...?' said Jarkowski.

'Zero-Eight, I don't like this,' said Fuller. 'Could be an ambush. I'm rolling left.'

'Roger, we have you covered.'

Fuller pulled back on the cyclic and rolled left in a steep turn just as VC machine guns opened up. Green tracers flew by the right door with Palmer helpless to return fire with his M60 staring up at the sky. They heard THUD, THUD as two rounds hit the right lower canopy. Palmer's right foot kicked forward. 'I'M HIT,' he yelled over the intercom.

More rounds hit the engine and the chopper struggled to climb and get away from the area. Meanwhile, Zero-Eight trailing thirty seconds behind found itself in a perfect position to return fire. Bryant turned slightly left to put Johnson who was on the right side of the aircraft in position to return fire with his M60. Johnson let loose with several three-second bursts, which shut down the VC firing.

Fuller called 'Mayday', and gave their position as 20 clicks north-west of LZ Baldy along the river. The chopper fought on for several minutes before the engine quit. Fuller slammed the collective down and entered autorotation, landing hard on a sandy point bar in the meandering river. Zero-Eight circled, covering the downed chopper.

Pelican Two-Three, a re-supply slick,[6] had just departed LZ Baldy. They answered the Mayday call and turned north-west from LZ Baldy. Five minutes later, Pelican Two-Three saw the circling OH-23G and landed on the river bar behind the stricken OH-23G. They picked up the threesome and called for another slick to haul the wounded 23 out of the riverbank.

Palmer's foot was bloodstained so Pelican Two-Three flew directly to the hospital at Da Nang. The following day Fuller and Tim Booth flew to Da Nang to see how Palmer was doing and learned that the bullet went through his foot and did NOT break any bones.

They found Sergeant Palmer with his foot suspended. A purple heart was pinned to the pillow.

'Palmer, you lucky S.O.B., I hear they are medevac'ing you to Los Angeles.'

'Yep, in a couple of days.'

'No worries, we will get all your stuff packed up and shipped home. I heard you got to talk to your parents.'

Booth said, 'The guys say hello; they'll see you back in the world.'

Palmer just grinned, rolled up his nose and replied, 'Booth, you stink.'

Chapter 11

Happy Hour: TINS Time

Americal Division Artillery Officers' Club
1745 hrs, 11 January 1969

It was Happy Hour in Chu Lai. Tonight most of the OH-23G drivers sat at the Div Arty Officers' Club with their favorite beverage in hand. One of the benefits here, if one could accept that there might be benefits to being in Vietnam, was the bar fare. It was 25 cents for a Dewar's and water, the pilots' drink of choice. You couldn't find Happy Hour prices like that anywhere.

No American bills or coins were supposed to be used by the US military in Vietnam. The currency consisted of Military Payment Certificates. The money was called many things by the soldiers: MPC, Military Script, Funny Money or Monopoly Money. The brightly-colored military money didn't look real, but it worked just like the real thing.

The Div Arty pilots in their worn, baggy jungle fatigues sat down at a large round table to play liar's dice to see who would pay for a round of drinks.

'Hey, what's for dinner tonight, James?' asked Lieutenant Lee Leffert.

'Chu Lai Steak,' replied the lieutenant, not looking up. He knew Leffert was trying to gig him a little. Leffert knew what was for dinner. Everyone knew because it was always the same, or nearly so: roast beef or some variation of it. James hated the roast beef. He used to love it, but getting the same thing over and over got old. Moreover, unfortunately, this roast beef was not his Mom's roast or even the roast served in a nice Stateside restaurant. The Div Arty pilots called the Club's roast beef CHU LAI STEAK.

Chu Lai steak is prime-cut cow butt from maybe Japan, or who knows where? It certainly didn't come from Wyoming, Kansas or Texas. If it did, the poor cow had to swim all the way here to get that tough.

James didn't order roast beef during his Philippine Christmas-time soirée to Jungle Survival School or at his R&R in Hawaii. Like most of the pilots, James hated the food at the Div Arty Officers' Club. The pilots ate virtually all their breakfasts and dinners at the Club, but every other Mess in the Division, it seemed, had better food.

'It must be like the old saying,' thought James, 'grass is greener across the street.' 'Nah,' thought the pilot, 'the food here sucks.'

This food or any food, on the other hand, didn't bother Leffert. He ate anything. Leffert was skinny as a rail but ate like someone twice his size. He drove his buddies crazy, not because he ate a lot but because he ate slowly and methodically, one anal-retentive bite at a time. Leffert often went back for seconds and sometimes thirds and took seemingly all day to eat. There was no way to embarrass or cajole him into speeding up either. They had tried.

Happy Hour often spawned storytelling: one of the favorite pastimes of the pilots. The pilots' tales, or TINS as they called them, were an important part of the culture and entertainment at Div Arty Air. The young men loved to tell stories, especially flying stories. The TINS were also a way of learning from each other's experiences and mistakes. Flying alone as they did, the tales sometimes didn't get out quickly.

Nevertheless, secrets were hard to keep at Div Arty Air and the important TINS were always told. Once someone started a story, others often poured out, making for a lively evening. It was like that this night.

Captain James Fuller, Div Arty's Section Leader, slowly pulled out three big fat cigars from his shirt pocket. Everyone watched as he passed one to the Flight Surgeon Doctor Cruz, who bit off the end of his stogie and lit up. Fuller did the same. Almost as an afterthought, Fuller handed the remaining stogie to Lieutenant Connor Dotson.

Fuller asked him, 'And how was your day, HONEY?'

'Huh?' he replied as everyone laughed, making him blush.

'Doc tells me,' said Fuller, 'that you got to peek up some cute young girl's skirt today. Is that right?'

Doc and Fuller smiled from ear to ear. The other pilots looked up curiously, wondering what in the world was going on.

'Well, yeah,' he said, a bit sheepishly.

'Well tell us, HONEY,' said Leffert. 'Tell us.'

Chapter 12

The Stork Flies to Div Arty Air

Earlier That Afternoon

'LIEUTENANT DOTSON, LIEUTENANT DOTSON,' yelled Johnson.

Staff Sergeant Willy Johnson was a lean, handsome African-American with a shaved head. He loved that 'look' and claimed it was not only a good 'look', but also cool in the tropical, humid climate of Vietnam.

'What's up, Willy?'

'Lin is sick.'

'What do you mean, sick? Sick like in throwing up, sick?'

Lin, the crew chiefs' hootch maid, was pregnant and pretty far along.

'She said she is going to have a baby.'

'We know she is going to have a baby, Willy. Everyone knows that. You mean she is going to have a baby, like today?'

'YES, YES,' Johnson said. 'NOW! I MEAN LIKE RIGHT FUCKING NOW!'

The three men took off in a run to the crew chiefs' hootches located across the road from the flight line. While all three men were running, Dotson decided to send Sergeant Perkins to the Admin Company Office.

'Perkins,' he said, out of breath, 'go get the duty driver and quarter-ton, we might need to get her to the hospital.'

'Right, Sir,' he said as he peeled off to the left.

The two remaining men continued running to the hootches. They rushed in the door and found Lin lying on one of the bunks. Sid Jones, one of the crew chiefs, held her hand. She cried out in pain, freezing Dotson in his tracks.

Dotson patted her forehead and said, 'It's OK Lin, Perkins is getting a jeep. We'll take you to the hospital.'

She relaxed as the spasm passed and smiled at him. In her eyes, Dotson saw a frightened, pretty, teenage girl reaching out desperately for help. To her, he was the head guy here: the Big Enchilada, as they would say in his hometown of Stephenville, Texas. The Big Enchilada was scared too. He had no earthly idea how to help, other than take her to the hospital. His only experience with this was when his wife, Nita, had their son, Connor Wade Dotson, at Fort Hunter. All he did was take Nita to the hospital when it was time, sit out in the waiting room until it was all over and pass out cigars.

Perkins and the jeep pulled up outside and he and the driver rushed in. The men gently helped Lin up from the bunk. They tried to pick her up. She shrugged them off and walked gingerly to the jeep.

'She's OK, Lieutenant. She's walking and everything. There is plenty of time; there is no problem at all. We will just take her over to the Chu Lai Hospital...'

Suddenly, Lin screamed!

'Oh shit,' thought Dotson.

He helped her into the right front seat and jumped in the back behind her. He rubbed her shoulders to comfort her. Johnson climbed alongside the lieutenant and held her hand. Dotson told the driver, who stood stunned like his feet were cemented in the pavement, to get moving. The driver jumped in and started the engine. The jeep pulled out and head south, driving fast on the two-lane black-top road.

Lin relaxed and leaned back in the seat. Dotson let go of her shoulders and sat back in his seat. Suddenly, she cried out again. The men all jerked up at the scream. The jeep swerved in the road and then came back straight. Then it swerved again as the driver screamed, 'LIEUTENANT, SHE'S ALL WET, REAL WET, EVEN THE JEEP'S ALL FUCKING WET!'

Distracted by this new, frightening development, the driver lost control of the jeep. It swerved off the pavement onto the shoulder and into a field. Lin screamed as they bounced across a ditch and slid out of control onto the grass. The driver slowed the vehicle, turned right into the direction of the skid, and regained control. He turned the jeep back onto the pavement.

'SHIT, ARE YOU TRYING TO KILL US?' Dotson yelled.

Lin screamed again, louder than before, 'IT'S COMING; DA BABY'S COMING.' Dotson now took his turn at getting hysterical and screamed, 'PULL OFF THE ROAD, NOW.'

The driver pulled over to the side of the road and came to a quick, jerky stop. The men jumped out and ran around the jeep to her side. She blabbered something in Vietnamese, oblivious to their presence. They grabbed her and gently turned her around until she faced out of the jeep's seat. Her black baggy pants were soaking wet.

She screamed again, 'HE'S COMING! HELP ME PLEASE, LOU-TEN-ANT.'

Dotson took off his shirt and told Johnson and the driver to do the same. He laid his shirt down and they gently took Lin from the seat and laid her on the ground on the crew chief's shirt. She tightened in another contraction. They waited a moment and then pulled off her baggy black pants. They immediately saw the baby's head crowning in the vagina. She screamed again with another contraction. Dotson watched as the baby's head came further out. She paused, breathed in a rapid animal-like panting and screamed again. This push did it and, like the miracle it was, a brand-new baby squirted out into Dotson's hands.

They cleaned off the baby's face with Johnson's shirt and after a few seemingly long moments, it cried, weakly at first and then strongly.

Johnson said, 'It's a boy, Lin, you have a son.'

They wrapped the baby in the driver's shirt and lifted the mother and baby, still connected by the umbilical cord, into the jeep. They drove off in the direction of the hospital.

Dotson grabbed the driver's shoulder and said, 'Wait a minute, turn here.'

The jeep slowed and then turned right.

'Let's go to the Division Artillery Aid Station,' said the lieutenant, 'it's closer.'

After the longest ten minutes of their lives, they reached Div Arty's Aid Station. Johnson leaped out of the still-moving jeep and rushed in. Out came two corpsmen pushing a gurney. One of the corpsmen inserted an IV into Lin's arm and called someone on the telephone. Fifteen minutes later, Doc Cruz rushed in and took over. Dotson, Johnson and the driver collapsed on the chairs in the outside room, neither man talking or moving.

Doc came out thirty minutes later and said, 'Lin and her son are just fine. Gentlemen, you did great. I am damn proud of you. An ambulance is on the way. The hospital folks want to look them over, but I am sure they are fine.'

The three sweaty bloodied men in olive-drab T-shirts smiled broadly.

'Oh, and guys,' said the Doc, smiling, 'Lin wants to see you three gentlemen.' He pointed to the backroom.

The men got up and entered the doorway. Lin was lying on a bunk covered by a sheet with her new son cuddled in her arms. She released her right arm and gestured to Johnson. 'Willy, come here.'

He leaned over and she planted a kiss on his cheek and said, 'Tank you Willy.' She rubbed his shiny shaved head. 'Willy, please tell Lin why you no grow hair on you head. Look, even my Baby san has hair. You head is like this new babe-ee's butt.' She giggled and added, 'Remember this, Willy, all girl like-ee hair.'

She next motioned to the jeep driver who, like Johnson, had tears in his eyes. She planted a kiss on his cheek, too. 'Sorry Lin and Baby-san ruin you nice shirt. Tomorrow, Lin wash for you.'

'That's not necessary, and besides, Lin, you need a day off.'

She gestured for Dotson and said, 'Lou-ten-it, please come too.'

He leaned over her, but didn't get close. He really didn't know Lin. He had only seen her a time or two in the crew chiefs' hootches. With surprising strength, she pulled Dotson to her and planted a kiss on his cheek.

'You num-ber one Lou-ten-it, boo-koo num-ber one. Tank you.'

'Honey, that was so sweet,' said Fuller. 'You really are a nice guy, in spite of what everyone around here says.' Everyone laughed.

Captain Fuller, the section leader, said to the pilots sitting around the coffee table in the bar, 'Girls, let's roll the dice for another round of drinks. There is plenty of time before dinner. Anyone know anything?'

'Well,' said Lieutenant Birmingham, 'I got an interesting call on the fox mike today at the Ops hut.'

Everyone turned to Birmingham, the unit's Operations officer.

'The XO out on LZ East called,' said Birmingham, 'to report a Twenty-three doing aerobatic maneuvers. I had to question him real close because I never thought a Raven could do AEROBATIC MANEUVERS.'

He paused for effect and looked around until he had everyone's undivided attention.

'Well,' he continued, 'the XO said that a Twenty-three was doing spins and twisty-turnee kinds of things, real low and slow-like, across his firebase. He didn't much like it because all his people stopped what they were doing and had to watch the show. He said his folks are lazy anyway, and he sure didn't need a Blue Angel act above his hill, good air show or not. The XO added that his First Sergeant was especially pissed getting his people's work interrupted like that and everything. Nevertheless, the sergeant was apparently real impressed.'

'The XO added that he didn't know much about flying, but it looked kind of dangerous to him. He was surprised because he thought only the Blue Angels always did stuff that looked that dangerous. The XO mentioned that it would be great if I could fix it so the Old Man could ride in the chopper for the next show. They would like to do something nice for the Old Man and give him a thrill.'

Birmingham paused again and smiled before saying, 'It must get boring up there on the hill.'

Birmingham then continued, 'Anyway, the XO asked me to check into it. I told him right off that we didn't have any Blue Angel-rated guys here, but I would try to find out which unit did and maybe I could get tickets for our entire section to watch next time.'

'Guys,' he added, 'it's got to be better than Bob Hope. Don't you think?'

'Anyway,' he continued, 'guys, I got to checking and it seems that only one of Div Arty's pilots was anywhere near LZ East today and that was Mr Lincoln.'

Everyone in the group but CW2 Lincoln rolled on the floor, laughing their butts off. Eyes turned toward the pilots' table. The Div Arty Air Group was creating a disturbance in the club and getting stern looks from a nearby group of non-rated Division field-grade types. Fuller hushed everyone down. When the room was quiet, he said softly, 'Mr Lincoln,' he paused, then continued, 'and what did you do at the office today?'

'Huh? Oh, ah, well,' said Lincoln, uncomfortably, 'ah, I did have a problem this afternoon.'

Chapter 13

Aerobatics on LZ East

Earlier That Afternoon

Sergeant Johnson strapped Mr Lincoln into the Raven and wished him luck. He checked in with Ky Ha tower and hovered to the active. Receiving clearance, he departed south over the South China Sea. Lincoln banked sharply left, descended down to 20ft and low-leveled over the bay and nearby fishing village. It was a nice, warm wintertime afternoon. Below him, he saw lots of fishing and crabbing taking place in the Chu Lai bay from fishermen in round reed boats.

Link, as his buddies called him, low-leveled across the marshes at a magnetic heading of 300 degrees. The helicopter flushed out nesting waterfowl as it sped overhead. The pilot's heading would lead him to Highway One just south of his destination, Hill 54. Lincoln banked sharply right over the highway and followed it north a short distance to Hill 54. He popped up sharply to an altitude of 500ft, circled once around the hill, and landed on a sandbag landing-pad, feeling sharp and frisky.

A lowboy truck moved toward the idling chopper with all kinds of gear on it.

'Now, where in the hell are they going to put all that stuff in my helicopter?' he thought.

Two bare-chested soldiers walked up to him. One said, 'Sir, we were told that you would take this stuff to LZ East.'

'OK,' yelled Lincoln over the noise of the idling chopper. 'It may take me two trips.'

They piled on boxes of small arms, a mail sack and boxes of who-knows-what in the right seat. They carefully strapped everything in with the seatbelt and rubber tie-down hooks. In the left seat, they had some kind of survey equipment, bundles of heavy-duty cotton rope and a large cargo net with a hook attached. They strapped the gear down and gave him the thumbs-up signal.

'Great, they fit everything in,' thought Lincoln. 'One trip and I am out of here. It's a big load. Need to be careful and make real sure this old gal can still hover with all this gear on board.'

He wouldn't want to be overloaded when landing on LZ East. The mountaintop LZ was on a sharp, knife-edge ridge with heavily-wooded steep slopes on both sides. Landing on the high, narrow ridge was tricky, especially with a heavy load. Lincoln would need plenty of contingency power to land with a margin of safety.

The warrant officer carefully picked up the loaded Raven to a hover. It hovered easily and the center of gravity felt fine, telling him he would have adequate power to land safely on the mountaintop.

'No problem…a piece of cake.'

He departed into the wind and turned north along Highway One climbing at 500ft per minute to an altitude of 2,000ft. He passed the province capital city of Tam Ky off to his left and noticed schoolchildren playing soccer in the large athletic field on the south side of the city. Some 10 miles past Tam Ky, Lincoln veered north-west into the highland forest, leaving the relative sanctuary of Highway One. As he climbed, he saw puffy white cumulus clouds threatening to build into afternoon thunderstorms.

Entering a pass through the mountains, the Raven picked up moderate turbulence. The small helicopter, pilot and cargo bounced vigorously. Link looked around and visually checked the cargo.

'Hmm, everything looks OK,' thought the pilot.

One item wasn't. A heavy-duty cargo net used by the large Chinook cargo helicopters to sling load/cargo worked its way loose from its tie-down on the left seat. Some of the net reached the floor and worked its way in between the pedals on the floor of the empty co-pilot's seat.

Soon LZ East appeared directly ahead. The heavily-fortified position with six 105mm howitzers and two quad 50 machine guns stood out distinctly on the horizon. The men on the LZ lived and worked in buried bunkers constructed from heavy timbers and sandbags on the bald ridge. Triple-canopy jungle and steep slopes leading into broad valleys surrounded it.

Lincoln squeezed the trigger on his cyclic and said, 'Ranger Zero-Four, Phoenix One-Niner approaching from the east, request smoke, over.'

'Roger, One-Niner, smoke is coming, over.'

The pilot needed the smoke to judge the wind for landing. Winds were tricky on these mountaintops, dangerous to small, heavily-loaded helicopters.

Link squeezed his trigger and said, 'Zero-Four, I have purple smoke.'

'Roger, purple smoke,' crackled the radio.

The small helicopter circled to set up for a normal pinnacle approach into the wind. The warrant officer smoothly lowered collective, added right pedal and eased back the cyclic, skillfully slowing the Raven down to 50 knots.

The Raven slowed to 40 knots approaching the white landing-pad. Seconds from landing, a sudden downdraft, a common occurrence in the mountains, pushed the helicopter down, dangerously shallowing the approach angle. Lincoln immediately corrected by adding power with his collective and pushing in left pedal to counter the additional engine torque.

The left pedal didn't move. Without the left anti-torque pedal, the helicopter suddenly yawed sharply right, providing the pilot an unwanted view out the left open door of the cockpit. The Raven descended sideways toward the LZ a mere 50ft from his landing spot. Experiencing an almost debilitating burst of stark, abject terror, the pilot pulled up hard on the collective to clear the ridge. This stopped his descent, but it also caused the helicopter to spin 720 degrees in a clockwise direction. Link saw LZ East appear twice as he spun over the narrow ridge. The Raven spun lazily, as if in slow motion, off in the thin air on the north side of the mountain ridge. Soldiers on the ridge stopped what they were doing and watched the Raven spin off in amazement.

Once clear of the ridge, Lincoln lowered the collective to slow the spinning and lowered the nose slightly. The spinning slowed and stopped. With the nose now pointing forward, he lowered it to gain airspeed. Reaching 75 knots, the pilot trimmed pitch and roll with the electric button on his cyclic and applied friction to steady the collective. With the aircraft now stable, he took his left hand off the collective and reached over to the left side of the cluttered cockpit and worked the net free from the co-pilot's pedal. This took some doing: long arms or not on the tall, lanky pilot, he could barely reach down to the pedals. He had to stretch and carefully tug, pull and shake on the net to free it. After several minutes of straining, he freed it.

He leaned back, took a couple of deep breaths and tried to relax. Turning toward the coast, he looked at his shaking left hand and thought, 'Shit, nearly bought the farm on that one. I don't know if I can even land this thing on LZ East right now. Screw them and their net. It nearly killed me today; I am going home.'

Lincoln finished his version of the story to his pilots, who smiled at him. Fuller stood up and said with a grin, 'Now wasn't that special?'

Everyone chuckled.

Chapter 14

Retreating Blade Stall: One of Many Ways to 'SCREW THE POOCH'

Retreating blade stall is a hazardous flight condition in helicopters where the rotor blade with the smaller resultant relative wind exceeds the critical angle. Balancing lift across the rotor disc is important to a helicopter's stability. In forward flight, the advancing blade has a higher airspeed than the retreating blade, creating unequal lift across the rotor disc. Excessive airspeed and/or turbulence can cause the aircraft to have retreating blade stall and roll to the left.[1]

American Division Artillery Officers' Club
1745 hrs, 11 January 1969

Captain Warren Fuller, Div Arty's Section Leader, said, 'We heard some good TINS tonight, maybe one more, huh, guys?'

He slowly pulled out two big fat cigars from his shirt pocket. He bit off the end of his stogie and lit up.

Almost as an afterthought, Fuller handed the remaining stogie to Lieutenant James.

Fuller asked, 'And how was your day, HONEY?'

James kind of flushed, a bit embarrassed. 'Ah, how did? Ah, ah, ah,' he mumbled. 'Oh well. Guys, I kind of messed up today. I came a little close to screwing the proverbial pooch. I guess I got real lucky.'

'You're always lucky,' said Lieutenant 'Pops' Baker. 'Come on. Tell us the damn story.'

'Well guys, I had the payroll duty today and…'

Early That Morning
James had been assigned to take one of the lowly lieutenants in Division Artillery Headquarters, Jack Ford, to visit Americal's southern LZs. Jack was given the mundane role of Pay Officer for Division Artillery. He had to go around to the artillery battalions to pay any of the men requesting money. This happened every month.

Being the Pay Officer was a boring job. It was always assigned to a junior officer. The Division Artillery Command Staff was loaded with field grades, captains and not many lieutenants. The few that were there got all the crappy assignments. 'Shit details', they were called. Ford, an assistant to the Assistant S4[2] of Division Artillery Staff, acquired many of the 'shit details'.

Ford had been in Vietnam nine and a half months and was getting 'short'. Short-timers were cautious and didn't want to tempt fate. This was the reason he requested that Div Arty Air Ops have Lieutenant James fly him that day.

'I want James,' thought the Pay Officer. 'I heard he's real safe to fly with. After all, he is the Unit's Safety Officer, and James has the reputation for flying high, away from the small-arms fire? He's got to be the most careful and maybe safest guy there.'

Ford knew, from experience, that James flew high. One day flying north along Highway One with him, the pilot kept climbing and climbing. It was freezing in the open cockpit. The Pay Officer didn't know that James had put on long johns under his gray cotton flight suit.

James asked over the intercom to his shivering passenger, 'Jack, would you mind taking my Mamiya Sekor 1000 DTL that's hanging from the first-aid kit? I want you to take a picture of the altimeter.'

'Huh? Oh sure, no problem.'

'Pilots always take stupid pictures,' thought Ford, 'but who would take a picture of instruments?'

Ford didn't know James was participating in a goofy Div Arty Air contest as to who could fly the highest this week. James didn't win. He gave it a good shot and came in third with Ford's picture of his altimeter showing 12,650ft.

James and Ford flew south to several firebases that morning. They left LZ Professional and turned south along Highway One at an altitude of 1,800ft. Jack's next stop was 'the Rock'.

The Rock was a prominent feature sticking up from the rice paddies of the coastal plain. The narrow spire of basalt rock looked something like a huge pillar. It stuck up prominently near the Quang Nai River along Highway One. It was a sort of navigation aid to the pilots, who labeled it the 'marble VOR'.[3]

The lonely spire was the lava passageway of an ancient volcano. The volcanic cone that once surrounded the neck had long since weathered away from eons of rain and wind.

An important Division OP[4] was established on top of the rock. There was no room for a helicopter to land on top. A sandbag helicopter pad was built at the base of the structure. A narrow winding road led up to the outpost.

James, the passenger's hand-picked pilot, the so-called model of aviation safety, was feeling bored that morning with this rather dull taxi-driving assignment. After departing LZ Professional, James decided to give his passenger a little thrill and auto-rotate to the base of the Rock. The OH-23G had low rotor momentum. When the engine stopped and entered auto-rotation flight, the helicopter would drop abruptly.

James glanced left and looked at the unsuspecting passenger. He smiled and rolled off throttle, then abruptly lowered the collective and shoved in right pedal. The chopper dropped like a rock and had the desired effect on the short-timer passenger.

Ford screamed. His stomach felt like it fell off a cliff. Instinctively, he looked for something to grab on to. He put his knuckles around the doorframe and squeezed them so tightly they turned white. It took him several seconds before he regained enough composure to work the intercom switch.

'What happened?' he asked. 'Did we lose an engine?'

James laughed. After Ford realized he was not going to die, he started laughing and said, 'You sorry sack of shit, you know how short I am? Don't do something like that.'

James continued laughing as he turned 180 degrees to point the aircraft into the wind. Just before touchdown, he rolled on the throttle and checked the tachometer to ensure that he closed the rotor and transmission RPM needles and didn't over-rev the transmission or engine. With the needles closed, he pulled in collective to bring the chopper to a hover over the pad. The pilot landed smoothly and shut down, feeling cocky.

Ford, with a case full of money, jumped into a waiting jeep which took him up the hill. James got out of the helicopter to stretch his legs. Young boys came around waving Cokes to sell. The pilot declined, but let two boys sit in the helicopter and took the youngsters' picture.

'There is a good size crowd of kids now,' thought the pilot. 'Where in the heck do they all come from so fast selling Cokes and cigarettes?'

Ford soon returned and climbed in. The feisty pilot decided to give the young Vietnamese boys gathered around a demonstration of his flying prowess. As his passenger strapped in, James said, 'Jack, I am going to low-level around the Rock one time to give these young rascals a thrill, so hang on and try not to brown your panties this time.'

'OK James, no sweat,' he said, a bit nervously.

James lifted the Raven to a hover and accelerated smoothly through transitional lift, keeping the nose low and power applied. The aircraft accelerated rapidly to 80 knots. He low-leveled counter-clockwise around the base of the Rock. The chopper came around the hill and roared over the heads of the kids. The kids yelled and waved. They loved it. James continued circling the Rock. His airspeed indicator indicated he was at VNE,[5] the maximum safe speed for the helicopter, but he never looked at it. As he continued his turn, a sudden gust of wind blasted the aircraft, creating severe turbulence. The nose pitched up abruptly and the helicopter rolled left almost out of control. The tip-path plane of the main rotor came very close to the ground. They were mere seconds from disaster.

Flying was often described as 90 percent boredom and 10 percent stark terror. The Raven's pilot and passenger were on the 10 percent side of the graph. The young, cocky pilot had entered into retreating blade stall, a condition that could be fatal.

The helicopter's main rotor was cambered like a wing to create lift as it turned in a counter-clockwise direction. When the helicopter was moving forward, wind came across the rotor blades from front to back. The lift force on the forward-moving rotor blade on the right side of the helicopter was always greater than the retreating blade on the left side. This differential lift occurred in forward speed. The helicopter compensated for this lift unbalance by the rotor system's design. The rotor system automatically increased the pitch slightly for the retreating blade to balance left. A problem occurred, however, when the helicopter's airspeed became too high. The retreating blade on the left side reached a pitch angle where it could not compensate enough without stalling. When it stalled, it created a sudden differential loss of lift to the left side. This caused the helicopter to roll left, resulting in a sudden loss of control. Turbulence aggravated the problem.

The pilot's savior from impending disaster was his recent flight school training. He reacted correctly, lowered the collective, inserted right pedal and eased back on the cyclic. Immediately the helicopter leveled and slowed. As it slowed, it came back under the control of the pilot, whose vascular system was now flushed with adrenaline. The Raven climbed away from the Rock.

'Well, cowboy,' thought James, 'you nearly screwed the pooch. Retreating blade stall is one of those things you were never supposed to let happen. You were lucky this time. You may not be, if there is a next time.'

A speechless, thoroughly shaken-up passenger was thinking to himself, 'And James is their fly-by-the-book, safe-as-shit pilot? I am too short for this shit. Just forty-four days, a wake-up, and I am out of here.'

'Great story,' said Fuller, 'A little birdie from the S4 Shop told me a little something about this incident.'

He held up his drink and said, 'To survive here, a pilot must be lucky enough to learn from his mistakes; he'll make some.'

'Hear, hear,' echoed the pilots.

'Girls,' said Fuller, 'I for one have had enough of these lies. Let's play another round of liar's dice to see who pays for dinner.'

Every night they played liar's dice to see who paid for each round of drinks and for the 10-cent service charge every officer gave to the Club for the dinner meal.

They rolled. Fuller had to pay. 'Great,' thought James. 'It is about time.'

Chapter 15

How Many PACs Can You Stuff in an OH-23G?

Division Artillery Officers' Club
1900 hrs

Dave Chambers, Bill Broderick and Mark Birmingham were gathered around the ping-pong table at the Officers' Club watching Doc Cruz putting a whopping on Lieutenant James.

'Darryl, you are like a brick wall. You return everything I throw at you.'

'Yeah, yeah, yeah, Doc,' replied James. 'You are toying with me.'

Cruz was indeed toying with James as he put lots of expert spin on the ball as he moved it all around the table, making James scramble to return his shots.

'He's killing you,' said Birmingham.

'We need Leffert to take on, Doc.'

'Heck, he's no better than me.'

'He's better than you,' replied Birmingham.

'Yeah, yeah,' replied James. 'Speaking of Leffert, Doc, did you hear what he did today?'

'No,' replied the diminutive physician, as he won another game from James.

'You should have seen what he did today, maybe by accident, probably, because he is a "peaches and cream" kind of guy.'

'Now you have my attention. Lieutenant Leffert seems like a nice guy,' replied Cruz.

'He is. Well, Leff dropped off a snake-eater[1] at this RVN[2] compound. You know, one of those triangular fort-like compounds in the boondocks?'

'Yeah, yeah.'

'Well, here's what happened.'

1645 Hrs That Day
Twenty Clicks North-West of Tam Ky

Lieutenant Leffert's radio in his OH-23G came to life. 'Phoenix One-Four, this is Ops, over.'

'Ops, this is Phoenix One-Four, go ahead.'

'Phoenix One-Four, Caspar just called and they need to transport some PACs to Tam Ky, over.'

'Roger that, Ops, proceeding to Caspar just as soon as I drop these supplies off at LZ Buff, over.'

'Roger, Ops out.'

Leffert dropped off the supplies at Buff and headed toward Caspar.

He was the last pilot in their unit flying the older OH–23s. Their unit was transitioning the new OH–6 Light Observation Helicopters into the unit, but he had not been transitioned yet. It made no sense for the newer incoming pilots to be checked out in the OH–23 only to be transitioned again a few weeks later. He was not happy about it, but it made sense.

He reported into Caspar about 5 miles out. They acknowledged the transmission and stated the passengers were waiting at the compound gate. There was no landing pad at the Green Beret base. Helicopters landed on a dirt road adjacent to the compound. He landed with rotor wash kicking up dust from the road. He was expecting a couple of 'Tiger Suits' (Green Berets) to come out for a lift to Tam Ky. Out came one Beret, followed by four Vietnamese carrying two crates of chickens!

He grimaced as he thought 'What…you have to be kidding!'

The Beret came up to him, shouted into his helmet, and said they had promised these folks he would take them to Tam Ky.

The pilot shouted back: 'I only have two frick'n seats; I can't take all these PACs!'

In an OH–23G, the pilot sat in the middle of a bench seat with the controls, and passengers could sit on either side. The Beret shouted back over the engine and rotor noise that it was imperative that these people get to Tam Ky.

Each weighed about 90-100lb soaking wet. He considered his options as he thought to himself, 'It's late. It will be dark if I make two trips. Weight-wise, I should be OK to take all four. I guess I could put two on the seats and two on the floor with their legs on the skids. The passengers on the seats could carry the chicken crates. I'm sitting on this road where I could make a long take-off run. I should have plenty of room. I could land in the soccer field; I will have enough room and have enough power to land. I can plan my approach to the ground with no hovering for safety. OK, then will I be able to land safely with this heavy load in Tam Ky? Yah, that should work, you one crazy-ass pilot, just don't tell anyone about this.'

He told the Beret 'Load 'em up.' There he sat with two strapped in the seats holding two crates of chickens, two sitting on the floor with their feet on the skids holding onto the legs of the seated passengers for dear life and chickens clucking away in baskets. All of this was in a three-place helicopter. 'If this works, maybe I will have some kind of record. I will have to tell James.'

As he prepared to take off, a Papasan[3] passed along the side of the helicopter on a bicycle. Leffert looked over at the passing bicyclist. 'I'll let him get farther down the road before I take off.' Because of the weight, he planned a 'running take-off'. This is a take-off where the helicopter is kept low to the ground until sufficient airspeed from transitional lift and rotor momentum is present for climbing. He brought the engine and rotor up to operating RPM and checked his instruments. The helicopter was grossly overweight and likely could not hover at a normal 3ft. He was being extra careful as he pulled in power and brought the helicopter up a couple of inches off the ground and started to creep forward. The helicopter bounced awkwardly on the dirt road.

He glanced ahead and saw the Papasan up the road. 'Plenty of room,' he thought. The helicopter crept ahead slowly, gaining ground speed but not wanting to climb.

'Crap,' he thought. 'The wind direction must have changed to a tail wind. I'm committed; I have to continue.'

He was gaining on the bicycle. Sensing the helicopter was gaining on him, the Papasan on his bicycle pedaled faster. Looking over his shoulder, he pedaled as fast as he could. The chickens squirmed in his passengers' hands. Scared, they started yelling and pointing at the cyclist.

With the helicopter gaining ever closer, the Papasan peddled with the passion of an Olympic cyclist! The helicopter started to climb. The cyclist, fearing an impending collision, bailed out. The bike ran into a narrow ditch just as the helicopter swooped over the prone Papasan face down on the road. The helicopter climbed, with its passengers yelling and chickens squawking.

As he climbed, the pilot prayed, 'Thank you Lord for not letting me hit that old man.' As he circled around, he looked back at the Papasan who was now standing and shaking his fist. Thirty minutes later, he made an approach to the ground at Tam Ky as planned. They hit the grass soundly with a bump and stuck on there. His passengers sitting on the floor scrambled out of the helicopter at a dead run. The others unstrapped and ran out of the helicopter with their chickens clucking wildly. All four ran out of the soccer field toward town.

Division Artillery Officers' Club
1915 hrs

'OK, Doc Cruz says "Leff is still a peaches and cream kind of guy. That incident wasn't premeditated."'

'Maybe, Connor Dotson better get him checked out in the Loaches, asap,' quipped Broderick. 'He's getting grouchy. We don't want him running over anyone else,' he chuckled.

'Shouldn't have told James,' mocked Broderick. 'He can't keep a secret.'

'There are no secrets in Div Arty Air,' said Chambers.

'New record at Div Arty Air,' shouted Birmingham. 'Five people and a bunch of clucking hens in an OH-23G; now that will be hard to beat.'

'Did he find any eggs?' cracked Doc Cruz.

Chapter 16

Shaking the Hornets' Nest

Div Arty Operations
0700 hrs

Leffert reported to Base Ops for the morning briefing on the pending missions.

'Leffert,' Captain James said, 'you need to go directly to LZ Young and pick up a PAC that has been granted emergency leave and bring him back here. When you get back, we will probably have something else for you.'

'That sounds good.'

Leffert went to his locker to get his M16, chicken-plate, helmet, gloves and maps. He carried a 45 semi-automatic pistol on a web belt buckled to his waist. He would twist the belt so the pistol would rest between his legs for added protection of his 'family jewels'. It also served as a resting platform for his chicken-plate. The plates weighed several pounds and would get increasingly heavy during the day if resting solely on his upper legs without the support of the 45.

Leffert had been transitioned into the OH-6. He compared the new OH-6 to the '23' as the equivalent of a Porsche to a Volkswagen bug. The OH-6 was stronger, faster and more maneuverable.

After pre-flighting the helicopter, he cranked it up and called the tower for taxiing and take-off instructions. The morning was completely overcast inland. The sky was clear from the coastline seaward. The bottoms of the clouds were about 200ft above the ground.

The pilot considered, 'I could either low-level just above trees under the clouds, or climb in the clear above the clouds with the risk of needing to find a hole in the clouds and safely descend.'

The LZ was about 40 kilometers north. It would be much easier to climb above the clouds and fly VFR on top[1] than low-level and take a chance on the ceiling dropping further. Low-leveling increases the risk of encountering enemy fire or running into another aircraft. He decided to climb out over the ocean and see how thick the cloud layer was.

He found the cloud layer to be only a couple of hundred feet thick. Flying on top, he could see the tops of the higher hills sticking above the clouds like islands in the sea.

He weighed his options and risks and decided to fly VFR on top. He sighed as he thought, 'I just hope the clouds break up enough at Ross so I can find and descend through a hole.'

He continued north. Flying on top of the clouds was beautiful! The bright sun shining on the pure fluffy white cloud tops made a kaleidoscope of colors and patterns. Pure green hilltops protruded at irregular intervals, allowing him to identify his location. The mountains looked beautiful, like tropical islands in the South China Sea. He smiled and thought to himself, 'This is what flying is all about.'

He was starting to get a bit nervous as he neared LZ Ross, which was located in the bottom of a large valley. The cloud layer showed no signs of breaking up.

He tuned the FM radio to LZ Ross frequency and said, 'Kilo One-Eight, this is Phoenix One-Four, over.'

'Phoenix One-Four, this is Kilo, go ahead.'

'Kilo One-Eight, I am inbound to your location to pick up a PAC.'

'Roger One-Four, the PAC is standing by, over.'

'Roger One-Eight, what is your current weather?'

'One-Four, current weather is a complete overcast. It appears as if the bottoms of the clouds are a couple of hundred feet above us. The winds are calm, over.'

'Roger, One-Eight. I'll see if I can find a hole in the clouds and proceed to your location, over.'

'Roger One-Four, keep us posted.'

There was a break in the clouds about the size of a football field. He flew above the hole and began a slow, tight downward spiral. Everything was looking good. He could see the tops of the trees below the clouds. Below the cloud layer, he turned to a heading of 270 degrees and intercepted a road that led to the LZ.

'I am home free.'

Suddenly hundreds of red and green tracers flew by his canopy. He had descended into the middle of a major fire-fight. He panicked; turning around would be suicide! Everyone seemed to be shooting at him and the hole in the clouds he dropped through was far behind him.

He dashed straight ahead below the clouds to get out of the melee. As he ran from the fire-fight, he remembered something he heard in flight school. He heard someone mention that slipping the helicopter sideways might mislead someone shooting at you by disguising the actual direction of flight. He decided to try the maneuver. He pushed in right pedal, forcing the nose to the right, and put in left cyclic, forcing the helicopter to fly about 45 degrees to the left of the direction his nose was pointed. It slowed him down, but he hoped it would help him escape. Dropping low behind a tree line, he escaped the tracers. He continued on flying out of the area as low and fast as he could go. He stayed low under the clouds and turned toward LZ Ross, carefully avoiding the fire-fight area.

He keyed the FM radio, 'Kilo One-Eight, this is Phoenix One-Four, over.'

'Go ahead One-Four.'

'Kilo One-Eight, I'm about a mile out for landing.'

'One-Four, be advised we just received orders for a fire mission. We will be firing to the east.'

'One-Eight, I'll stay west of you.'

He watched the 105mm howitzers fire their mission, which lasted several minutes.

'Phoenix One-Four, this is Kilo One-Eight. You are clear to land.'

'Roger One-Eight, I am circling to land on the west pad, over.'

On the ground, he told Ross Operations that he was shutting down to wait for the clouds to break up. He did a walk-around inspection for possible bullet holes. There was not a single hit.

He went to the mess hall for a cup of coffee and had the PAC meet him there. A young PFC was waiting for him. He had a sad, forlorn look about him. Striking up a conversation, he stated that he had been in country for a little over ten months and had just received a 'Dear John' letter from his wife. His commander was sympathetic and granted him emergency leave to go home to try to rectify the situation.

'Dear John' letters were common in Vietnam: a young serviceman in a relationship with a young woman who, after a few months of absence, found the relationship non-sustainable and wanted out.

About a half-hour later, the clouds began to break up. Leffert and the young soldier climbed in the helicopter and ascended through the broken cloud layer. He dropped the PFC off at Chu Lai an hour later.

In the middle of the fire-fight, Leffert did not have time to be scared. That evening at the Officers' Club, the fire-fight experience started sinking in and his hand quivered around his glass of Dewar's White Label as he related the story (his TINS) to his 'Band of Brothers'. He had come close to 'buying the farm'.

'Such is life in Vietnam,' offered Broderick.

Years later, the fire-fight melee became etched in Leffert's memory, as the *Star Wars* incident. A scene in the epic movie had tracers surrounding the space fighter aircraft, a feeling he experienced looking back at descending through the clouds to land at LZ Ross.

Chapter 17

Saving a Snake–Driver's Life

Ky Ha Heliport
Chu Lai, 1969

Captain Jim Minter pre-flighted his Cobra gunship with an inexperienced warrant officer looking over his shoulder. They climbed in and the crew chief helped them strap in. To the right of them in a separate revetment, another Cobra gunship cranked up. Minter keyed his cyclic radio switch and said, 'Ky Ha, Tower, Blue Ghost Flight, with a flight of two, request permission to taxi to the runway for take-off.'

'Blue Ghost One-Zero, your flight of two has clearance to runway Two-Seven-Five and cleared for take-off.'

'Roger.'

'Craps,' thought the pilot, 'we have to take off west and clear the hill with these heavy gunships.'

The two heavy Cobras burdened with weapons and full fuel tanks were over maximum gross weight and could barely hover. They bounced awkwardly in a 1ft hover to the active. The lead Snake reached the active, pedal turned to the right, and Minter gently pushed the cyclic forward, urging the helicopter into transitional lift. The overweight helicopter slowly began to climb. Warrant officer Donald Sledge in the front seat keyed his radio and said, 'This heavy ol' bird is sure straining to get in the sky.'

Minter double-clicked on his radio in a boring acknowledgment.

Sledge adjusted his chicken-plate as he sat in the co-pilot/gunner seat up front in the Snake. The slender Texan from Plano was excited and apprehensive. Today was his first real mission in the Snake and he wanted to perform well. This was the real thing, not some training drill. His primary function was to accurately fire a 7.62mm mini-gun located at the front of the aircraft directly underneath the front of the Cobra. Minter, as aircraft commander, was to fly the aircraft, work the radios and in an attack, position the aircraft to fire the 2.75in folding fin rockets from tubes located on both sides.

Captain Minter grew up in Metuchen, New Jersey and went to college at Oglethorpe University in Atlanta, Georgia. He began his tour flying the OH-23G observation helicopter with their unit's neighbors, the Americal Div Arty Air Section. Now he was with the Americal 123rd Aviation Battalion flying the latest and greatest chopper. The Snake was like a Corvette: sleek, fast and deadly.

The two helicopters turned north along Highway One, staying below 200ft out of the fast-movers' control zone. Once far enough north, Blue Ghost White climbed to 2,000ft above the ground. Rattler One-Five followed in a trailing formation. They followed Highway One until they reached the city of Tam Ky. They then turned inland toward the mountains. Their mission was to support the infantry operating in the lowlands west of Tam Ky.

Minter keyed his mike and spoke over the FM Operations channel, 'Blue Ghost flight over Station Zebra.'

'Roger Blue Ghost Flight, stand by.'

The two Cobra gunships entered into a racetrack pattern waiting for a fire mission. Minter looked below at the plush, rolling terrain. It looked peaceful, but he knew the enemy was hidden below. They circled lazily for several minutes, then the radio crackled, 'Blue Ghost flight, stand by for a fire mission.'

'Roger!'

'Friendlies will pop smoke, and you must ID smoke.'

'Roger. I have green smoke, north-east on a ridgeline.'

'Correct smoke ID, place rocket fire in tree-line two clicks west of green smoke.'

'Wilco, two clicks west of smoke in tree-line.'

'Roger.'

The two Cobras dove on an enemy position at the edge of a field ready to release a four-pair salvo of 2.75in folding fin rockets. Upfront in the lead Cobra gunship, Sledge held his hands on the joystick controlling the 7.62mm mini-gun. Suddenly several rounds hit the diving helicopter from the side. Minter was hit once in the thigh with an AK-47 round. He jerked, pushing the left leg hard on the left pedal, causing the Cobra to nose sharply to the left out of trim. The projectile tore through flesh and punctured the large artery supplying blood to his leg. Blood gushed throughout the cockpit, splattering the canopy.

Sledge in the front seat felt several heavy thuds as the helicopter skidded left. Momentarily, he froze. The gunship continued diving toward the ground, skidding to the left out of control. Sledge looked above him and saw mud splattering on the plexiglass canopy. 'Mud?' he thought. 'How in the hell can mud be hitting us up here? Then he knew. 'Blood!' He looked behind him and saw blood everywhere. He keyed his mike and yelled, 'Captain, are you OK?'

The gunship dove toward the ground, turning to the left. Sledge turned forward and grabbed the miniature control sticks on the sides of his front-seat cockpit. He pulled back on the cyclic stick on the right, added pedal to trim the aircraft and pulled the Cobra out of the dive.

He rarely got to fly using these miniature controls. They were difficult to use and had no 'feel' to them. They were only used in training or during an emergency.

He pulled the sleek gunship up sharply and smoothly transitioned in a high-g turn to the east.

'Where will I go? I can't call anyone here up front. Chu Lai? Too far. Two–Niner, I think there's a medevac.'

'Hill Two–Niner, that's it; it's our best chance.'

The startled crew of the Cobra behind them called on the emergency radio, 'WHAT'S WRONG, ONE-ZERO? WHAT'S WRONG?'

The rookie pilot flying the wounded ship never heard the frantic calls. He had a single purpose and that was to get his aircraft commander help.

In back, the captain, barely conscious, grabbed his thigh and squeezed it to stem the flow of blood. He began to feel a heavy warm darkness slowly filling his body, giving him a feeling of floating.

Sledge landed straight in on the first landing pad he saw, the VIP pad. The co-pilot quickly shut down the helicopter. With the blade still turning, he opened up the canopy and jumped out. He climbed up and put pressure on the captain's leg. Soldiers from Hill Two-Niner rushed out to see why a gunship landed on the VIP pad. Seeing the emergency, they called for a medevac chopper, which fortuitously was parked nearby with the crew inside, ready on-call. The medevac chopper started up and hopped over to the VIP pad. Medics pulled the wounded aviator out of the helicopter, applied a tourniquet and started an IV. He was flown to the large Chu Lai hospital and operated on. He was flown later that evening to Japan where he received additional treatment.

A week later, he was flown home to the States.

Div Arty Air Section
Recreation Room

Later that evening several of the Div Arty aviators were gathered in the rec room listening to Doc Cruz. 'Guys,' explained Doc Cruz, 'Jim nearly lost his life and nearly his leg. He's one lucky Buck. He can thank his front-seater for saving his life and the doctors for saving his leg. I understand they took a vein out of his left leg and used it to repair the artery in his right leg.'

They raised their drinks in unison and said reverently, 'To Jim, thank the Lord.'

Jim Minter subsequently reported: 'The bullet, a 7.62 armor-piercing, passed through my left leg just below the knee, destroying the artery junction that supplies blood to the lower portion of the leg. Several years ago, at a BLUE GHOST reunion, the medic who got to me and ultimately saved my life told me this, 'When I got to you I knew that you had ten minutes left to live because of the massive blood loss.''

Jim Minter had a successful career at the Federal Aviation Administration. He suffers from chronic pain in his wounded leg, but gets around just fine. Many years later, he reclaimed friendships with his former fellow aviators at Americal Div Arty Aviation Section and meets annually with them.

Chapter 18

The Rescue

Div Arty Air Hootches
January 1969

Lieutenant Darryl James laid in his bunk a moment, looked up at the plywood ceiling of his hootch and thought about his nickname, Yoz. You had no control over what your buddies decided to call you in Vietnam. His nickname was after the character Yossarian in Joseph Heller's book *Catch-22*. In the book, Yossarian thought everyone and everything in the war were trying to kill him. They jokingly claimed James felt that way too.

He hated the nickname, but pretended he loved it. If he told them he hated it, they would keep on using it to tweak his sensitivities. If he told them he loved it, they would keep doing it because they liked him. It was a 'Catch-22'.

Breakfast was black coffee, a couple of eggs and two pieces of bacon. It's good, but then it's hard to screw up breakfast. James looked over at Lee Leffert. The blond-haired slender lieutenant, as usual, was putting away the groceries. Leffert was 120lb soaking wet, but he would eat like someone triple his size. The skinny pilot was methodically putting away three eggs, a stack of pancakes and five strips of Canadian bacon. 'He must have the metabolism of a sex-starved hummingbird.'

Lieutenant John Duffy sat next to Leffert. 'Duff-man', as he was called, was Div Arty's Maintenance Officer. Duffy was the kind of guy you wanted around if you got into a card game or knife fight. He was tough as nails. You could always find him at the pilots' recreation room on Thursday nights in the weekly poker game. Duffy was known to exaggerate all his previous sexual exploits and other noteworthy events in his life. The Div Arty Air Flight all knew he was a bullshitter, and he knew they knew. It did not matter; he still bullshitted with the best of them.

America's Div Arty Air Section was excited about the arrival of the Loaches to replace their aging Raven helicopters. The Ravens were reliable and rugged, but they couldn't carry much. The OH-23G pilot sat in the center on a bench seat and only two passengers or small pieces of cargo could be carried. The Raven was also hard to fly. Whenever the pilot added power with the collective, the throttle had to be increased to keep rotor and engine rpm constant. When the pilot reduced power, he did the opposite and reduced throttle. The new jet-powered Loaches had a governor that maintained a constant rpm.

The OH-23G had other shortcomings. The Raven had low rotor momentum, which meant that if the engine quit, the pilot had to get the collective down and add right pedal fast to preserve rotor rpm. The OH-23G had only two poor-quality radios. The Raven pilot seemed vulnerable. He sat on an aluminum padded bench seat with a plastic bubble-like canopy around him. Div Arty Maintenance put a piece of armor-plating under the OH-23G pilot's seat to protect him from below. The pilot's back was against the transmission wall and he wore a ceramic bulletproof vest which was called a chicken-plate. The Loach pilot would be safer in its built-in ceramic armor seat.

Most helicopter pilots had one more safety feature. Most of them carried a 45-caliber automatic sidearm strategically placed between their legs with the chicken-plate resting on top. This was theoretically to keep stray shrapnel in the cockpit from making the pilot a soprano in the choir. Instead of a 45, James elected to carry a 38-caliber revolver as a sidearm. He was more comfortable hitting a target with it. The Safety Officer tried placing the 38 revolver between his legs. It didn't work. It hurt him in a place he wouldn't tell Mom. James carried the revolver in the more conventional manner in a holster around his hip, forgoing the special between-the-legs safety feature.

'I see on the schedule,' said Leffert with a twinkle in his eye, 'where I am flying for MACV in our darling 23s, but you two pukes are training with Dotson in the new Loaches.'

'Tough shit,' Duffy and James said in unison.

'Somebody's got to do, right, Yoz?' said Duffy as he began giggling.

The Loaches were big news at Div Arty Air. Lieutenants Connor Dotson and Mark Birmingham had hitched a ride on the Division's Otter to Cam Rahn Bay two days earlier to pick up two of the sexy-looking eggbeaters. The Loaches were brand-new. They even smelled new, like the fabulous smell of a new car. They were jet-turbine powered, fast, maneuverable and supposedly quite survivable in a crash.

The day before, Duffy and James each received two and a half hours of flight time in them. They were surprisingly easy to fly. 'Felt like a damn sports car,' Duffy later said. They had four radios and flight and navigation instruments such as an ADF (automatic direction-finder), a radar transponder, a large artificial horizon on the right where the pilot normally sat, and an extra artificial horizon for the co-pilot on the left.

James looked down at his coffee and thought, 'My first approach yesterday was ragged. I came barreling into Ky Ha hot. I had a heck of a time getting it stopped and overshot the heliport pad. It was damn embarrassing.'

Yesterday Dotson, the check pilot, just laughed and said, 'Remember, this isn't a 23. Be sure to look at your airspeed indicator and slow down to 60 knots when you begin your approach.'

After an hour and a half of dual instruction, Dotson got out so James could get some solo time. He loved it. It was a dream to fly. He and Duffy needed to get an additional hour and a half each, five hours total, to get qualified. They planned to get that time today.

The pilots left the Officers' Club. Duffy headed on down to the flight line ahead of James.

'See you in about thirty, Duff,' James said.

'Right, Yoz.'

Duffy was scheduled to fly another thirty minutes dual with Dotson and then James would fly thirty minutes dual. Afterwards, they would both fly a few more hours together, with each getting time in the right pilot-in-command seat.

The rest of the group turned on the path to Operations. James lingered a few minutes in Operations then went to the pilots' ready room, got his gear and walked down to the flight line.

As usual, Ky Ha Heliport was a beehive of activity with slicks and Snakes hovering, refueling and queuing up in line for take-off. A Rattler gunship slithered by so heavily loaded it bumped awkwardly across the tarmac, struggling to hover. The Cobra gunship had teeth painted on the front akin to General Chenault's Flying Tigers of Second World War fame in China.

James sat on his helmet by a revetment and waited. He looked over the only other Div Arty Loach sitting on the tarmac. The unit's two Loaches were training aircraft. They did not have armor seats and armor protection in the engine compartments. Tonight, Lieutenant Birmingham and their boss, Major Fulton, would be bringing two mission-ready Loaches from Cam Rahn Bay.

The pilot stared at the lonely Loach with his survival instincts stirring. 'It is a little spooky sitting in an aircraft here resting your butt on only an aluminum nylon seat, but no sweat, Battalion maintenance will have them fitted with all the combat embellishments within a week or so. Relax. NO ONE WILL BE SHOOTING AT US. WE WON'T FLY MISSIONS IN THESE TRAINING BIRDS.'

Training ships or not, by rote, the new Safety Officer for Div Arty Air had his chicken-plate, M16, 38-caliber sidearm and holster, survival knife, a bandoleer of ammunition and a survival kit with an emergency beeper radio. He looked at his watch and waited for Dotson and Duffy to return.

Ten minutes later, the new Loach descended onto the runway and hovered up to the waiting lieutenant. Duffy stepped out of the right seat and climbed in the back. Connor waited for James to get in and connect his helmet to the intercom.

'Go get 'em, Yoz,' the check-pilot said.

James called Ky Ha tower and received permission to taxi. He picked the Loach up into a hover and found himself over-controlling the unfamiliar sensitive aircraft. Connor sat in the left seat, seemingly oblivious. Duffy, in the back seat, chuckled. 'He never could hover.'

James settled down and smoothly hovered to the active runway. He received clearance from Ky Ha tower and took off north over Div Arty's Hootch City. He leveled off at 200ft. Almost instantly, the quick aircraft accelerated to 110 knots. They flew over to Arty Hill located nearby on Highway One outside the village of Chu Lai and did a few pinnacle approaches. Then they low-leveled across the tidal flats north of Chu Lai until they reached the South China Sea. James did a couple of approaches to the beach. He was enjoying himself and began feeling a mite cocky about his Loach flying skills. Twenty minutes later, they landed back at Ky Ha and refueled. The check-pilot got out and gave James the thumbs-up. Duffy climbed in the co-pilot's seat. James took off and spent an hour and a half flying formation with large waterfowl around the tidal flats.

They returned to Ky Ha, refueled and Duffy and James switched seats. The Loach departed north with both pilots feeling puffed up with their Loach flying ability. They were confident and comfortable with the new aircraft.

'Yoz, you mean they are gonna pay us to fly this thing?'

'You got that right. Almost better than sex, huh?'

'Let's not get carried away. Never bullshit a bullshitter.'

'No one alive could out-bullshit you.'

They were flying along the safety of Highway One at 1,700ft just north-east of Chu Lai having a large time when the UHF radio crackled. 'Salvation Control, this is Red Hawk One.'

James wondered, 'Hmm? I hadn't heard that call sign.'

'Red Hawk One, this is Salvation, over.'

'Salvation, I'm over a downed Oscar One with two survivors lying on the wing. They appear wounded. They are in a tight, heavily forested ravine about 15 clicks north of Chu Lai. Looks bad for a pick-up. Do you have anyone nearby to help? Over.'

James hit the trigger on his cyclic and said on the intercom, 'Duff, that's close.'

They next heard, 'Roger, Red Hawk One, stand by.'

'Phoenix One-Six, Salvation, I see you are nearby, can you assist Red Hawk One?'

James pushed the trigger on the cyclic to the second click and transmitted on UHF, with Duff's call sign, 'Salvation, Phoenix One-Six, yes, we can help, over.'

'Phoenix One-Six, this is Red Hawk One, say position, over.'

James replied, 'Roger, Red Hawk, we are over Highway One, 10 klicks north-east of Chu Lai, over.'

Then they heard, 'Red Hawk One, Salvation, can you give position and altitude?'

'Roger, Salvation, Red Hawk One is three-one nautical miles on the Chu Lai Two-Niner-Five radial. We are circling at four and a half grand over mountains.'

'Whoa,' James said over the intercom. 'Listen to that shit, Duff. Does this guy think we are the Air Force? We're Army; we don't have those fancy instruments. Shit, we work for a living down in the trees and mud.'

Before Duffy could reply, James pressed the switch to transmit on the UHF, 'Red Hawk One, this is Phoenix One-Six. We do not have VOR nor TACAN, can you give map grid coordinates?'

'Roger, Phoenix One-Six, wait one.'

The radar operator at Salvation control grabbed the mike and pressed the trigger, 'Phoenix One-Six, I have you on radar. Squawk Two-Four-Five-Zero.'

James placed 2450 on the transponder and hit the ident button. A moment later, 'Phoenix One-Six, Salvation, I have you. Come to a heading of two-eight-five.'

'Roger, Salvation,' James replied in his mike. Duffy banked the Loach sharply left heading into the mountains and pulled up the collective to climb. He leveled from his turn on a heading of 285 degrees and continued climbing.

'Phoenix One-Six, this is Salvation. Red Hawk One will be One-Four nautical miles directly ahead.'

'Roger Salvation,' replied James.

James switched to Div Arty Air Ops and reported their position and intentions.

He looked at the beautiful, rugged mountains below and took a deep breath. 'I have my M16, ammunition, sidearm and survival pack. All Duff brought was his damn forty-five. Nice going Duff. Well, we are certainly armed to the teeth.'

He pressed the cyclic switch one click to transmit over the intercom. 'Duff, do you feel naked here in the mountains?'

'Huh?'

'Remember, Bud, we are only sitting on NYLON WEBBED SEATS held up by aluminum frames with NO ARMOR-PLATING!'

'No shit,' he replied.

'Thanks for bringing your M16,' James replied sarcastically.

'I don't need it, shithead, I'm flying.'

'Thanks pal.'

James pulled his M16 off the first-aid kit on the wall between them. He felt the triple assembly of three twenty-round magazines and thought, 'Bless you, Jenkins.' The crew chief taped the triple clip assembly together for him last week. The pilot looked back over his seat and saw a bandoleer of M16 ammunition and a survival radio strapped in the back seat, right where he couldn't reach them.

'Isn't that special? Someone is in real trouble and we are to help?'

They flew over the heavily forested mountains west of Chu Lai into the teeth of Indian country, feeling vulnerable in their training aircraft. Off in the distance, they saw an OV-10 Bronco with mini-guns and two rocket pods under its wings circling ahead.

'That will be Red Hawk One, Yoz.'

James hit the toggle switch and transmitted, 'Red Hawk One, Phoenix One-Six, we have you in sight, over.'

'Roger, One-Six, tally ho Phoenix.'

James looked below and hit the intercom switch, 'Duff, there they are.'

He pointed as Duffy turned toward the crash site. The Loach descended, turning below the Bronco and flew directly over a very bent-up airplane. The Bird Dog was crunched in a narrow gorge in thick jungle. James looked out the door as they passed. He hit the intercom, 'It's stuck in the trees, Duff, two hombre are laying on the wings; one is waving.'

'Roger, Yoz.'

The radio crackled, 'Phoenix One-Six, can you get in there?'

'Red Hawk One, I don't know. There is no place to land, and the crash site looks tight. We will go down for a good look and give it a try.'

'One-Six, my wingman is only zero-four mikes out. Suggest you wait until he's on station. I can escort you down; he can provide high cover.'

'Roger, Red Hawk.'

The Loach circled as they waited for the second OV-10. Duffy mentally planned his approach. James glanced out his side door and saw another lethal-looking OV-10 approaching. He noticed the large word 'MARINES' painted on its side.

James hit the radio switch and said, 'Red Hawk One, we are going in, over.'

'Roger.'

Duffy lowered the collective and descended in a racetrack pattern to the crash site. Red Hawk One moved in alongside in formation off the right side of the Loach and descended with them. James looked out Duffy's open door and was momentarily startled. The OV-10 was close and 'all dirty', with full flaps and gear extended to allow it to fly as slow as possible while he escorted them down.

'These jarheads are all right,' thought James. 'He could have stayed overhead. Coming in low and slow with us makes him a pretty juicy target.'

James laid the M16 across his lap and chambered a round. Duffy concentrated on the tricky approach into the gorge and crash site now dead ahead. Gradually the Bronco crept ahead as the chopper slowed below 60 knots in the final portion of its approach. The Loach descended to 100ft in the air on short final to the gorge. Suddenly, James saw gun flashes ahead directed at the Bronco 200 yards ahead.

'Red Hawk One, taking fire and breaking right.'

Watching from above, his wingman replied, 'Red Hawk Two, is rolling hot, Phoenix One-Six we're coming in off your right, stay on present heading or break left, over.'

James hit the radio trigger with his left hand. His right hand remained tightly around the butt of the M16 as he said, 'Roger, ONE, we are low and slow on short final. We ain't going anywhere.'

The second OV-10 swooped by above them. As it passed, they heard the screech of its mini-gun firing ahead of them to their right. The firing abruptly stopped and the OV-10 pulled up smartly into a turning climb to the right.

Lieutenant James holding an M16 with an M203 grenade-launcher attached.

OH-6A and UH-1D parked on mountain fire base pad. Landing on the mountain fire bases was always tricky.

CH–47B Chinook dropping a sling-load on a hilltop. This workhorse of the Vietnam War was nicknamed 'Shit Hook' by the soldiers. It delivered 'shit' by a so-called 'hook'. Chinooks delivered supplies routinely to our fire bases in Americal Division.

Lieutenant Birmingham flew an Artillery officer and water cans to a new, hastily-prepared landing-pad on a mountaintop observation post (OP).

Unloading ammo delivered by Chinook sling-load.

A pair of Loaches at Hill 29, which is south of Da Nang near the town of Tam Ky.

Lieutenant James dropped off the battalion commander at this battery fire base. Artillery officers watched as soldiers calibrated a 105mm howitzer's firing position.

M107 self-propelled 8in howitzer positioned in place on fire base.

105mm M101 howitzer on firing mission.

M107 155mm self-propelled gun in position on a fire base.

F-4 dropping napalm below the flank of an artillery fire base.

Shutting down a Loach at sunset in a Ky Ha Heliport revetment. A crew chief is leaning into the side of the aircraft to assist. Helicopters were parked in revetments to protect adjoining aircraft from damage in case of mortar attacks.

A hovering Loach at Ky Ha Heliport.

Looking back through the tail of the LOH-6A in flight. The observer riding in the back seat perilously leaned out of the side of the aircraft to take this interesting photo.

Lieutenant James loading a Loach preparing for a mission. This Loach was named 'California Dreaming'; its crew chief's wish to get home.

Lieutenants James and Duffy posing in front of a Loach at Ky Ha Heliport.

Lieutenant James allowed some Vietnamese kids to have their picture taken in his Loach.

Lieutenant Birmingham hovering in his Loach.

Lieutenant James preparing to climb into his assigned Loach.

OH-23G Hiller, 'Raven'. The pilot sat in the middle with observers on either side. On some scout missions, an M60 machine gun was hung on the right side.

Above left: *Lieutenant Fuller preparing to start his OH-23G.*

Above right: *Lieutenant Fuller and Warrant Officer Lincoln preparing for a mission. Note Fuller is holding a Thompson machine gun, his coveted weapon of choice. Lincoln is wearing a ceramic bullet-proof vest with an M16 strung over his shoulder.*

Then: Warrant Officer Broderick, Lieutenant Birmingham, Lieutenant Duffy, Lieutenant James and Warrant Officer Lincoln, circa 1968. Now: Bill Broderick, Mark Birmingham, John Duffy, Darryl James and Steve Lincoln, circa 2012.

Up on the stage at the Division Officers' Club singing We Gotta Get Out of This Place *by The Animals. Captain Fuller, Captain Dotson, Captain Duffy, Captain Doc Cruz, Warrant Officer Broderick and Lieutenant Leffert.*

Warrant Officer Booth and Lieutenant Gilyard ready to watch a band perform in the Division Officers' Club.

Maintenance Officer Lieutenant John Duffy in front of a Loach at Ky Ha Heliport.

Captain James posing in front of a Loach.
The Loach was named 'Whale' after its
crew chief's nickname.

Back row: Lieutenant Birmingham, Warrant Officer Broderick, and Warrant Officer Booth. Next row down: Warrant Officer Lindauer and far right Warrant Officer Morris. Next row: Captain Cruz. Lieutenant Baker (in center). Bottom: Lieutenant Leffert.

Lieutenant James constructing a shelter at Jungle Survival School in the Philippines during Christmas 1968.

Lieutenant James brought two Green Beret soldiers to this fortified Montagnard compound. Families lived with these indigenous guerrilla fighters who fought alongside the Green Berets.

A secluded Vietnamese compound.

Lieutenant Dotson with cigar and hat playing poker. 'I bet two beers!' Poker was played every Wednesday night in the Div Arty Air recreation room.

Lieutenant Leffert posing with a First World War Snoopy leather hat, goggles and survival knife in his teeth, ready to take on the Red Baron!

Duffy struggled to hover down into the crash site: a tight, deep ravine with steep, vine-covered walls.

The Loach drivers, nervous and tense, looked out left and right as the Loach sank lower into the ravine.

James looked up through the helicopter's rotor blades and watched the hillside climb higher and higher.

'How can so much stuff grow on such a sheer cliff?' he wondered.

Over the intercom, Duffy said, 'Craps, this is a hole, not a ravine, watch my tail.' He continued shakily, 'You have to help us stay clear.' He yelled, 'Watch my fricking tail.'

'You're OK,' James replied nervously, with his head full out the door. 'I'll keep us clear.'

They descended deeper into the gorge. Trees were all around them. Some had been bent over by the impact of the crash. James looked out the door again to the rear to ensure their tail rotor was clear and then he looked to the side and then down into the blood-streaked faces of the wounded men now only 10ft below them. They stared up with ashen faces, waving weakly. James saw the ground and a small stream below the wreckage and trees. He glanced back up the steep hillside in horror. 'Shit, if I have to fire at anyone poking their heads over the top of the cliffside, I'd shoot through our own rotor blades. We are sitting ducks.'

James keyed his intercom switch and said, 'Duff, this is bad, I can't shoot up the hill without hitting our rotor blades.'

Duffy remained silent as he hovered down to 4ft above the wounded fliers. They couldn't go lower. Trees and bushes encased the Loach in a cocoon, leaving no margin for error. If their tail rotor hit the trees, they would crash and kill the wounded pilots below and maybe themselves.

Several feet above the broken wing of the Bird Dog, James motioned with his left arm for the guys below to climb up onto the skids and into the back seat of the Loach. They lay there, not responding. If they stood up, they could grab the skids. They couldn't move; they were hurt badly. They covered their bloody faces with their hands, protecting themselves from the rotor wash.

James motioned with his left hand to come on as he screamed, 'CLIMB IN. CLIMB IN.'

They did not move. James keyed the intercom switch, 'Duff, it is no use; they must be hurt real bad. They can't climb in.'

James could not get out of the helicopter to help them. The collective on his left side was up high in hovering flight, blocking him. He also could not reach into the back of the Loach to pass them a radio or ammunition. He felt helpless.

'Duff, we can't do any good here. Let's get out and cover the top of the hill and try to protect them.'

Duffy hovered out of the hole and they heard the familiar call sign of their neighbors at Ky Ha Heliport.

'Red Hawk One, Rattler Three with a flight of two ready to help. I see a Loach down there, can we assist, over?'

'Roger Rattler, that's Phoenix One-Six. We took small arms as we covered the Loach's approach to the downed bird, I don't think Phoenix can get them out.'

James keyed his radio, 'Red Hawk One, this is Phoenix One-Six. We couldn't land, and they couldn't climb in. They are hurt real badly. The plane is in the trees about 20ft off the ground but it looks stable. We would have placed our skids on the wing, but we couldn't get down far enough. We will protect the area around them, out.'

'Roger, Phoenix.'

Red Hawk One in the OV-10 remained in control of the rescue operation, but was glad of the two Rattler gunships. They could provide down-in-the-bushes close-in support, the kind that might be needed.

'Phoenix One-Six, this is Rattler Three with eyes on you. We have your backside covered, little buddy. If anything moves down there let us know. We are cocked and ready to rock and roll. Stay safe, over.'

James keyed his cyclic twice in the familiar 'double squelch' OK.

Rattler Three-Five selected two 2.75in folding fin aerial rockets from his left and right pods with the selector switch on his console and told his wingman to be ready.

'Phoenix One-Six, this is Red Hawk ONE. Salvation has a Pav Low on the way from Da Nang. They'll be here in One-Eight mikes, over.'

'Roger Red Hawk.'

A new call sign joined in. 'Red Hawk One, this is Dolphin One-Two off to your south in an empty Slick. Ready to help, over.'

'Tally ho, Dolphin, be advised we have two Broncos, two Snakes and a Loach low-level. We have a Pav Low inbound.'

'Roger, we'll stay clear and high and on call, over.'

James and Duffy heard the double squelch break of Red Hawk acknowledging.

'Damn, it must be getting crowded up there,' James thought as he silently thanked Jesus for all the eyes on them.

They were too busy to look up. Hovering slowly, they saw the jungle floor, knowing there were a million places to hide down below them. They hovered at the treetops to the south side of the ravine.

James looked through the trees from the slowly hovering Loach. The Loach moved back and forth along the sloping contours of the narrow ravine. Water reflected sunlight through the trees to the left of the Loach below. A flicker caught James's attention. 'Was that movement?'

'Duff, swing around back toward that spring, I thought I saw movement.'

The Loach moved toward the mountain creek above and leading to the crash site further down the slope. James's eye moved to the left again sensing movement. 'Could it be an animal? They have tigers, deer, and lots of other creepy things here.'

'Come left again, Duff, I thought I saw movement again; I am just not sure.'

Duffy radioed to the covering aircraft, 'Rattler Flight, Phoenix One-Six, possible movement off to our left.'

'Roger, Phoenix,' replied Rattler Three.

'Yoz, fire off a few rounds,' Duffy barked over the intercom. James fired off a couple of three-round bursts in the direction of the stream. He watched the tracers, waiting.

Gunfire erupted around the Loach. James fired back, spraying the area on full automatic as Duffy lowered the nose and accelerated over the trees.

James keyed his mike, 'TAKING FIRE, TO THE LEFT AND BEHIND US IN A SMALL CREEK.'

'Roger, Phoenix One-Six,' replied the OV-10 lead. 'Rattlers are coming hot behind you, climb and continue to the north.'

'Wilco,' replied James.

James and Duffy could hear the roar of the gunships' mini-guns and then a salvo of rockets behind them as they climbed.

A new call sign broke the air. 'Red Hawk One, this is Angel One-Niner, four klicks north-east. We have been monitoring your situation and request permission to approach from the south for a rescue approach.'

'Roger, Angel One-Niner. Permission granted,' replied the lead OV-10. 'We have had occasional small-arms fire. Your assistance is appreciated.'

'Phoenix One-Six, this is Red Hawk One, continue scouting north of the area. Rattler flight will provide support. Red Hawk Two will cover the approach of Angel One-Niner.'

James replied, 'Wilco, out,' as a huge Sikorski CH-53 helicopter gracefully swooped over the wreck and stopped in a high hover. Moments later, a jungle-penetrator descended from its belly with a specially trained airman holding on. The airman's camouflaged face looked down as he hugged the heavy base of the penetrator. He had lots of gear hanging around him. The airman hit the ground within the gorge up slope of the wreckage. He skillfully drew a machine pistol and looked around carefully for danger. Sensing none, he made his way along the creek to the aircraft in the trees. Trees were bent from the crash delicately holding the wreckage above them. He climbed 20ft into the damaged trees to reach the wreckage. The airman carefully sprung his lean body onto the wing. Anxious bloody faces looked out to him for help.

The airman said, 'We will get you out of here, like real quick.' He quickly but skillfully examined each soldier. He assured them all was OK.

He pulled out a small radio from his belt and said softly, 'One-Niner, Zero-Six here. We have multiple broken bones; I need the penetrator with litter and assistance. Aircraft in trees seems stable; suggest you send penetrator down over us.'

'Roger Zero-Six, One-Niner, out.'

The jungle-penetrator descended this time directly over the broken wing of the aircraft. Another warrior in camouflage got off on the wing of the crippled Bird Dog. It moved uneasily under the additional weight. A litter came next. In five minutes, they had the more wounded pilot strapped into a vertically-hanging stretcher and on the way up. Another four minutes and the second pilot was strapped in and hoisted up. On the third trip up both Air Force medics came up together, sitting on small metal seats straddling the jungle-penetrator on opposite sides. They each held their weapons ready and searched below for danger.

'Red Hawk ONE, Angel One-Niner is outbound for Chu Lai hospital.'

'Thanks, Angel, we appreciate your help.'

'Roger Red Hawk, ditto from us.'

The Loach climbed to a safe altitude and joined several circling helicopters breaking off to return to Chu Lai. The Red Hawk flight headed north to Da Nang.

'Phoenix One-Six and Rattler Flight, thanks for your help, guys. Good work.'

'Roger One,' replied James. He continued, 'Rattlers, thanks for covering our butts.'

'Roger, Rattlers are always ready to strike. Call anytime. We are in the Yellow Pages listed as "Have gun, will travel".'

After landing at Ha, Lieutenants Duffy and James were ordered to report to Major Fulton in Operations. Fulton was a lean, tall Texan, greatly respected by the unit.

The major looked into the faces of the two men braced before him and said, 'Duffy, just what in the hell were you guys doing in an unarmed Loach, in webbed seats hovering over the trees in Indian country with what, four hours each in that eggbeater?'

Duffy kept his mouth shut, figuring it was better to say nothing.

'Did you guys know what in the hell you were doing?'

Duffy answered this one, a bit sarcastically. 'Yes, Sir. We were using hunter-killer team tactics taught to us at Hunter.'

'That's the biggest bunch of bullshit I heard today. They don't even teach that in Flight School.'

'James, what do you think? What was going on out there? What tactics do you think you were using?'

'Well Sir, we kind of made them up as we went along.'

'That's what I mean; you guys didn't know what the hell you were doing, had an unarmed aircraft that neither of you were signed off to fly. You could have gotten your asses shot off.'

'Tell me,' he said quietly, 'why did you do it?'

Duffy answered, 'Sir, we were there and they needed us. And Sir, I thought we flew pretty damn well.'

'Well guys, the CO from the Rattlers called me. For some reason unbeknownst to me, he thinks you two no-counts deserve a citation. I can't imagine why. GET OUT OF HERE, GENTLEMEN!'

The pilots turned, but the major then raised his hand, stopping them in their tracks. 'Wait, one.' He let out a shit-eating grin. 'Tell you what, Girls. I'll buy you each a Scotch at the club.'

'YES SIR,' they replied.

The two of them quickly left. Leffert waited for them outside the Ops shed and gave them each playful shoulder blocks. 'How did it go?' he asked.

'No problem,' Duffy said.

The three of them headed to the Officers' Club as James said, 'Lee, did I ever tell you how the Duff-man got his name?'

'Oh, let me think,' replied Leffert, as he continued with an old, familiar routine. 'Hmm, does his name have something to do with a low frontal assault on a pretty woman with a full gainer in the layout position, and does it rhyme with a covering to keep a pretty girl's hands warm in the winter?'

'Yes,' replied James as Duffy smiled. He loved his nickname.

Chapter 19

Midnight Requisitioning

Virtually every military unit had a character in it who was especially adept at acquiring desirable hard-to-get goods through purchases, trades and midnight requisitioning. Midnight requisitioning was a kind of military borrowing where one unit stole something from another unit. The practice was generally acceptable to the military powers-that-be as long as a few rules were followed: (1) the theft must be benign to everyone and not done for profit; (2) the borrowing was not recurring; and (3) the goods borrowed were more or less surplus to the so-called aggrieved party.

All of the plywood the Division Artillery Air Section pilots used to build their recreation room was acquired from the Navy Seabees through various trades and some midnight requisitioning.

Div Arty Air's trader and chief of midnight requisitioning – aka grave-robber – was Sergeant Jenkins. Some of Jenkins' trades had become legends. His mother-of-all trade was the acquisition of a Huey-load of live lobsters. Jenkins traded two flight jackets, two AK–47s, a bloody NVA flag (made and bought in the local village and decorated with chicken blood) and ten cases of Coke to the Navy Chief in charge of a lonely radar station billeted on a small island off the coast of Chu Lai. The chief in turn traded the Coke to the villagers for the lobsters. The lobsters were placed in hand-made bamboo cages that were stacked four high in the C & C Huey. The critters were probably scared to death on what would be their first and last helicopter ride. They arrived in great shape, anxious to jump in the hot water and be eaten.

Jenkins' monster trade allowed the Div Arty pilots and crew chiefs to have quite a feast. It was a big party. Pilots from sister flight units filtered in. Two non-rated majors from the hill above called 'Silk Stocking Row' even ventured down into Div Arty Air territory to partake of the feast. Later their Commanding Officer, Colonel Jones, heard about the soirée and asked Captain Fuller about it. A few days later, the colonel asked Fuller if he might be able to get the handy Sergeant Jenkins to obtain lobsters for one of his senior officer calls. Fuller told him he would be glad to relay his requisition request to Jenkins.

Trades were by far the best ways to obtain things in the military. In contrast to trades, midnight requisitioning could become embarrassing, and sometimes it could become a serious punishable offense. It required experience and finesse to do it well. The key consideration in midnight requisitioning was never to get caught, and if by chance you did, then have a clever explanation.

One recent incident of Div Arty Air grave-robbing backfired awkwardly. This incident involved Div Arty's colorful, mature Lieutenant Baker, affectionately known as 'Pops'. Ol' Pops was quite a character. He was older than dirt, but didn't act like it. The man was always cutting up and acting goofy. He was fun to be around and the brunt of many jokes. Pops was beloved by his peers.

He was a 32-year-old first lieutenant with a wife and four kids. He had been a non-com who went to officer candidate school and flight school.

Two months earlier, the 32-year-old former non-com and a crew chief, Buck Sergeant Perkins, decided to steal some plywood to use for hootch improvement. Perkins had heard there was a bunch of new plywood pallets over at Artillery Hill being pretty much ignored.

Two months earlier

'Heck, Lieutenant, we won't even be stealing it from the Navy,' said Perkins. 'This stuff belongs to the 325th. They are Artillery pukes just like us. What's the difference?'

Lieutenant Baker sat thinking as Perkins continued. 'Heck, Lieutenant, we are in Division Artillery Headquarters; those guys really work for us. We can drive up there, pick up a load and be back within an hour. No one will even miss it.'

After some serious inward deliberation, the lieutenant said, 'It sounds like a good idea to me.'

They borrowed a three-quarter-ton truck from the flight line and drove across the sprawling Americal Division. The Division area covered 8 square miles and butted up against the even larger area of the Chu Lai Airfield.

The two vagabonds passed through the main gate, drove across Highway One and turned onto a 3-mile paved road that led up Artillery Hill. They asked, rather brazenly, at the Battalion's security gate where the plywood was stored. The guards directed them down the road to the supply area. They carefully looked around and tried not to look suspicious. They got out of the truck near some PFCs unfastening pallets. The grave-robbers shared cigarettes with the soldiers and made a little conversation.

'We're here to pick up some plywood for the Old Man,' said Perkins.

'Uh-huh,' said one of the PFCs, a huge bare-chested black guy. 'You'll need to get your paperwork straight with Sergeant Cramer.'

'No problem,' replied Perkins. 'The guy's a friend of mine.'

'Uh-huh,' said the PFC.

The men directed Perkins and Baker to the supply hut a quarter-mile up the road. The grave-robbers drove partway up and stopped at a place in the yard filled with ¾in 4 by 8ft plywood sheets covered with tarps. They filled the enclosed truck bed with plywood. They loaded quickly, but not carefully. Instead of laying the sheets down flat on the bed of the truck, they leaned the plywood sheets against the side of the cargo bed. The grave-robbers jumped in and drove quickly down the hill past the two soldiers.

Baker sighed, relaxing a bit now that they had pulled off their plywood heist. They hit a bump. The lieutenant bounced in his seat and bumped his head on the roof of the truck cab. He yelled, 'SHIT, SLOW DOWN, PERKINS.'

The truck continued downhill, bouncing. The load shifted in the back and Perkins felt the truck suddenly pull to the left.

'SHIT, I CAN'T KEEP IT STRAIGHT, LIEUTENANT!' he yelled.

Perkins fought the wheel and slammed on the brakes. The truck swerved. He had it back under control when suddenly it swerved again to the left. He turned the wheel right and it skidded. He swung the wheel back to the left, attempting to regain control. The truck skidded on the left shoulder of the road, then bounced and slipped off the road. It slowed in the brush and rolled slowly over on its left side. Inside, the two felt like they were on a TV camera in slow motion as it rolled and stopped.

Baker and Perkins climbed out, unhurt, but both knew they weren't going anyplace without help. They heard a quarter-ton jeep approaching from the hill. Inside was a large sergeant. He appeared to be smiling.

'Shit,' said Perkins. 'They made us.'

'Don't worry,' said the lieutenant philosophically. 'What can they do? Send us to Vietnam!'

Jenkins laughed, guardedly.

About a half-hour later, Captain Fuller at Div Arty's Operations heard the phone ring. Fuller picked it up and said, 'Captain Fuller, Div Arty Operations.'

'Captain Fuller, this is Captain Malkovich, 1st of the 3rd S4. I have a Lieutenant Baker and Sergeant Perkins here. They claim they belong to you. It seems that they have had a slight driving accident. Don't worry, Captain, they're unhurt, but it seems they rolled over a Div Arty three-quarter-ton that was full of OUR PLYWOOD!'

'Shit,' thought Fuller. He took a deep breath then said, 'No kidding Harry, surely there must be some mistake. Let me check this out and call you right back.'

Fuller hung up and told Sergeant Jenkins the Baker-Perkins saga. Jenkins digested this information then said, 'Sir, hmm, what do we have to trade?' He thought some more and then said, 'How about those two extra cases of steaks? You know, Sir, those that were left over in that shipment we brought back from Cam Rahn for Colonel Jones?'

'Yeah!' said Fuller. 'That could work.'

'Right, Sir! Those guys on Arty Hill surely would like a BBQ. While you call back the Captain, I'll call their Operations Sergeant and then their Supply Sergeant. Their Operations Sergeant is a buddy of mine. Owes me!'

'Hate to lose those steaks, Jenkins, but they have us by the short hairs and they know it.'

Fuller picked up the phone and dialed a number. He said, 'Captain Malkovich, this is Fuller. Say, friend, I checked out that little incident you mentioned. Now it is my understanding that our Operations Sergeant, you know Sergeant Jenkins, the guy who gets you all that hook and slick support every day. He's a great guy, runs the place over here. You know what I mean?'

'Uh-huh.'

'Yeah, right! He's always doing favors for you guys. Goes the extra mile for the Battalions. Somehow, he always finds a way to get your artillery Batteries out in the field with a little extra chopper support. Well, I was told that he made a trade with your Operations Sergeant or maybe it was your Supply Sergeant. I'm not clear on that. Anyway, I think it was something about two cases of filet mignons or something like that.'

Fuller paused to give the captain a moment to think about those delicious, prime-cut steaks. 'They are probably thin and tough as hell,' Fuller thought.

'I didn't know anything about the steaks,' said Captain Malkovich. 'You did say filet mignons?'

'Sure did. They are being placed in a quarter-ton as we speak.'

'Well, there is really no problem, Fuller. I'll get the truck rolled back upright and will send the two gentlemen back your way with the plywood. Hell, we have plenty.'

'Thanks a bunch. Malkovich, you are a real sweetheart. Call us anytime if Div Arty Air can help you.'

'You know I will.'

'Jenkins, have Lieutenant Baker and Sergeant Perkins report back to me when they get here. They just cost us a BBQ. I am going to cut them a new one.'

'Yes Sir.'

Chapter 20

The 'A, B, Cs' of Shooting Down a Loach

0800 hrs, 8 June 1969
Div Arty Air Operations

Captains Mark Birmingham and Darryl James sat in the Operations hootch with Sergeant Jenkins reviewing the morning's scheduled hook sorties and pilots' missions. The Operations room had two metal desks, a couple of extra chairs and a large map of I Corps glued onto the back wall. A UHF radio sat on a crude wooden shelf by the map. Sergeant Jenkins, the Operations Sergeant, sat behind one of the desks. Jenkins, the guy who ran the day-to-day activities of Operations, chatted merrily on the phone. Birmingham sat on top of a corner of Jenkins' desk reading the pilots' flight schedule. He had his always-present pipe stuck in his mouth. It filled the room with a sweet smell of hickory nuts. Captain Birmingham had been the acting commanding officer of Div Arty Air for six weeks. Major Barnes, their former boss, went home in February. Division Artillery filled the Air Section's slot for a couple of months with a non-aviation artillery major, Major Phillips. The pilots respected Major Phillips, but he wasn't a pilot and that just didn't work too well. Division gave up trying to fill the slot and allowed Birmingham, the senior captain at Div Arty, to become acting CO. Captain Dotson, the second senior officer, was busy as the unit's check-pilot. Captain James, the third in line, was made the Operations officer.

Warrant Officer Tim Booth strutted into Operations full of his usual piss and vinegar. 'Morning, douche-bags,' he said cheerfully, as he belched and farted as if on cue.

'SHIT, BOOTH,' shouted Birmingham, 'you're going to be barred from Operations.'

James said, 'Nice one, Booth.' He and Jenkins held their noses and laughed.

The 5ft 6in chubby pilot shot them the finger and walked out the back door. The short pilot had a baby face that made him seem more like a high school student than a 20-year-old helicopter pilot flying a $500,000 helicopter. Booth came from a well-to-do, church-going conservative Methodist family in Tacoma, Washington. The boy-pilot grew up a rich kid who could have easily found a way of not going to Vietnam. He tried college for a year and did well academically but dropped out, which really upset his parents. He heard about the Warrant Officer Program and easily qualified. He wanted to fly.

Booth had arrived at Div Arty Air several months earlier, fresh out of flight school. The baby-faced pilot quickly acquired the colorful language at Div Arty Air. Prior to Vietnam, he rarely uttered a cuss word. Now the colorful character could not say two words without sounding like a seasoned Marine drill sergeant. As if fitting with his new image as a hell-on-wheels-didn't-give-a-fuck-Wobbly-One, Booth let everyone know that he had little if any respect for any non-rated officer. He, along with most of the aviator warrant officers in Vietnam, avoided saluting a non-rated officer below the rank of lieutenant colonel. Actually, they didn't even salute rated lieutenants, captains and sometimes majors.

The colorful aviator had an adventure or two at Div Arty that only added to his hell-on-wheels-didn't-give-a-fuck-Wobbly-One reputation. One happened back in January. His engine quit in his OH-23G while cruising at 1,700ft over the Quang Ngai River. Booth crashed, destroying the aircraft. Luckily he and his passenger walked away virtually unhurt. As the old saying goes, a good landing is one you walk away from. The Raven, however, didn't fare well; it would never fly again.

Lieutenant Jim Farley, a non-rated artillery observer who had flown enough combat hours with the section to earn a couple of air medals, followed Booth through Operations. Birmingham saw him and yelled, 'HEY FARLEY, hold up a minute.' The artillery first lieutenant stopped at the door. Birmingham continued, 'You and Booth are off to Rocket Ridge for the 82nd today, I see.'

'Yeah, we are going to tool around the hills today for a look-see.'

'Be careful guys. Activity reports showed up on today's morning report.'

'Yeah, I know. We discussed it last night at G2; that's why we will be doing the scouting.'

'Remember you are not armed and flying alone; avoid getting low.'

'You know Booth,' said Farley. 'He's crazy, sometimes.'

'Not really. His reputation sometimes, ah.... Oh, forget it! Booth's all right. Listen, Farley, be careful.'

'Roger.'

Farley and Booth walked down to the flight line. A Loach pulled up and Warrant Officer Bill Broderick got out and walked up with his gear. Broderick said, 'I came in on fumes. You will need to taxi over to the refueling station. I jumped over to the Qui Nhon airbase and guess what? Those damn Air Force pukes wouldn't fill me up. They ignored me and some Alpha Hotel[1] took my picture sitting on the tarmac. I heard they did the same darn thing to Lieutenant James last month when he flew in there in a 23. Wouldn't give him Av gas and took his picture. They must have a nice gallery of pictures over there.'

Booth got in and started up the Loach. He noticed the low fuel warning light was on. He picked it up to a hover and requested permission to taxi over to the refueling station. As he taxied out on to the active, he found himself sitting on the runway with a whole armful of collective pitch and a loud beep-beep warning with the master caution light on.

'Holy shit! I've run out of gas.'

The Loach has such high rotor momentum that he had conducted a hovering auto-rotation and didn't even know it. In the OH-23G that the Loaches replaced it would have been a different story. The timing of the collective pull in a hovering auto-rotation was crucial to landing softly. It was easy to bend the skids on a 23 and often damage the tail boom on a hovering engine failure.

'Tower, this is Phoenix Two-Six, I've run out of gas. Sorry about that. Please send a fuel truck.'

'Roger,' said the tower. The tower controller covered his mike and suppressed a chuckle.

Farley turned to Booth and asked, 'What the hell; the engine quit?'

'That, my friend, is running out of gas.'

'Let's not let that happen to us.'

'No worries, Amigo. NOTHING IS GOING TO HAPPEN TO US! Jump in; let's go.'

1445 hrs, 8 June 1969
Rocket Ridge

The four-man VC patrol moved stealthily through the elephant grass surrounding a small village in the valley below the foothills of the scarred Chu Lai Highlands. They had inspected the village for the presence of any young men and obtained their monthly tribute of rice from the villagers' meager stores. The squad moved carefully. Here, low in the valley, they were in danger. They were headed for sanctuary, just a few kilometers away in the mountains.

The second-in-command, Sergeant Soo-Dong, walked in front of the squad. He was discouraged. Recently their leader, Commander Ro Kwan, had kept him from being reassigned to a tactical unit. The VC sergeant wanted to get away from the tiresome, often boring job of carrying rockets. He knew Commander Kwan hated him ever since the incident months ago when they shot down a helicopter lost in fog north-west of Quang Ngai. Soo-Dong watched the beating of the helicopter's crew with distaste. Although he said nothing, his disapproving manner embarrassed Kwan. Since that time, he and Soo-Dong had said little to each other. The young sergeant felt he had to get away from this man at all costs.

Recently, Soo-Dong and Kwan received several days of training from the North Vietnamese Regular Army at a hidden camp in the jungle. One part of the training involved shooting at low-flying helicopters. Commander Kwan became a bit haughty at this phase of the instruction and had to tell their brothers from the north how they shot the helicopter down. Their comrades were less impressed when they learned the helicopter was hovering, an easy target. They told the trainees that shooting down helicopters was difficult. They learned the helicopter was most susceptible coming in to land or taking off and the pilot was the most vulnerable part of the helicopter. They were taught to aim ten helicopter lengths in front of a fast low-flying helicopter and to shoot a series of three-round bursts.

'Be patient,' their instructor added, 'and wait for the helicopter to fly into the hail of bullets.'

Tim Booth and Jim Farley flew from LZ Artillery Hill along the outer perimeter of Rocket Ridge. Rocket Ridge referred to a series of heavily-forested hills north of Chu Lai where the VC routinely fired rockets at the division. As they scouted, the two coordinated by radio with the various infantry units in the field. The morning was uneventful. Booth and Farley stopped at Artillery Hill for an hour's lunch break. During lunch, an infantry second lieutenant on the G2's staff asked for a ride out to Charlie Company located 18 klicks to the north-west. They dropped the lieutenant off and departed Charlie Company's small clearing in the jungle and turned south-west. Booth elected to fly low-level and follow what they called Ho-Chee's creek as they returned to Artillery Hill.

Booth's decision to fly low-level had advantages and disadvantages. It gave Farley a better chance to gain intelligence in the area. If they climbed to 1,500ft above the ground to safety from small-arms fire, they couldn't see as much ground detail. Flying 10ft off the ground also provided cover. A Loach was difficult prey to hunt as it passed in and out of the tree line at 110 knots. However, if the helicopter came through cleared areas without cover, shooters nearby would get a good target. Another part of Booth's decision to fly low-level was that it was a rush for the 20-year-old. Loach pilots tended to be aggressive with a feeling of invulnerability. Cobra pilots often said that you had to be one taco short of a combination plate to fly a Loach.

Booth and Farley raced at low level, following a creek through the heavily-forested foothills north of Chu Lai. The Loach enjoyed plenty of cover until the creek cut across a broad rice field.

Up ahead of the helicopter, the four-man VC squad moved down near the creek bank. Closer now to refuge in the mountains, they relaxed and rested their AK-47s on their shoulders as they walked along the creek. Sergeant Soo-Dong, the point man, raised his hand and stopped them where the trail forked. One trail went south-west to a village located a couple of kilometers north along rice paddies in the valley.

The point man looked back at their leader. Kwan, annoyed, waved at Soo-Dong to take the west fork. Suddenly they heard the familiar drone of the small helicopter behind them. The VC looked back toward the sound and pulled the assault rifles off their shoulders.

'It is another of those egg-shaped devils,' Kwan said excitedly. 'Move back, Comrades, quickly.'

He motioned them back several feet out of the creek into the jungle edge in excellent cover. The VC leader directed them to take up firing positions. 'Shoot in front of the helicopter,' he said, 'not the ten lengths. Use three to five lengths. I know more than those NVA Cadre,' he whispered. 'I have experience with this helicopter type. Three to five lengths only!'

The noise grew in strength to their left. They saw the helicopter approaching for a brief instant then lost sight of it as it dipped below the trees. The egg-shaped helicopter should pass from left to right, hopefully within range. The enemy helicopter reappeared and approached directly towards them, then veered away. The men sighed, greatly disappointed; they would miss it. Suddenly, the helicopter turned back and, as if on cue, lined up along the creek within range in perfect position to try their technique.

'FIRE,' screamed Kwan.

Three men aimed slightly ahead of the helicopter and fired three-round bursts at the fast low-flying helicopter. Their initial bursts missed. Tracer rounds passed well behind the Loach. Soo-Dong aimed ten lengths in front and fired. The initial burst missed. Tracer rounds passed well behind the Loach. Soo-Dong's initial three-round burst passed in front of the helicopter. His next two three-round bursts were closer.

The Loach traveled at 108 knots, a mere 10ft off the ground, seemingly invulnerable. The pilot's eyes blinked, surprised at the tracers passing off the aircraft's nose. His cyclic had been trimmed with slight back pressure for safety in low-level flight. Any reduction in forward pressure from his right hand and the Loach would climb on its own. Instinctively, as the green tracers passed in front, the pilot reduced forward cyclic pressure and the helicopter rose. The aircraft seemed to shudder as it took hits. The OH-6A was tough, designed to withstand small-arms fire and continue flying. Not this time; the fire was devastating. One round bounced off Booth's chicken-plate, breaking the windshield in front of Farley. Booth lunged sideways in his armored seat from the impact, locking his seat's inertia reel. He struggled to keep his hands and feet on the controls as another bullet missed his right foot by inches. The projectile cut through the thin aluminum in the floor, shearing off the control linkage to the pilot's right pedal. A third AK-47 round broke one of the control linkage rods to the main rotor, causing Booth to lose fore and aft control of the helicopter. He eased back on the cyclic to keep the Loach's nose up with no response. The stricken craft veered slightly out of trim to the left. The pilot lowered the collective and tried to add right pedal. The pedal wouldn't move. He knew they were doomed.

The airstream moving past the craft pushed the Loach back to the right into trim, facing forward. Amazingly, as if willing itself to survive, the helicopter's nose pitched up and the airspeed decreased to 50 knots. The Loach settled. Its landing gear hit a rice paddy dike, breaking off part of the skids. What little remained of the landing gear dragged along the wet rice paddy, sending up a high brown rooster tail of water, mud and rice grass. The skids then sheared off completely, slowing the helicopter. The Loach slid to its left, sending up a new spray of mud and brown water. Then, as if in slow motion, the stricken craft rolled over on its right, disintegrating the main rotor. The aircraft twisted and the tail boom snapped off, sending pieces high in the air. What remained of the aircraft slid further, rolled one last time and, miraculously, landed upright in thick mud.

Soo-Dong saw the stricken helicopter go out of control and lost sight of it. Moments later he heard the impact and saw a plume of mud and water shoot up high in the air down the valley. One of the men cheered loudly. He was immediately hushed by Commander Kwan's fierce look. They were in danger here, and it was too dangerous to investigate. With an arm wave, Kwan directed them off the trail into the jungle. The squad quickly departed.

1545 hrs, 8 June 1969
Div Arty Air Operations

'Div Arty Ops, this is Dolphin Two-Four, over.'

Captain James picked up the mike from the UHF radio and said, 'Go ahead, Two-Four.'

'OPs, one of your Loaches is down one-five klicks north-east of Arty Hill, over.'

'Holy shit,' thought James. He pressed the mike and said, 'Two-Four, this is Div Arty Ops, SAY AGAIN.'

'Roger, one of your birds is down. I am over the position now; it looks bad, Amigo. Real bad.'

Birmingham and James rushed to the wall and checked their flight following board. 'It fits,' said James, 'that could be Booth returning to Arty Hill.'

As they studied the map, Sergeant Jenkins picked up the mike and said, 'Dolphin Two-Four, did you hear a Mayday from them, over?'

'Negative, Ops. Maybe Salvation did.' James and Birmingham rushed out the door and shouted to Jenkins, 'WE ARE ON OUR WAY OUT THERE. WATCH THE SHOP.'

'Roger,' he replied. Jenkins pressed the mike and said, 'Two-Four, we will be there in one-five mikes or less.'

James and Birmingham grabbed their flight gear and ran down the hill to the flight line. They found a ready Loach and jumped in without pre-flighting. They received emergency clearance from Ky Ha and departed toward Arty Hill. Ten minutes later, they saw the circling Huey. A gunship was also circling now. James was at the controls, while Birmingham worked the radios.

'Holy shit, Mark, look at that,' said James over the intercom.

'Yeah,' replied Birmingham, 'I see.'

Below, a 200-yard broad path of debris and flattened rice field revealed the skid path of the crashing aircraft. At the south end of the debris field, a form that looked to the pilots like a pile of metal junk stood upright in the mud like a statue at a modern art show. Villagers flocked toward the wreck, attracted to the metal and plastic debris. As James and Birmingham came closer, they saw that the villagers were carting off pieces of the Loach.

'I'm going right in,' James told Birmingham.

Birmingham nodded and relayed their intentions to Dolphin Two-Six. The villagers scattered as they landed. Birmingham dashed out with his M16 as James applied friction to the controls and foolishly followed, leaving their Loach idling and vulnerable. A gunship swooped over their heads, loudly letting everyone know he was there and meant business.

The two pilots rushed up to the wreckage, relieved to see no bodies nearby or inside. However, their optimism evaporated as they examined the wreckage. It was a shell of muddy junk with no glass, no tail boom nor rotor blades. The cockpit and passenger compartments were devastated. They looked up front and gasped. There was no cockpit floor. The front seats and seat belts were virtually all that survived. Both cyclic control sticks had been ripped out of the cockpit. The pilot's right side collective was gone. The co-pilot's collective was pushed all the way down. The back seats and floor remained intact.

'They couldn't have survived this,' said Birmingham, shaking his head slowly. 'No fucking way they could have.'

James remained silent and looked around, sadly agreeing with Birmingham's assessment, but something didn't look right to him. 'Where were the bodies?' he asked himself. James looked off toward the bush at the departing villagers, wondering if they had carried off the bodies. 'They wouldn't do that. They would be afraid to do anything like that. The men must have walked or crawled off. That's got to be it.'

James looked up at the cowling above the crew compartments and saw the words, 'California Dreaming'. 'Jenkins will be pissed.'

The two walked back along the crash path looking left and right. They stopped and looked up as they heard the whop-whop of a Huey coming toward them in a slow landing approach. It landed 20ft away from the wreckage and the door gunner waved for the two Loach pilots to come over. Birmingham walked to the Huey and climbed up to the co-pilot's door. The co-pilot yelled over the rotor and engine noise, 'SALVATION JUST SAID THAT MARINES CALLED FOR A DUST-OFF[2] FROM A LOCATION NEAR HERE. IT'S EN ROUTE NOW TO THE HOSPITAL. MAYBE IT WAS YOUR GUYS.'

Birmingham patted him on the shoulder and turned away from the Slick smiling. He yelled, 'JAMES, JAMES!'

1552 hrs, 8 June 1969

Booth raised his head slightly off the floor of the Dust-Off Huey. He sighed and thought to himself, 'Shit, what happened? Everything happened so fucking fast.' Steve Lincoln looked back from the left pilot's seat. He was smiling back at him with his thumb up in the air: the 'You're OK' sign. Booth laid his head back on the floor; he felt dazed. 'Shit,' he thought, 'I'm on Link's Slick. The crazy fucker should be home in the World; the land of Whoppers and round-eyed-women.' Booth tried to move his right arm. It hurt badly and felt heavy. He turned to his right and saw Farley laying near him and looking back with sunken eyes.

Booth laid back and tried to remember the crash and aftermath. He remembered unstrapping himself and falling through the missing floor into the soggy bottom of the rice field. Farley had fallen heavily, favoring his left wrist. He remembered that their M16s, survival radio and gear were gone, thrown and scattered from the wreckage. Their 45-caliber automatic pistols remained strapped to their bodies. He recalled limping away from the wreckage, frightened and hurt, knowing they had to hide. They moved off in the direction of their destination, seeking the safety of friendly troops they knew were ahead somewhere. The two walked about one half-mile when they heard shouts ahead of them.

'TROOPERS, STOP RIGHT THERE. FREEZE, YOU ARE IN A MINEFIELD.'

They stopped. A squad of Marines fanned out in front and partially around them. Their M16s pointed toward the trees on all sides. A gunnery sergeant walked a careful path out to them and said to follow him and step only in his footprints. They did as he said. The Marines had them lay down and checked them over. They applied a heavy splint-like bandage to Farley's wrist and immobilized Booth's shoulder with a sling. Another Marine spoke into a PRC-10 radio and in ten minutes a beautiful Huey arrived with red crosses painted on the sides.

Booth would learn that he had a shrapnel wound in his right foot and had strained his left arm from when the collective was torn out. The cyclic bruised his thighs badly as it, too, was ripped out. The pilot also had bruised ribs from the impact of the AK-47 round against his chicken-plate. Farley was bruised all over too, but his most serious wound was his wrist, broken in three places. This wound would take him to Tokyo in the morning for surgery. He was going back to the States.

Chu Lai Hospital
1600 hrs, 8 June 1969

The UHF crackled in the modern air-conditioned emergency room, 'Chu Lai hospital, Dust-Off Niner-Niner, over.' Major Lincoln, recognizing her brother's voice, dashed out of the break room to the radio.

She pressed the button and replied, 'Niner-Niner, Chu Lai Hospital, Bro, what do you have?'

'Tally Ho, Sis, I'm zero-five mikes out with two PACs[3] with some broken bones and shock. They seem stabilized.'

'Roger, Bro.'

'Sis, these guys are friendlies, Div Arty Air amigos.'

She paused, concerned, then stuttered, 'Ah, ah, do I know these friendlies?'

'Roger that! They both seem stable. Ah, take good care of them, Sis.'

'Roger, Bro. That you can count on.'

The Next Day

James and Leffert left the driver and jeep and walked into the Chu Lai hospital entrance. A young nurse wearing the gold bars of a second lieutenant rushed out into the hallway. She had been having a bad day, losing a burn patient in Bravo Ward. She saw two soldiers strutting in carrying a package. She ran up to them and spoke in a snappy, authoritarian voice: 'It's not visiting hours, Captains, you can't go in there until nineteen hundred hours; they're having supper.'

James and Leffert glared at the nurse, instantly thinking her to be a tight-ass, schoolteacher type with a big chip on her shoulder. They ignored her, grunted and continued walking down the hall. She followed and shouted, 'I SAID STOP.'

James turned around, looked her in the eyes and said, 'Lieutenant, we're going to Ward Three. Call the MPs if you want, but we're going.'

'Captain, we have plenty of majors here.' She stared back at their backs fuming, turning red: 'I mean it!'

Leffert felt his anger slowly building inside. He stopped and turned smartly to face her, holding a stealthy finger against his chest. Only she could see the one-finger salute. She scowled back; he smiled.

They walked into Booth's room. He had two black eyes and black and blue areas across his arms. His leg was out straight, wrapped in a bandage.

'How you doing, Amigo?' said Leffert.

'I had a few stitches,' replied the smiling patient. James looked at his pillow. A Purple Heart was pinned to it. Leffert saw it and admired it with James. Booth noticed them looking at it and said, 'Oh, some tight-ass Full Bird came by earlier to pin that to my pillow. Pretty, ain't it?'

Major Barnett burst in the room and said, 'What in the hell are you two doing with my nurses? They're volunteers here, you know, and should be treated with dignity and respect.'

'Sorry, Dede, I mean, SORRY, MAJOR,' said James. 'It was entirely my fault. We had a little communication problem.'

'Communication problem? She said one of you shot her the finger.'

'Ah, sorry, Ma'am,' said Lieutenant Leffert, standing at attention. 'I shouldn't have said, ah, I mean done, ah, anything.'

'Listen to me, Lee, she just lost a patient and was.... Oh, forget it.' She turned to Booth and said, 'How are you feeling, Tim?'

'Like a boiled owl, Major.'

Chapter 21
Doc's Boondoggle

1900 hrs, 15 June 1969
Div Arty Air Recreation Room

Doc Cruz walked into the pilots' private lounge. James looked up from his chair where he was reading a John D. McDonald novel. He set the book down to study their flight surgeon, one of the real characters from Division Artillery. The flight surgeon helped himself to a beer. 'Heck,' thought James, smiling to himself, 'the Doc must be the shortest cotton-picking officer in all of Americal Division. Shoot, he might be the shortest guy in all of I Corps. I guess it depends on whom you're counting because I bet there are some Charlies out there shorter. Well, no matter, the Doc would be right there in that pissing contest, even if counting the Gooks.'

Captain Cruz was 5ft 4in in his stocking feet. He told everyone he was 5ft 6.5in and most believed him because there was power in that small frame and enough personality to go around for a half a dozen guys. Doc was loquacious and witty; an all-round likable guy. He had a thick, bushy black mustache and wore thick dark-framed glasses. The glasses, however, did not hide the dark, sparkling bright eyes that revealed intelligence. He loved movies, reading, ping-pong and Scrabble. He was excellent at ping-pong and Scrabble, but movies and novels were his passions. He spent lots of time in verbally dissecting the current movies and books. His favorite movie was *2001: A Space Odyssey*. He especially enjoyed discussing and interpreting the symbolism and admiring the special effects of the science fiction epic.

Doc and his wife of six years graduated from the Medical School at the University of Pennsylvania. They both went on to medical residencies at Los Angeles General, a public hospital.

Doc was drafted in 1967. He took the Flight Surgeon's course at Fort Sam Houston in San Antonio and subsequently found himself in Vietnam. He made the best of it and never complained. Most doctors opted for the experience of working in the high-tech Chu Lai hospital. Cruz volunteered to work at Division Artillery. He was a people doctor and wanted the day-to-day contact with real people, not cases.

Although the Army trained him as a flight surgeon, Cruz was board-certified in gynecology. A lucrative practice in gynecology awaited him when he would leave the Army in two years.

Lieutenant Duffy, Div Arty Air's maintenance officer, once noted that Doc Cruz had the wrong specialty. 'He should be in obstetrics,' said Duffy. 'He's just at the right height to catch those babies sliding out.'

Dr. Cruz ran the medical clinic at Division Artillery Headquarters but hung out with the aviators. This surprised both his medical colleagues and the many career-officer types found at Division Artillery Headquarters. They considered the pilots to be the 'unwashed'. Cruz, a bit unconventional himself, fit in with the group. Another reason Cruz liked the gaggle of aviators was because of his own love of flying. He thought that maybe, just maybe, he might learn to fly when he got back to the world and made some real money. The flight surgeon frequently hung around Operations or Maintenance to bum a ride.

The previous day, Cruz had finagled a reason to fly with Div Arty. He wrote a memo to Div Arty's Commanding Officer Colonel Jones, stating that he needed to inspect the field mess and sanitation facilities on some of the firebases to comply with some such regulation or another.

That evening, Captain Birmingham announced that Lieutenant Leffert, one of the Doc's closest friends, had the job of taking Cruz on his sanitation inspection tour. When Leffert learned what he was to do, he broke into an uncontrollable fit of laughter. As Leffert laughed, James asked, 'You mean Doc is really going to inspect the shit houses?'

Birmingham and the rest of the aviators, comfortably consuming adult beverages in the recreation room, roared with laughter. Doc ignored them, paying attention only to the Scotch and water in his hand.

Leffert asked, 'Just how does he do that? Does he get a flashlight and look down the double holes, or does he lift the trap door around back and check out the shit tub?' Cruz joined in as everyone laughed again.

The so-called 'shit tub' was actually a steel barrel cut in half. Vietnamese laborers or unlucky GIs on KP removed the drums daily and poured kerosene into the mixture of paper, feces and other unidentifiable organic substances. The mixture was then burned, resulting in a thick black smoke. Out on firebases, the burning waste gave the chopper pilots a wind direction and was in that regard a helpful albeit smelly daily occurrence. The burning tubs of crap were one of those unforgettable smells known by all who visited the field in Vietnam. Most REMFs[1] never had to experience this real smell of the war. Most of them got to sit on wood and porcelain and hear the sweet sound made by a flushing toilet.

Everyone in the air section considered Doc Cruz to be one of the guys, but they were always just a bit suspicious of his medical abilities. After all, real doctors wouldn't have anything to do with pilots. They lived in some pretentious ivory tower near the hospital and chased nurses. The pilots would tell him that they would sooner go to see a veterinarian if they were sick than ask him for medical advice. Cruz took the Div Arty ribbing well. He, like everyone, learned quickly that you had to have a thick hide to survive the constant kidding and insulting comments the pilots made to each other. Two incidents, however, were to change what might be called their somewhat suspicious medical opinion of him.

Several Weeks Earlier

One especially hot day in early May, James and Leffert had an LRRP[2] insertion along the trails at Rocket Ridge. Door-gunners with M60 machine guns protected the Loaches. Leffert and James dropped off a four-man LRRP team in a small bomb-induced clearing in the mountainous jungle. Birmingham, in an empty ship, acted as back-up and scout for the insertion. It was a quick in-and-out mission. Several days later, they would pick up the team at another site. The mission went smoothly and they all returned to Ky Ha Heliport by 0900 hrs. Birmingham gave James and Leffert the day off.

The two of them went to the beach. Leffert liked to work on his tan whenever he could. The beautiful Chu Lai beach had yellowish-brown soft sand that would rival the beaches of many resorts with its beauty and charm.

The two pilots tossed around a football at the water's edge. James took a 3-mile jog along the beach while Leffert worked on his tan. Tired, hot and sweaty, James joined Leffert and sat on the sand watching the frequent helicopter take-offs directly overhead and listening to Radio Da Nang. They laughed as the announcer said, 'Good Morning, Vietnam; it's time for another Chicken-man episode. He's everywhere, he's everywhere.' Chicken-man was a farcical super-hero spoof loved by the pilots.

As they walked back for lunch, James complained of not feeling well. He said, 'I think I'll skip lunch, Leff, I think I got too much sun.'

'You look a little pale, Darr. A nap would do you good. I'll bring you something later from the club.'

'Thanks Leff.'

James walked up the hill to the water fountain to get a drink. He felt weak and thirsty. He laid down on his bunk for a nap, but could not sleep. The pilot felt nauseated. 'Definitely don't feel well,' he thought to himself. 'I need to get another drink.' He got up to walk up the hill but felt too weak to make it. The pilot sluggishly returned to his cot and tried to sleep.

Lieutenant Leffert returned from the Officers' Club, looked at his roommate and became suddenly concerned. He rushed to his side and touched his shoulder, 'Darryl, you look terrible.'

Leffert felt his friend's forehead. It was hot and dry. 'This is not right,' thought Leffert, 'something is definitely wrong.'

'Help me up, Leff,' said James, 'I feel weak and I need to get another drink of water.'

Leffert helped him up, practically carrying him to the door. He stopped and led him back to the bunk and said, 'This is no good, Darryl. Lay back down on your bunk. I'll be right back.'

He rushed to the next hootch and found Lieutenant Dotson. 'Connor, James is ill, real ill, I think we need to find the Doc.'

'Let me go see him.' They both returned to James's hootch. Dotson felt his head. James was becoming listless and not very responsive. 'Stay here, Leff,' said Dotson. 'Watch him; I'm going for help.'

Fifteen minutes later, Dotson returned with Doc Cruz and a corpsman in a quarter-ton jeep. They ran up the hill to the hootch. Leffert and Bill Broderick stood over the ailing aviator. Cruz brushed them aside and felt James's head. He looked at the pale, dry skin and sick eyes and made an immediate diagnosis. He grabbed a bag of saline solution and put an IV into the captain's arm. James closed his eyes. Several minutes later, he opened his eyes and told the flight surgeon that he felt better.

'You had heatstroke; you should feel even better soon.'

Cruz turned to Leffert and said, 'Leff, go up to the Club and get a pitcher of ice water and bring a whole shitload of salt tablets back with you.' Leffert rushed out the door.

'Doc, I am real thirsty,' said James. 'I just felt too weak earlier to get up the hill for a drink.'

'I know. We'll have something for you to drink in just a bit. Feel strong enough to sit up?'

'Yes, I am feeling better.'

Cruz noticed the pilot's complexion was returning and a few beads of perspiration appeared on his forehead. Good signs, he told himself.

'Your electrolyte balance in your body was totally out of whack, Darryl. Did you eat breakfast and have any fluids this morning?'

'Yes.'

'What did you do today?'

'Leff and I flew a mission and then we spent three hours at the beach.'

'It was especially hot today,' replied Cruz. 'You probably sweated a lot and didn't take in enough fluids. You are definitely doing better now, Darr.'

'I am feeling much, much better, Doc.'

Leffert came in. Cruz poured James a full glass of water and made him take four salt pills with it. He also encouraged him to drink two more glasses of water. The corpsman removed the IV solution. Before they left, Cruz said to everyone in the hootch, 'Guys, this can happen to any of you here. It's hot and humid and we all need to drink lots of fluids and take the salt pills every day. I need to impress on you how serious this can be. James could have died without medical treatment. You can't go without water on these hot days. This can sneak up on you frighteningly quick like it did on him today.'

The dozen gathered pilots were impressed. James stood up and smiled. 'I'm feeling fine, guys. It's amazing. A little while ago, I thought I was going to die right here on this cot. I really did.'

'You might have, Shithead, if Doc hadn't come along,' said Broderick.

'Sit down, James,' several of them said.

'Are you hungry?' Dotson asked.

'Yes, I could eat.'

0800 hrs, 16 June 1969
Operations Hootch, Sanitation Flight

Dotson and Birmingham watched Leffert and Dr. Cruz grab flight gear and head down the hill to the flight line. The diminutive flight surgeon struggled to carry his helmet, M16, bandoleer of ammunition, survival radio, medical bag and chicken-plate.

'Looks like Mutt and Jeff,' Dotson said to Birmingham. Sergeant Jenkins sitting at the desk, chuckled.

The two approached the flight line as Cruz whined, 'Leff, you sure I need all this stuff?'

'You ain't flying with me if you don't take a chicken-plate, helmet and M16.'

'But I have all this medical stuff.'

'Doc, you ain't getting your short, skinny butt shot off on my watch.'

'I am merely staturely challenged, NOT SHORT! I don't know why they assigned you to my flight anyway. You couldn't find your ass in the closet with two hands and a flashlight.'

'You better be nice to me; I'm driving.'

'Yeah, yeah.'

They departed Ky Ha low-leveling north across the marshes and water inlets. Cruz was getting a great ride. He felt a rush, as the ground seemed to flow all around him in a blur. He noticed he was clutching his seat tightly with his fingers. The flight surgeon forced himself to relax and enjoy the exhilarating flight at low level. The Loach crossed over the beach and low-leveled just above the surf. The helicopter turned inland and they traveled west until they crossed Highway One. Leaving the relative security of the lowlands, the pilot eased back on the cyclic and the Loach climbed swiftly and leveled off at 1,800ft above the ground. Cruz looked out his left door at the bright blue sky and puffy cumulus clouds above the mountains to the west. The view provided him a horizon with picturesque quality. The lush green Hawaiian-like mountains of the Vietnamese highlands awaited them.

Ten minutes later, they landed at Hill Three-Niner 22 kilometers west of the city of Tam Ky. Captain Cruz climbed out and met the battery commander. They shook hands and went into the mess tent. Leffert followed along behind. The battery commander introduced Cruz to the mess sergeant. The chubby sergeant with a dirty white apron looked on nervously as Cruz looked around and made a few notes. The commander asked Cruz if he would check out one of his men on sick call. At the Aid Station, Cruz checked the soldier over and gave him antibiotics. A sergeant poked his head in the bunker and asked the captain if he would mind looking at a hootch maid's hand. Cruz spent the next hour helping several people with minor ailments. Many wanted just to talk with the doctor.

Lieutenant Leffert thought to himself, 'He's not out here to check shit houses; he's here to help and provide a little moral support.'

Two Weeks Earlier
Div Arty Hootch City

The pilot remembered an incident when he and James accompanied Doc Cruz up the hill from their recreation room to see an Artillery second lieutenant. The lieutenant was shaking in his bunk when the trio entered his room. This lieutenant was having some kind of a nervous breakdown. He had been the manager of the Div Arty Officers' Club. That morning, the Division Artillery's Executive Officer had fired him and was sending him to Charlie Battery at Arty Hill. It was a relatively safe area; as safe as anywhere in Chu Lai.

Cruz talked to the shivering lieutenant softly and held his hand. He gave him a sedative and stayed with him for some time. The spectacle made Leffert and James disgusted. They waited outside for Cruz to finish, not saying a word to each other but what they were thinking was written all over their faces. Cruz came out and the three walked up the hill.

Cruz said softly, 'Everyone is different; we all handle stress and fear differently. This boy has been chewed out. He's had a real bad day. He's real scared. Does that make him a coward? I don't know, and you don't know. Maybe he'll be all right. I think he will recover, but I don't know. Even if he is sent home, I for one will not judge him or his character based on this. I wish him only well, not because I am a doctor but because it is the right thing to do.'

Leffert and James never said another word about the incident, but it troubled them.

Remaining Inspections
Cruz finished his work on Hill Three-Niner. He spent the remainder of the day visiting five different firebases. At each, he checked the mess tents and tended to minor ailments. On LZ West, for his pilot's benefit, Cruz looked in one outhouse. Leffert watched as Cruz talked to the men about their concerns, their fears, their

living conditions, problems at home, how long they had left in Vietnam, etc. He made some laugh and seemed to cheer everyone up. 'Doc is a fine guy,' thought Leffert.

Returning home, Cruz entered the dimly-lit room of his hootch and took off his flip-up sunglasses. As his eyes adjusted to the low light, he noticed something unusual. 'Huh, what the...?' Suddenly alarmed, he did a double-take. 'A BOMB?' He opened the door to back out and stopped. It took him a few more moments to see the 55-gallon drum in the center of his room. 'What in the hell...?' It was a drum, like those used in the outdoor crappers. The drum was thoroughly decorated with toilet paper. Rolls of toilet paper were wrapped around the sides and crossed up and down. A crudely-tied bow made from the paper was at the top. There was a sign that said, 'R. Cruz, M.D., Doctor of Sanitation', and underneath the title, in bold letters, 'HOPE YOU HAD A CRAPPER JACK TIME!'

Chapter 22

The Rocket Attack

2330 hrs, 22 January 1969
North-Eastern Perimeter Americal Division

Lieutenant James climbed in the front of the jeep alongside the duty driver. Tonight he was pulling officer-of-the-day duty. Sergeant Markowski, who had the duty as sergeant-of-the-guard, was in the back seat of the jeep. They had these duties between 1800 hrs and 0600 hrs. During their duty, both men were responsible for defending a portion of the perimeter defense. Their sector was called Kilo and was located 200 meters north of the Div Arty Officers' Club close to where James lived.

Sergeant Markowski came from Division Artillery's Headquarters Company and pulled this duty regularly. James, however, being a pilot, didn't have this duty often. The Division could not afford to have pilots pull this duty often as it made them unavailable to fly the next day.

James wore a light gray cotton flight suit, unusual attire for guard duty. Most pilots opted for combat garb. James wanted the guards to be able to see him in the dark as he approached their bunker. Captain Fuller told him it was better to approach the bunkers talking and singing in your flight suit so that there would be no doubt as to who you were.

Flight suit or not, James felt he looked like a warrior of sorts because he was wearing his 38-caliber Smith and Wesson with a Western holster and belt. The holster and belt, which were made locally, did not look military. The belt had twenty-eight 38-caliber rounds hooked into bullet sleeves and the holster had fancy Western stitching. A large survival knife and sheath were attached to the gun belt. The sheath was made in the same cowboy style. The gear seemed better suited to a Pancho Villa movie than a helicopter pilot on guard duty.

Like most of the helicopter pilots in Americal Division, he liked to look different. The non-rated[1] staff officers in Division Artillery hated this attitude of the pilots. James was wearing some government-issue gear. He had on a standard steel pot and carried a flak vest in his lap. The pilot also cradled an M16 assault rifle in his arms. The weapon had three twenty-round magazines taped together by electrician's tape into a Y-shape. The shooter could empty out one magazine, flip it over and slide in another magazine and then the last, giving him sixty rounds in total. The pilot's left upper sleeve had a band around it with a black 'OD' printed on it. Markowski had a similar band labeled 'SG'.

When James reported in earlier to the Operations bunker, Sergeant Markowski looked him over with some disfavor. Holy cow, thought Markowski, what in the hell do we have here? Looks like a damn cowboy. These pilots think they're John flipping Wayne.

Lieutenant James had just returned from R&R in Hawaii, surprised at the changed atmosphere at Americal Division. While he was enjoying the sunny beaches of Waikiki, a major enemy offensive had developed throughout Vietnam. The campaign coincided with the Vietnamese Lunar New Year called Tet and had been labeled the '69 Tet Offensive by the media. When he returned, James found the previous secure atmosphere within Americal Division's confines had evaporated.

Rockets had hit the Division hard. He learned that these had destroyed a slick helicopter and damaged several other choppers at Ky Ha Heliport, a mere 100 meters from their hootches. Rocket attacks, which had occurred twice a month or so before Tet, now happened daily. Some impacts had been close, too.

The previous week a Russian- or Chinese-made 123mm rocket hit 60 meters from the pilot's hootch. The rocket killed a soldier and wounded two others. Tet gave the perimeter guard duty tonight a new urgency.

The driver started the jeep, turned on the lights and looked toward Lieutenant James for orders. The pilot motioned for him to go and, as they left, Markowski reported on the FM radio that they were moving toward the perimeter. The jeep bounced along. As he peered into the darkness, James thought back to the close encounter he had yesterday with one of those dreaded 123mm rockets.

The Previous Evening
1900 hrs

James rode in the duty driver's jeep along with Captain Cunningham, Division Artillery's Perimeter Defense Commander and Sergeant Thomas Johnson. They were heading to the Division MARS Station to try to call home. The MARS station utilized a radiotelephone system that placed calls through a wireless radio system that connected into the conventional telephone system in the United States. Soldiers would stand in line for the chance that they might get through with a call to home. About half the time, they were successful.

The facility was located in the middle of the Division area, adjacent to the commanding general's house.

There was a long line of soldiers waiting to call when the two officers arrived. Rank had no privileges at the MARS station. They signed up into a queue. James's turn came after waiting forty-five minutes. He spoke into the phone, which was set up as a two-way radio. He had to say 'over' after each sentence. He gave the operator his wife's telephone number in New York. It was 2.00 am in New York, but he got no answer.

Hmm, he thought, it's late there, wonder where she is? Surely her mother would have answered; it's not that early. Puzzled and disappointed, he left the booth, gave a thumbs-down signal to Captain Cunningham and said, 'Didn't get through, Bill. Hope your luck is better.'

The lieutenant's attempts to call later did get through to his wife. Short-wave radio operators monitored the frequencies for the American soldiers to help whenever they could. One would later call his wife to let her know Lieutenant James tried to call. Bill Cunningham got through to his wife.

The three soldiers walked out in the parking lot. They heard a faint noise and looked instinctively up into the night air. In seconds, the noise grew in volume to a loud swoosh. They ran to the jeep as a hot blast of air followed by a loud 'KABOOM' knocked the three men to the ground. The air was heavy and thick with dust.

James shook his head. It ached and he had a loud ringing in his ears. He smelled the somewhat sweet, musty odor of high explosives, which reminded him of a Fourth of July celebration back in New Jersey.

'Holy Shit!' said Cunningham, getting to his feet. 'Darryl, Johnson, are you all right?'

'Yes, I think so,' replied James.

'That rocket was close,' moaned Johnson.

'NO SHIT!' said Cunningham, getting to his feet.

The area was chaotic. Soldiers were running every which way. Vehicles were speeding on the road. Other soldiers were getting off the ground. Luckily, the 123mm rocket had impacted harmlessly behind the general's quarters. They saw windows knocked out at both the general's quarters and the MARS station. Sirens wailed around the Division. In the distance, they heard other rockets impacting.

'I need to get back to Div Arty asap,' said Cunningham.

'Right,' replied James, 'let's go.'

The three ran to the jeep and leaped in. The jeep driver handed the mike to Captain Cunningham. The captain learned everything was OK on the perimeter and he told Operations he would be there in zero-eight minutes.

'Boy, that was real close last night,' thought James as he unconsciously rubbed his right elbow that was skinned up the previous night as he hit the hard pavement during the attack. 'We are getting more and more rocket attacks. The Snakes can't seem to find those guys shooting them either. Just one time, I would like to see those Snakes put some of our rockets up the butts of those guys firing those rockets in the hills.'

James, the sergeant and the duty driver slowly made their way along the dirt road that connected the bunkers and tower along the perimeter. Sergeant Markowski pointed off to Kilo sector's wooden tower with four spotlights shining outward toward the perimeter.

Markowski was a brute of a man. The 26-year-old blond-haired 6-footer weighed 220lb. His thick muscular chest, narrow waist and rugged features gave him the appearance of a man that no one would want to make angry.

The sergeant came from parents who were Polish emigrants who settled in Philadelphia. The big man had the reputation of being a good sergeant, a fair man well-respected by his men and officers.

The area out beyond the road was well lit from searchlights along the perimeter. No man's land, thought James, and bright enough that night for a football game.

Markowski brought along an M79 grenade-launcher with a bandoleer full of exploding rounds. The M79 looked like a sawn-off shotgun and opened downward at its breach like a shotgun. It fired a grenade shell in a low-velocity hyperbolic arc that could be followed by the shooter's eye. It was fun to shoot.

Tonight the sergeant planned to lob a few rounds out beyond the barbed-wire perimeter just to let anyone out there know that no one was asleep out here in the bunkers.

'I'll ask the lieutenant to shoot the M79,' thought the big sergeant. 'Those flyboys always love to shoot it. Hell, I will give the cowboy a thrill. What a lightweight!'

The three arrived at the first bunker, making plenty of noise with the jeep and their movements. They did not want anyone to misidentify them as enemy. This bunker, built several feet above ground for better visibility, was constructed from heavy timber crisscrossed for strength. The bunker portion of the structure was made from plywood with two layers of sandbags on the outside. The roof was constructed from heavy timbers, plywood and two layers of sandbags. Other bunkers along the line were at ground level; some were partially underground. The formidable structures were roomy enough for three fighting positions, a cot and two chairs.

The sergeant and lieutenant approached the bottom of the ladder leading to the dark bunker above.

'Mighty,' a soldier whispered the challenge from the bunker.

'Purpose,' replied the big sergeant correctly on the bottom of the ladder.

'Advance.'

The sergeant, followed by the lieutenant, climbed the ladder legs into the bunker.

'Hello, men,' said the sergeant.

'Evening, Sergeant,' said one of the soldiers.

James recognized one of the men in the bunker as Spec 4 Ferguson from the Admin Company.

'Good evening Ferguson,' James said.

'Evening, El Tee,' he said.

'Men,' said the sergeant, 'remember we are on Yellow Alert right now. One man can be sleeping, but two men must be awake.'

'Roger that, Sarge,' the men echoed.

The sergeant turned toward the lieutenant in the darkness of the bunker. 'Sir, how about if we fire a few M79 rounds out beyond the perimeter?'

'Go ahead,' said the lieutenant.

The sergeant took the mike from the bunker's radio and said, 'Red Horn Zero-Zero, this is Red Horn Zero-Two, be advised that we are going to lob some Mike Seventy-Niners out toward the perimeter.'

Markowski waited until all stations acknowledged, then he and the lieutenant climbed down the stairs.

One of the men came down with them.

'Sir,' said Markowski, 'would you do the honors?'

'Love to, Sergeant.'

Sergeant Markowski handed the M79 to the lieutenant. It was bent open, exposing the empty chamber. He gave James a grenade round. The lieutenant inserted the round and closed the weapon. He adjusted the sight and aimed across no man's land.

The sergeant said, 'Try 175 meters, Sir.'

'Roger, Sarge.'

The lieutenant sent off a round and tried to follow its flight, but lost it as it rose above the lights into the darkness.

'Short,' thought the sergeant.

The grenade impacted at the wire.

'Sorry, Sergeant, that was a bit short,' said the lieutenant.

'No shit,' thought the sergeant. 'We need our wire intact, Lieutenant. Let's not do that again.'

James's next round was better placed beyond the wire. He lobbed two more that landed more or less where he intended them to go. At least they were beyond the wire. He handed the M79 back to the sergeant.

'Good shooting,' said the sergeant, diplomatically.

'Thanks, Sarge. I really enjoyed shooting the M79.'

The lieutenant and sergeant left the three men at Bunker 1 and moved down to check the remaining bunkers in Sector Kilo.

The Marines manned the last bunker. These Marines were support personnel, not combat troops. Sometimes these support units contained the malcontents, goof-offs and jerk-offs. The best people always seemed to be out in the field.

As the sergeant and lieutenant walked into the Marine bunker, they got a heavy dose of marijuana smoke.

'Jesus,' said the sergeant. 'You men better not be doing what it smells like in here.'

'No Sergeant, we ain't doing nothing in here but what's we supposed to be doing.'

'That's a bunch of crap,' said the lieutenant. 'I'm high just coming in here. You men back off over here. The Sarge and I are going to look around.' They found nothing.

'Listen, men,' said the lieutenant, 'I can see that you hid or swallowed your shit. The Sarge and I know you have been doing it. You can get your asses court-martialed for that. I have been on six courts-martial panels since I have been here. Do you want to guess what these Special Court-Martial panels were for?'

There was no reply.

'Marijuana,' said the lieutenant. 'We will come back here later tonight. This bunker had better smell as sweet as a baby's freshly diapered and powdered butt. Get my meaning?'

'YES SIR.'

The sergeant then said, 'If there is any problem here, I will personally come back and kick every one of your ugly asses. Do you get my meaning?'

'YES SERGEANT.'

The sergeant's estimate of the value of the flyboy lieutenant's stock just went up.

'He can't shoot too well, but he handled himself real well in there. This El Tee ain't too bad. I certainly have seen worse.'

Two Hours Later

As the lieutenant, sergeant and jeep driver approached Bunker One, they realized something was wrong.

'Lieutenant,' said the driver. 'I don't see movement; something doesn't seem right.'

Instinctively the lieutenant grabbed his M16. Markowski did the same and hopped out of the jeep.

They waited outside the bunker at the foot of the ladder. Nothing happened. They were not challenged.

'Hello to the bunker,' called the lieutenant.

There was no answer. The lieutenant looked at the sergeant. Even in the darkness, he could see the scowl on Markowski's broad face.

The sergeant climbed up the ladder, followed by the lieutenant. They entered the dark bunker and in the dim light saw that everyone was asleep. One man was resting his head on the M60 machine gun sitting at the firing position facing off into the perimeter, dead asleep. Another man slept on a chair leaning his head against the plywood wall. The third man slept on the cot on his back, snoring peacefully.

The sergeant and lieutenant took the M60 and three M16s and carried them to the jeep. No one stirred in the bunker. They remained sound asleep. One of the men was allowed to be asleep in the Yellow Alert Status, but two must be awake at all times. This was a serious breach of security.

The man sleeping in the cot was Spec 4 Ferguson.

'Ferguson is probably allowed to be asleep,' thought the lieutenant as they put the weapons in the jeep, 'but I don't know for sure. Shit, they must be drunk or high on drugs to be that asleep and allow us to walk in and take their weapons like that.'

The sergeant turned to the lieutenant and asked, 'Sir, I would like your permission to call headquarters for replacements and place these men under arrest.'

'Go ahead, Sarge,' said James.

Another fifteen minutes passed. The men in the bunker remained sleeping. James looked up as he heard vehicles. Two jeeps approached. One had three new guards. Two MPs rode in the other. The men in the bunker finally woke up as the vehicles approached. They knew they were in serious trouble.

As they were relieved, Ferguson said with pleading eyes to the lieutenant, 'Sir, I was allowed to be asleep.'

James patted him on the shoulder, and said, 'You will be OK then, Fergie, hang in there, soldier. Tell them what happened!'

James and Markowski got back in their jeep and headed to headquarters. James patted the driver as the jeep approached the main lookout tower and said, 'Stop here! I am going to spend some time in the tower.'

James got out of the jeep with his steel pot and flak jacket. The sergeant got the radio and alerted them that the lieutenant was coming up to them.

The tower was 40ft in the air and constructed like the bunkers with heavy reinforced crossed timber, plywood and sandbags.

James climbed up a one-storey ladder to a turn-around platform, then another ladder, then another turnaround until he came to a trap-door. He banged on the door. It opened and the three occupants let the lieutenant into their dark sanctuary.

'Morning men,' said the lieutenant.

'Good morning to you, El Tee. We have some nice hot coffee, Sir.'

'Great, I would love some.'

PFC Roberts poured the lieutenant a cup and said, 'Don't get many visitors up here, Sir.'

'Just wanted to see how the other half lived.' The men laughed.

'What was that all about in Bunker One, Sir?' asked Roberts.

'Sleeping on guard duty.'

'Shit,' someone said. 'That's a bad one, real bad.'

0445 hrs
Perimeter Tower

The lieutenant was on his third cup of coffee. He was tired. He looked at his watch and thought, 'Only one hour and about fifteen to go until this is over and I can turn all this good stuff over to good ol' Bill Cunningham and hit the hay.'

It had been a troubling night with the men being relieved in Bunker One. Sleeping on guard duty was a very serious offense in wartime.

'Those poor fuckers,' he thought to himself, 'they would be court-martialed for sure. Maybe Ferguson will be all right.'

His thoughts were interrupted by the crackle of the radio: 'Red Horn, this is Red Horn One-Four. The Division alert status is now Green. I say again, Green.'

'Well,' thought James, 'now that guard duty is almost over, they change the alert status so two guys can be asleep in a bunker.'

The sky was showing a twinge of light. The lieutenant took a sip of tepid coffee. He cringed at the bitter taste of the tepid, strong black coffee. Looking out the window, he saw an orange streak shoot upwards from the mountains. 'What the...?' he thought, as another streak followed and then another. James grabbed the mike just as he heard the radio crackle in an excited, hurried voice, 'Red Horn, INCOMING, INCOMING.'

The lieutenant placed his steel pot on his head and slowly set his coffee cup down. There was nothing he could do but watch the two yellow streaks in the early-morning dark-blue sky fly directly toward his position. He braced for the inevitable. Time seemed to stand still.

One rocket seemed to be coming directly at him. 'A golden bullet,' he thought, 'with my name on it. That's what they say anyway; fate gets you with that one golden bullet.'

He waited, said a silent prayer and thought of his wife and daughter. Then it hit with a loud retort, 'KABOOM.'

The tower shook but remained standing.

'THAT WAS FUCKING CLOSE,' said PFC Robertson.

The three men in the tower looked out to their left and saw that the rocket impacted below them. Dust and debris hid the impact site.

Robertson pointed, 'HOLY SHIT, BUNKER ONE TOOK A DIRECT FUCKING HIT.'

He screamed on the radio, 'RED HORN ONE-EIGHT. ARE YOU ALL RIGHT?'

No answer.

'RED HORN ONE-EIGHT, ARE YOU OK, OVER?'

The radio remained silent.

'ONE-EIGHT, ONE-EIGHT, ARE YOU OK?'

Finally, the radio crackled and a weak voice responded, 'This is Red Horn One-Eight, we have two men down, I say again, two men down. NEED HELP, OVER.'

'Roger One-Eight, this is One-One, help is on the way, out.'

James looked out and checked the perimeter; it seemed quiet. They were not under a ground attack. He said to Ferguson, 'Call for help. Stay on the radio; I am going down to the bunker.'

The lieutenant opened the trap-door and rushed down the ladder. Sergeant Markowski came up in a jeep and stopped to pick him up. They rushed toward the bunker.

They saw that the bunker was heavily damaged. The rocket impacted on the bunker's right side, blowing away its sandbagged side and a portion of its roof. Markowski grabbed the jeep's first-aid kit and he, the lieutenant and the driver climbed up the ladder.

Two men were lying on the floor of the living quarters. The third man was down on his knees holding bloody hands against the throat of one of the men on the floor. Blood gushed from the man's neck through the fingers of the man helping him. Markowski grabbed a battle dressing from the first-aid kit and held it against the man's neck. James looked at the other man on the floor. The soldier was still, with one arm bent at an unnatural angle. The lieutenant felt for a pulse. There was none. He put his head against the man's chest and said, 'He's dead.'

A three-quarter-ton truck with a Red Cross painted on it rushed up to join them. A team of medics climbed up the ladder and took over. The medics worked over the man still alive on the floor. James and Markowski climbed down the stairs and waited. Soon a medic helped the third soldier down the stairs. The man was shaken but didn't seem to be seriously injured.

They didn't seem to be hurrying, thought James. The other guy must be dead, too.

Minutes later, they lowered two dead men to the ground on stretchers. They loaded the bodies onto the truck.

'Shit,' thought James, 'is it better to be court-martialed for sleeping on duty or do your duty and be dead? I can't believe this. What a night.'

Several Minutes Earlier

The short, stocky man in rough, well-worn fatigues looked down from his position on the ridge to the men scurrying towards him. The men, mostly boys, carried AK-47 Chinese-made rifles. The man wore a seasoned North Vietnamese cap; his face and mannerisms suggested a tough, experienced soldier. The seasoned guerrilla fighter was 24, old for a VC but stronger than most of his younger comrades. Thirteen round trips from their supply point located 35 kilometers in the mountains had hardened his body. The freedom fighter grew up in Phu Bai in a middle-class family. His schoolteacher parents, who doted on him, died when he was a boy. He migrated north with an uncle when only a teenager, where he was trained to become a guerrilla fighter.

The man's broad face with a square jaw widened into a deep grin as he saw the four rockets arcing toward the huge base at Chu Lai.

Their attack occurred dangerously late; it was almost light, a dangerous time to be shooting the rockets. They had difficulty preparing the weapons tonight.

Commander Ro Kwan looked up and saw that dawn was breaking; they had to hurry now before the American gunship helicopters came.

He waved to his men and said, 'Hurry comrades, it is time, past time to depart!'

'Comrade Ro,' said the tall, slender VC, 'all four of these magnificent fire swords flew straight and true to the Imperialists. No failures.'

'Wonderful, Comrade Tran, but we must go now.'

A teenager pointed, 'Comrade Ro, look, I see the helicopters coming.'

The squad scurried away into the jungle, leaving behind evidence of their deadly efforts that morning. Eight long slender poles stuck into the ground remained for the Americans to find. The poles, carefully chosen for their straightness, were crossed and tied to form an 'X'. The VC leaned the rockets on the upper joined portion of the 'X'. Small batteries were hooked to each rocket to ignite them. A crude aiming instrument made from two equal-length sticks allowed them to position the rockets on the crude launchers to an angle of 45 degrees. This angle provided maximum range to reach the Americans' Air Base and Americal Division spread out before them like a city. The large area target required no sophisticated equipment to aim the weapons.

The crudely-aimed rockets were not important in any strategic sense. The missiles generally fell harmlessly, doing little damage. Their purpose was to harass and terrorize. Kwan's men didn't know this. They thought each rocket killed many Americans. That morning they were right; several Americans died in the attack.

Kwan's squad walked swiftly along the mountain trail. The six teenage boys were recruited from the villages in the nearby area to fight the Imperialists. Most would not live long; the dangerous life of a VC guerrilla was short. Many would die, not from the bullets of the enemy but from disease and injuries in the harsh jungle. Their lives were devoid of healthy food and medical care. Their harsh existence took its toll.

The VC squad carried AK–47 rifles held loosely by a sling over their heads as they trotted into the shadowy, dark world of the jungle.

No two men in the squad dressed exactly alike. They clothed themselves with whatever was available. Most wore black pants and shirts and the large reed hats of the Vietnamese farmer. These hats were useful in the rice paddies in the valleys below them, but here in the shadows of the mountain jungle, they were less useful. The more experienced guerrillas wore baseball caps; a more practical jungle hat.

The baseball-style caps had a variety of origins. Some came from dead Americans, the South Vietnamese Army or from their ally in the north. Commander Kwan's cap was an NVA regular issue cap. He wore it proudly and it brought respect from his men, a reminder of his valuable training in the North.

All the men but Ro wore sandals constructed from leather and rubber. Ro's brown boots came from the North Vietnamese Army.

Kwan's second-in-command was Sergeant Tran Soo-Dong. The slender 19-year-old had a boyish face devoid of facial hair. His dark eyes sparkled with intelligence. Soo-Dong wore green NVA fatigue pants, a fatigue shirt and an NVA cap like his commander. The second-in-command worked under Commander Kwan for more than a year. The 19-year-old received rudimentary training at camps run by NVA instructors along the Cambodian border. Commander Kwan recruited his sergeant from a farming village near the city of Tam Ky prior to the previous year's monsoon season. Kwan recognized the potential of this intelligent young man and promoted him quickly.

The squad hurried along the trail. They had to get to the safe area quickly. Helicopters, American patrols and the dreaded American LRRPs were their biggest fear now. The LRRPs hid in the jungle for days along trails waiting to ambush the VC. They killed quickly and disappeared.

Kwan looked up through the trees. It was getting lighter. Behind them, he heard helicopters, but none of the sounds seemed threatening. He looked up ahead to Soo-Dong and said, 'Tran, move the men more quickly. We almost waited too late to fire our rockets. The daylight is our enemy this close to the launching point.'

'Yes, Comrade Ro.'

Soo-Dong replied to the squad, 'Comrades, you heard our leader, move more quickly now or your head will adorn some Imperialist's gate post.'

The squad increased their pace. The sergeant had heard of American bases with the skulls of their brothers on stakes. This was offensive to him. It showed no respect and disgraced their memories.

They penetrated deeper into the darkness of triple-canopy jungle. In less than an hour, they reached their destination, a sanctuary consisting of a small hidden tunnel. The men carefully inspected the tunnel for any indication that the Americans may have been there to set booby-traps. Kwan looked down the dark hole. It was frightening to enter, but it provided safety during the day. The men entered after raking away footprints and other signs of their presence. They did this carefully; their lives depended on it.

The tunnel contained a small room barely large enough to hold the seven men. Three narrow crawl spaces led out from the room to three escape exits. The tunnel stored rice, water and ammunition. The squad would eat and rest in the sanctuary all day. In the evening they would head west through the mountains.

The guerrilla fighters learned to travel at night, but the jungle trails were dark and dangerous. In the darkness, men sometimes walked off cliffs to their deaths. The jungle came alive at night with dangerous predators like tigers, leopards and deadly snakes such as the banded krait, king cobra and Russell's viper. Ro's men knew these dangers well, but moving at night allowed them to avoid the enemy, the greatest predator of all. They would only travel at night for the first three days. From then on, they could travel during the day at a more leisurely pace to their turn-around staging area. The staging area complex consisted of caves holding rockets, supplies, food and medical supplies. A larger staging area located about a seven-day walk west near the Cambodian border had an underground hospital. These supply stations and the myriad of trails connecting them formed an effective supply system. This system supported the needs of the freedom-fighters as they fired rockets, blew up bridges and set mines.

Resting comfortably in their tunnel, the men ate rice and talked quietly. The rice was turning rancid but the hungry men ate it without comment. They used their meager medical supplies to tend to an assortment of minor ailments.

Kwan turned to his second-in-command and said, 'Tran, you did well today.'

'Thank you, Comrade Ro.'

'I have other plans for you Tran, besides carrying these rockets down the trail. I am creating a select group of operatives to maintain regular contact with certain loyal people in the villages. They will help us watch the activities of the enemy and supply us with information about the enemy's intentions and weaknesses. We will also collect tribute from the more isolated villages. These villagers must be allowed to help support our noble effort. I have decided to allow you to help me in these efforts.'

'I am honored you have selected me, Comrade Ro. I will do my very best for you, Sir.'

'I know you will, Tran. I have faith in your abilities and your loyalties.'

Late that morning, the Americans found the poles, wires and batteries used by the guerrillas. There was no trace of the VC. The frustrated Americans gathered the materials and placed them on a helicopter to be transported to Division intelligence.

Three Weeks Later
Americal Division Headquarters

Lieutenant James and Sergeant Markowski waited outside the courtroom on wooden chairs in a stark hallway. The door opened; a sergeant appeared and asked for Lieutenant James. The lieutenant walked up to the panel of officers, stopped in front of the senior officer, a full colonel, and saluted.

'Lieutenant James reporting as ordered Sir.'

'Swear the lieutenant in,' directed the senior officer.

James was sworn in and told to sit. He looked out nervously. Seated in front of him at a table to his right were two of the men on guard duty that night. Specialist Ferguson was not among them. The lieutenant had heard earlier that Ferguson was released.

James glanced at the two dejected soldiers sitting with their heads down and thought, 'You lucky assholes. You could have – maybe you should have – been killed.'

'Lieutenant,' asked the officer representing the prosecution, 'you were the Officer of the Day on 22 January 1969? And, you…'

The court-martial took all day. The two men illegally asleep on guard duty that night received six months' hard labor in Saigon. They would only serve three months because of good behavior and would finish their tour in the rear echelon of Saigon, a much safer place than Chu Lai. They would then return to the States and receive a general discharge from the Army.

Many would say they were lucky fellows.

Chapter 23

How Not to Enter a Helicopter

Over the months, Lieutenant Leffert settled into the daily routine. Missions were going smoothly, with few major incidents. Pilots would complete their daily missions and congregate in the Officers' Club every evening for drinks and chow, as the 'mess hall' was in the same building. The ritual served several purposes. One was to let other pilots know some of the problems and/or incidents encountered during the day (i.e. lessons learned), and another was just to tell tales – 'TINS' (This Is No Shit) – of their daily exploits. The TINS one evening was 'the Tale of the Bent Barrel'.

'Guys,' said Leffert, while rolling the daily evening ritual of liar's dice to see who paid the 10-cent surcharge for dinner, 'I got a story to tell.'

'OK,' said CW2 Bill Broderick. 'What's up, Big Guy?'

Calling him 'Big Guy' was actually Broderick's attempt to gig him a little. Leffert was in fact a little guy, about 5ft 7in tall and weighing 130lb soaking wet.

'Guys, I had been flying for several hours already that day, completing a variety of missions.'

May 1969

Lieutenant Leffert was flying over Highway One south of Tam Ky when he heard over the Ops frequency 'Phoenix One-Four, this is Ops, over.'

'Ops, this is Phoenix One-Four, go ahead'.

'One-Four, you are to go to LZ Buff and pick up a PAC and transport him to Caspar, over.'

'Roger Ops, One-Four out.'

Leffert turned toward LZ Buff and took out his book strapped to his vest to find the frequency and call sign of the LZ. He contacted them and they affirmed there was one passenger waiting by the landing pad. A Green Beret in his specialty tiger-patterned camouflaged fatigues worn exclusively by Special Forces was waiting by the pad. Leffert motioned for him to come over and strap in the seat beside him. The soldier was carrying a small knapsack and his M16 rifle. He stored his equipment on the floor between his legs. They took off for LZ Caspar, a Green Beret compound twenty minutes to the south-west.

Leffert landed outside the compound on an adjacent dirt road.

When they were firmly on the ground, Leffert rotated the throttle to flight idle and pressed the intercom switch on his cyclic and said, 'It's safe to get out. Be careful and good luck.'

'Roger, Sir. Thanks for the ride,' was the cheerful reply.

The Green Beret unbuckled his seat belt and shoulder harness, grabbed his pack and rifle and hopped out. He was standing next to the door of the idling Loach when he saw a friend waiting for him near the compound entrance. The arriving Green Beret raised his rifle in a greeting. The soldier, a novice to riding in a helicopter, forgot about the whirring rotor blades above him.

WHAM! He was thrown to the ground and rolled repeatedly, crying out in pain. His M16 also went flying. It hit the ground about 100ft from the aircraft and tumbled to a stop in a cloud of dust. Green Beret soldiers ran up to their stricken comrade to help.

The helicopter also was stricken. It started vibrating and a whistling sound emanated from the rotor blades.

'Oh shit,' thought the pilot. He immediately shut down the aircraft.

The young Green Beret lay with an injured shoulder. He, at first, did not comprehend what had just happened. A medic came over and examined his shoulder. It was swelling. The medic did not think it was broken, but they would have to get him to a hospital for an X-ray. After a head-to-foot examination, they sat him up and put his arm in a sling. They radioed for a medevac helicopter, which promptly arrived and flew the shaken up Green Beret to Chu Lai.

When the rotor blades slowed to a stop, Leffert climbed up on top of the aircraft to survey the damage. One blade had a 2in-deep, V-shaped dent in the leading edge. Airflow over the dent caused the whistling sound. He suspected the damage was too severe and the helicopter could not be safely flown. He went inside the compound and contacted Operations for help.

Lieutenant Duffy, the Unit Maintenance Officer, decided to bring a new blade out and change the blade on site.

In about an hour, the maintenance helicopter landed with a new blade and a couple of mechanics.

When changing a blade, protocol dictates the new blade is to be 'tracked' so it is in line with the other blades. If not in line, the rotor system would vibrate, much like a fan with one blade bent.

They completed the replacement in about an hour. Duffy started the damaged helicopter and adjusted the rotor head. Once he determined the tracking was good enough to fly the helicopter back to the Chu Lai Heliport, he said, 'Leff, you take my chopper with our two guys and I will fly your chopper back.'

He told his mechanics to leave the damaged blade there and climb in Leffert's chopper.

Both Loaches safely landed at Ky Ha Heliport. Duffy placed the hastily repaired helicopter on the maintenance pad adjacent to the maintenance facilities. Mechanics and crew chiefs were waiting to begin the process of a complete aircraft inspection and tracking of the new blade.

'OK, nice story, Leff,' said Lieutenant Dave Chambers. 'What happened to the dumb ass Green Beret?'

'Well, Doc told me he dislocated his shoulder but was going to be alright.'

They raised their glasses. 'To the Green Berets,' Leffert quipped, 'even if they do something dumb occasionally.'

'To the Green Berets,' the other pilots repeated in unison. Glasses clinked, drinks were chugged, a new round was bought and everyone was ready for dinner.

Following the incident, the M16 with the barrel bent at a 30-degree angle and the damaged rotor blade were placed on the wall in the Berets' Operations room. The display was a stark reminder of what NOT to do when entering and exiting a helicopter with turning rotor blades.

Chapter 24

Harrowing Day at LZ Professional

0730 hrs
Div Arty Operations

Captain Birmingham spoke hurriedly on the phone as the new Assistant Operations Officer, Lieutenant James, walked into the Operations hootch. James was not scheduled to fly today. Birmingham wanted him to sit in and learn the Operations business.

Birmingham hung up the phone and said, 'James, sorry, but I need you to get to the Admin pad and pick up Lieutenant Colonel Stakowski and another passenger and take them to Professional. The LZ was hit hard last night and yesterday afternoon. Shit, we lost a Hook[1] from mortar fire on the hill. Sorry about giving you this unscheduled mission. Be careful, Darryl.'

'Always careful,' said the pilot. He went to the door, turned back to Birmingham and said, 'Which ship, Amigo?'

He checked his paperwork and said, 'Ah, take 245.'

'The Whale?'

'Yeah.'

James grabbed his gear and walked down to the flight line. Spec 4 Wallace met him and saluted.

'Morning, Sir.'

'Good morning, Whale. How's it going?'

'Great, Sir. Are you taking my ship?'

'Roger, that.'

'She's all set, Sir.'

The crew chief helped James pre-flight and helped him get strapped. He held the fire extinguisher as James started up the helicopter with the blue whale painted on it. He smiled at the lieutenant and gave him a thumbs-up as the 'Whale' hovered away.

The Loach departed Ky Ha and turned south for the three-minute run to the Admin pad. An odd-looking pair stood hatless leaning against a quarter-ton jeep. One figure was short, slightly built with gray hair and wore the uniform of a lieutenant colonel. He held a steel pot in his hand and had a 45-caliber automatic strapped to his waist. An M16 rested on his leg as he stood in a classic *contrapposto* pose like a Greek statue.

Colonel Stakowski was 42 years old and on the full colonel's promotion list. It was his second try to make the list, his final chance, but he made it. Not making this list would have been a career-ending event for the West Point graduate.

He watched the Loach land, then said to his companion, 'This has to be it, Bob.'

The colonel climbed out of the jeep followed by a bear of a man wearing the stripes of a sergeant major. The man was over 6ft tall and weighed 250lb; a man few would want to upset. The sergeant major, about the same age as his colonel, was almost bald. He, too, carried a steel pot, an M16 and had a sidearm strapped to his side.

Both men walked up to the helicopter and stowed their steel pots and M16s in back. Their driver brought them flight helmets from the jeep. The two waved a noiseless 'Hi' to the pilot and climbed in. The colonel climbed in front and the sergeant major struggled to put his large frame in the left rear seat.

'Good morning, Colonel,' said the pilot over the intercom, 'I'm Lieutenant James.'

'Hi, James,' replied Stakowski. 'They told me you are driving today.'

'That's Sergeant Major Bob Stevens in back holding down the fort.'

'Good morning, Sergeant Major.'

'Morning, Lieutenant.'

The pilot turned to his left seat companion and said over the intercom, 'Are you ready to go to Professional, Sir?'

'Roger. It's our first trip out there, Lieutenant, but we don't have time for a tour. We lost thirty-four men last night. I need to be there as soon as possible. How long will it take?'

'About thirty minutes, Sir. We lost a Chinook on that hill yesterday.'

'Yes, I know. It's bad out there.'

The Loach lifted off from the Admin pad and departed north along Highway One. After about fifteen minutes, the Loach turned through a pass in the mountains and steered toward LZ Professional. The lonely aircraft followed a valley partly obscured by a morning ground fog. As they ventured west, the morning sun broke up the ground fog, revealing a lush green valley, a valley dotted with peaceful-looking mountain villages. However, the peaceful look was misleading, for this valley was territory infested with NVA activity.

On Professional, a chief warrant officer and a Spec 5 were exhausted from lack of sleep. They spent a harrowing night enduring an onslaught of mortar, small-arms and heavy-caliber fire. Technically guests, the two had joined in for an all-out defense of the perimeter the previous night. The guests were artillery technicians, not combat soldiers, but they gave a good account of themselves.

The hill's advanced new counter-fire radar had been down for several days. It was used to direct counter-fire from enemy artillery and mortars. The two techs had come out three days earlier to get the advanced radar going again. Although the hill had been under heavy fire. The new system was not a high priority to the battery commander. The radar was more effective against conventional artillery, not the highly mobile light mortars that were bringing misery to his men on the hill. The two technicians had the radar working that morning. It was time to get off this hill. They sat on cots in the Operations bunker, dirty and tired, drinking hot black coffee. Their duffel bags and spare part cases sat at their feet. They declined breakfast. The men planned to eat a quiet hot meal in Chu Lai. The two had been promised an early ride off the hill.

At the moment, LZ Professional was the hottest spot in American Division. The mountain fire base took heavy casualties during the night and was licking its wounds in the early morning sun. Two Dust-off helicopters braved the mortar fire and darkness to evacuate some of the wounded. The dead soldiers would be removed that day if helicopters could land.

The FM radio clicked into life in the Operations bunker. 'Tiger Two, Phoenix One-Three, over.' The two radar men, sitting in the radio hootch, looked over at the olive drab radio as the Battery's XO picked up a mike and answered, 'Go ahead, Phoenix One-Three, this is Tiger Two.'

'Phoenix One-Three is approaching your position from the east. We are about zero-eight mikes out. Be advised I have an Oscar five on board.'

'Roger Phoenix One-Three, we currently have a fire mission pending. We have our guns in a check fire for you to land. We will hold the check fire for your immediate departure. We have two PACs for you. They will be waiting at the West Side pad. Be advised we have been taking mortar rounds periodically.'

'Roger Tiger Two.'

'THAT'S OUR RIDE,' replied the chief warrant officer.

In the approaching Loach, Lieutenant James pressed his intercom switch and said to his front seat passenger, 'Sir, that's LZ Professional out ahead.'

'Roger,' said the colonel as he studied the smoking hill.

Even in the distance, they sensed the significant damage on the hill. Smoke drifted slowly up from various points along the hill. The east side of the hill seemed the worst. A dark outline of burned debris was all that remained of the CH-47 Chinook helicopter.

James slowed to 60 knots and began a tight left descending turn.

Below an NVA soldier watched the Loach descend in a graceful spiral, turning to the left. It reminded him of an eagle circling to dive in to catch a fish in the marshes, a scene he witnessed many times in his homeland to the east. He studied the helicopter. It seemed to tighten its turn and descended more rapidly.

He caressed his mortar tube and whispered to his ammo-bearer, who was holding the rocket in his hand, 'Soon.'

The chopper passed in front of them at an altitude of 300ft. Suddenly, machine-gun fire opened up well off to their left, reaching up to the turning helicopter. 'Shit,' he thought, 'don't fire and scare it off, Comrades. It is my kill today.'

As sparks erupted out of the Loach pilot's open right-side door, James tightened the turn and dropped lower to fall away from the gunfire.

James transmitted, 'TIGER, ONE-THREE IS TAKING FIRE!' He paused, then continued, 'No hits, we are OK.'

'Roger, Phoenix, our grunts are returning fire.'

The Loach continued down and flattened its descent on short final. Some 50ft in the air, James slowed the Loach to 30 knots to land. The pilot noticed soldiers moving toward the landing pad carrying bags.

He thought to himself, 'Shit, I know you're anxious to leave, guys, but back off and let me land this thing.'

The pilot blinked as a burst of white light erupted in front of the Loach's windscreen. Gray dirt and debris leaped into the air, hiding the landing-pad from view. A loud crackle followed by a shock wave buffeted the Loach.

Adrenaline rushed through the Loach driver as he added full power from his collective. The nimble Loach abruptly nosed forward past the pad and rose quickly as another explosion erupted behind the helicopter. He felt the tail buzz from another shock wave. The helicopter climbed swiftly to the safety of the sky.

'Shit,' thought the pilot, 'that was close, too close!'

'Phoenix One-Three, Tiger Two, are you OK?'

'We're OK, Two,' James said with a shaky voice over the Fox Mike radio.

'Roger, One-Three, stand by.' Seconds later, the radio crackled with 'One-Three, we just took two casualties by the pad.'

'Colonel,' James said over the intercom, 'did you hear that, Sir?'

'Roger.' He asked, 'Lieutenant, can we evac those casualties?'

'Not if they're serious; not in a Loach...'

The radio interrupted, 'One-Three, I am afraid your PACs are Kilo-Indian-Alpha,' said a shaky voice.

'Sir,' replied the pilot in a shaky voice over the intercom, 'they're gone. I saw them out front waiting for me. I, I, ah, I suggest we abort, Sir, and could try to land later. The Gooks, they were, I mean ARE, THEY ARE OBVIOUSLY WAITING FOR US TO LAND AND HAVE ZEROED IN ON THE PAD.'

'Lieutenant,' replied the colonel in a calm, casual voice. 'I really need to be there. These are my men; they're hurting. They need me. Let's try again.'

The radio crackled, 'Phoenix One-Three, this is Tiger Two. Stay east of the hill. We have a fire mission west.'

'Roger, Two-Six.'

One 105mm howitzer fired three rounds to a close-in target to the west of Bronco. The rounds left the guns in a high arcing flight path.

'One-Three, be advised our guys are firing machine guns to the west and east.'

'Sir, OK,' James replied over the intercom, 'I am willing to try again, but I can't hover or stay sitting on the pad. I'm going to bounce in; you'll both need to jump off, IMMEDIATELY.'

'No problem, Lieutenant. Let's have a go as soon as they give us another check-fire.'

'Roger, Sir, will give it our best shot.'

'Phoenix One-Three, this is Tiger Two; we have a check-fire again for you. State your intentions, over.'

'Roger, Two, we're coming in.'

The colonel removed his flight helmet. The sergeant major handed him his steel pot from the back seat. The colonel put it on and fastened the chinstrap. In the back seat, the sergeant major did the same and then carefully strapped down both flight helmets on the vacant rear right seat.

The Loach spiraled out of the sky in a steep, aggressive diving tight turn as if daring the enemy to shoot at them. The pilot looked left and saw tracers flash by the colonel's profile in the left seat. He was about to transmit this information to the hill when to his amazement, the colonel unfastened his seat belt and shoulder harness and deftly climbed over the collective and stood on the skids, looking back at the source of the machine-gun fire. The Loach dove in a steep left turn as the colonel held on. He glanced up briefly at the pilot, smiled and then stared back down. 'This guy is Effing John Wayne,' thought the pilot. Unbeknown to the pilot, the sergeant major also climbed out on the left skid, holding on with one hand. His other large meaty hand was inside the cabin balancing the two M16s on the seat. The Loach spiraled in jerkily to land. A few feet from the pad, the colonel and sergeant major jumped off the skid and fell into a paratrooper's roll. The oversized sergeant major amazingly rolled instantly to his feet holding the two M16 rifles and helped pull the colonel up away from the landing-pad. The Loach bounced off the pad into the air and, with full power applied, swiftly took off.

Two minutes earlier, the high-tech radar that had been repaired by deceased techs painted the mortar rockets' arcs and back-calculated their firing position. This data automatically fed into the FADAC computer. The battery commander immediately gave authority to shoot three 105mm HE (high-explosive) rounds with radar-controlled air-burst fuses. Everything worked as it was designed. Data fed into the computer was correct and accurate. The gun settings obtained from the computer output were correctly set by the gunner to gun #1 and then rechecked by their second lieutenant. The fuses were properly set and worked as the manufacturer said they would. The first round exploded 75ft directly above four camouflaged men disassembling the mortar. Shrapnel from the exploding warhead rained down on the bush that so effectively hid them from sight. Now it provided little protection from the steel pouring down. By the time the second round came down, they were already dead.

The commanding general sent reinforcements to Professional. Slicks brought in fresh infantry to relieve the weary perimeter troops and pull out the American KIA. Fresh supplies and hot chow were sent. Gunships and fast movers peppered the hillsides around Professional all day. The sky above was filled with aircraft.

Later that day Captain Dotson was to witness yet another tragedy on the hill. He came out in the late afternoon to retrieve the colorful colonel and sergeant major when directly ahead of him he saw a helicopter pilot's worst nightmare, a mid-air collision. Two Slicks carrying supplies to the men on the hill collided explosively, killing everyone. Debris rained down on the west side of Professional. It was a chaotic debris of metal and men: the debris of death.

Chapter 25

Friendlies on LZ Ross?

Officers' Club
0700 hrs

Four of the Div Air Section pilots were having breakfast and discussing their morning meetings. Captain Fuller had DEROS'd[1] back to the States and Captain Birmingham was the new Operations officer.

CW2 Broderick looked over at Lieutenant Leffert chomping down on a huge breakfast. 'I'm just amazed at how much you eat, Leff. What are you, a buck-forty soaking wet?'

'I'll have you know I am a buck-thirty.'

'He has the metabolism of a hummingbird,' wisecracked Captain Duffy. 'I've heard a hummingbird is always one hour away from starvation. The boy needs to eat.'

Captain Dotson quipped, 'The quartermaster has a special entry in his ledger, marked "Leffert", to ensure that there are enough groceries to go around.'

Captain Birmingham unhurriedly joined them. Birmingham was never in a rush. He sat down slowly and looked at Dotson: 'Connor, I know you and Leff had the morning off, but the XO called and wants us to fly by LZ Ross for a look-see.'

'A look-see? How come?' asked Leffert.

'The 23rd moved a battery off yesterday, lock stock and barrel. They want to make sure the hill looks OK and everything was taken off. So how about you two hotshots look and make sure the area is "policed up"?[2] You know the old boot camp proverb, "Gentlemen, pick everything up. If you can't pick it up, paint it. If it moves, salute it"?'

'Yeah, yeah,' lamented Leffert. 'I've heard that somewhere before.'

Leffert was a blond, slender Coloradan who loved to talk about skiing in nearby resorts: Angel Fire, Ski Apache, Purgatory, Copper Mountain, etc. He promised his hootch mate, Captain James, to teach him to ski when they returned to the world.

Leffert and Dotson went to their hootches to fetch their M16s, sidearms, ammunition and survival radios. They passed through Operations and asked Sergeant Jenkins what ship they could take. '451 is available, gentlemen,' he said.

'OK, my man,' replied Dotson.

They passed through to the backroom, picked up their helmets and chicken-plates and walked with their weapons, bandoleers of ammunition, survival radios and a survival kit down to the flight line.

'Can you manage all that heavy gear, Mr 'A Buck-thirty'?'

'Shut up! Just for that, I'm flying, you take the left seat, shut up and observe, Dick-head.'

'OK, I didn't know you were so sensitive about your skinny, hummingbird metabolism ass.'

'You're pretty skinny yourself, you know.'

They found the '451' Loach and pre-flighted the aircraft with the crew chief. Leffert hung his M16 over the first-aid kit between the pilot and co-pilot seats. There was no room for Dotson's M16 up front, so he strapped his weapon in the back along with the survival radio and kit. They both strapped in and Leffert started the helicopter. As he did, Leffert thought about his first flight in Vietnam eight months earlier. He had just arrived at Div Arty Air and was preparing for his orientation flight with Connor Dotson.

September 1968
Div Arty Air Operations

Div Arty Air's Operations Officer Lieutenant Fuller greeted the unit's newest pilot.

'Lee, I want you to meet our instructor pilot, Connor Dotson. Take note, he's a Texas Longhorn, thinks he's funny and talks constantly.'

'Hi Lee,' said Lieutenant Dotson, shaking his hand, 'I understand you have no time in the OH-23G "Raven".'

'Yep, I learned in the TH-55A at Wolters and the UH-1D at Hunter-Stewart. Thought I'd be starting here as a co-pilot in the Huey.'

'We all did,' replied Fuller, chuckling.

Connor added, 'So you flew the good ol' Mattel Messerschmitt,[3] huh? No worries! We'll get you checked out in the Raven. Oh, and don't listen to ol' blow-hard Fuller over here. He's mostly full of hot air, as are most of the pukes in this gaggle of chopper-drivers.'

They walked down to the flight line and met the maintenance officer and a couple of the crew chiefs.

'Now this here is John Duffy, our Maintenance Officer,' said Dotson. 'He thinks he's cute, but he is likeable. Be careful, he can get you in serious trouble. Stay away from the poker table with him. He's notorious, and about the best poker-player in Division. He has a wad of MPC mostly taken from the majors and colonels up on Silk Stocking Row directly uphill from our hootches. It's where all the field grades stay and their accommodations are considerably nicer than ours.'

Duffy shook Lieutenant Leffert's hand and looked him in the eye with his ever-present shit-eating grin. 'Remember this, Lee, Connor is known for hyperbole and it's HE who carries around a bucket of "horse pucky".'

Connor laughed and said, 'Duff, don't bull shit a bull-shitter.'

'What a bunch of goofiness. I think I can fit in here just fine,' thought the FNG[4] pilot at Div Arty Air.

Lee was introduced to several of the crew chiefs, who he noticed immediately were treated with deference by Lieutenants Duffy and Dotson.

'Lee,' Dotson said, 'these guys keep us safe. Always treat them with the utmost respect.'

Following the pre-flight inspection and a briefing on heliport operations, Lee cranked up the helicopter under the guidance of Dotson. He performed several 'touch-and-gos', followed by a short orientation of landing zones and support pads in the local area. They then turned south following Highway One to Qui Nhon, where Connor had said a Green Beret unit was operating. Dotson directed Leffert to a landing-pad in the middle of a square, surrounded by buildings with nearby electric and communication cables.

'Let me have the controls, Lee. I'll show you how to get into this pad. It has wires along the usual approach path that need to be avoided.'

Lieutenant Dotson demonstrated the approach while chatting with the Special Forces on the FM radio. When they were about 50ft off the ground, a large waft of dust and debris erupted about 100ft at their two o'clock position. Seconds later, another closer explosion rocked the helicopter sideways.

'Mortar attack!' shouted Dotson over the intercom as he turned sharply left when a third explosion came, seemingly following their vulnerable small chopper.

Connor pulled maximum power as they turned steeply, struggling to climb. They skirted within inches of power lines as they hastened to fly out of the kill zone of the mortar attack.

Leveling off at 2,000ft, out of harm's way, Connor spoke into the intercom. 'These attacks usually involve three quick mortar fires. What they do is sneak in close at night to a planned firing position and wait. The firing position is where they did their homework to zero in on the landing-pad. When they have a target, they drop three quick rockets in the tube, run and hide. Obviously, we were the target of the attack. We just happened to be in the wrong place at the wrong time. We were lucky.'

'Holy shit!' replied the shaken new pilot.

'Shit happens, Amigo, let's go home.'

The events of the day spun wildly in the new pilot's head on that early flight. 'We were almost blown out of the sky on my first day; what are the next 360 days going to be like?'

Ky Ha Heliport
0745 hrs

Leffert keyed the radio switch in his Loach, 'Ky Ha Tower, Phoenix One-Four is ready to taxi to the active for take-off.'

'Roger, One-Four, you are cleared to the active for an east departure.'

'Roger, Ky Ha, cleared for departure to the east.'

Leffert and Dotson took off over the blue waters of the South China Sea and headed south. The sun was shining brightly over the sea with white puffy clouds. It was gorgeous weather, but that would change with the coming monsoon season.

Dotson keyed his intercom switch on his cyclic, 'Beautiful day to fly, Leff.'

'Right you are.'

'Say, Leff, did you hear the one about the two Aggies who wanted to go to the Aggie UT Football game at College Station?' asked Dotson.

'No,' replied the blond Colorado wannabe ski bum, knowing that a corny Aggie joke was coming from a UT Longhorn. The Longhorns were the traditional must-beat rivals of the Aggies.

'Well, they were worried because they came to a football game last year in their Volkswagen bug and parked it in a vast parking lot. Many other Volkswagen bugs were there too. The game was out of hand, so they decided to be smart and leave early. They could not find their car and had to wait until all the other Volkswagens had left before they found it and could leave.'

The smarter of the two said, 'Not to worry, Cowboy. I work on an exotic animal ranch outside of town and we have camels. It's only 10 miles to College Station, so we can ride in on the camel. No one else will have a camel. Smart, huh?'

They rode in on the camel, tied it to a tree on the edge of a grass parking lot and went into the stadium to watch the game. UT was handily beating A&M, so again they decided to leave early. Little did they know that a circus was coming to town. What a surprise when they saw a host of camels tied up at the edge of the field near where they tethered their charge. They were despondent. How could they ever find their camel?

Well, the smarter one said, 'I know how, Cowboy, follow me.' He went around lifting the tails of the camels, one by one. 'What are you doing?' asked Cowboy.

'This is how we will find our camel.'

'Huh?' replied the second Cowboy.

'Didn't you hear them say when we rode in, "Hey, look at the two assholes on that camel"?'

'Oh, good grief,' said Leffert. 'What a groaner.'

'I thought it was pretty good.'

'You would, you Longhorn puke.' Connor Dotson was the UT graduate and loved to tell Aggie jokes if he found someone to listen. Driving the helicopter next to him on his right, Leffert was a captive audience.

They climbed to 2,500ft and headed inland, passing Highway One. Turning inland toward the mountains, they continued climbing to 5,000ft at an altitude where it was cool.

Leffert reflected back on another time when he was cruising at 5,000ft in the mountains.

'Connor, did I ever tell you the time I flew formation with an F-4?'

'Huh?' Connor replied, puzzled.

April 1969
20 miles south-west of LZ Baldy

Helicopters normally flew at one of two altitudes. They either flew low-level, below 50ft, where they were a fast-moving target that was very hard to hit, or at an altitude above 1,500ft, essentially out of range of small-arms fire. Anything between these altitudes was considered 'no man's land' and avoided. Another advantage of flying higher than 1,500ft was to cool off. The helicopters flew without doors and windows and the air temperature was 10 to 20 degrees cooler at 5,000ft, a welcome relief from the hot, humid air on the surface.

There was another hazard in flying above 5,000ft. It was not the threat of surface-to-air missiles or anti-aircraft guns, it was F-4s!

F-4 Phantoms were the Air Force, Navy and Marines' state-of-the-art fighter-bombers. They were capable of carrying 18,000lb of ordnance at supersonic speeds exceeding Mach 2. Whenever they flew a mission, they would fly in pairs: a lead and a wingman. The jet pilots sometimes played games with helicopters. Whenever they would see one alone at altitude, they often would 'buzz' it. Following a second or so behind, his wingman would buzz by.

Leffert was flying near LZ West in the mountains south-west of Da Nang one day in April when WHOOSH, followed closely by another WHOOSH, two blurs out of his right open door of his Loach. He cussed under his breath and flew on toward LZ West. This time, rather than disappearing in the distance, one started a sharp left turn in the distance.

'What in the world is this guy doing?' Leffert thought.

He continued on his heading and altitude, thinking, 'Once isn't enough, this bozo has to circle around and buzz me again?'

Off in the distance at his 11 o'clock position he saw the jet's landing gear drop and his wing flaps extend. 'What in the world is this guy doing?'

He then heard, 'Helicopter, this is Phantom Two-Four-One on Guard.[5] If you hear me, come up to 126.0 megahertz, over.'

By this time, the F-4 was outside Leffert's open right door, about 50ft away. He could see the pilot and his back seat WSO (Weapons Systems Officer) in their cockpit, smiling. Leffert gave a 'thumbs-up', acknowledging his transmission. He keyed the radio switch and said, 'Phantom Two-Four-One, this is Phoenix One-Four, over.'

'One-Four, sorry to bother you, little guy, but I always wanted to fly formation with a slow little feller. Do you mind if I tag along for a few minutes?'

'Sure.'

'Phoenix One-Four, can you speed it up a bit, I'm about ready to stall.'

'Roger.'

Leffert was flying at about 100 knots (about 120 miles an hour). He increased power and nosed the helicopter over to 120 knots (about 140 miles an hour). This speed seemed OK for the F-4. They proceeded with small talk. He told him that if he got over to the Air Force's Officers' Club in Chu Lai, to look him up and he would buy him a drink for allowing him to fly formation. After a few more minutes, he said, 'OK, fun's over, thanks for the ride.'

May 1969
5 Miles East of LZ Ross

'Are you trying to unload a bucket of horse pucky on me because you didn't like my Aggie joke?'

'No, no, I really flew formation with an F-4.'

'Come on, Leff, you have to be shitting me. You're telling me you actually flew formation with a bad-ass F-4 in a Loach?'

'Yes, not bull-shitting, Connor; this is a definite "TINS". And we flew in formation for at least ten minutes or so.'

'You didn't tell any of the guys?'

'Nah, well maybe Chambers. He is about the only one around here who can keep a secret. Well, Amigo, this has to be officially recognized by Div Arty gaggle. You have to look this F-4 driver up at the Air Force Officers' Club.'

'Wilco![6] He promised me a beer.'

Leffert reported in on the Operations frequency, 'Ops, this is Phoenix One-Four, over.'

'Go ahead, One-Four, this is Ops, over.'

'One-Four is descending into LZ Ross for a quick "look-see". We will give the hill a once-over and report back, over.'

'Roger One-Four, Ops, out.'

They began their descent and made a casual 'straight-in' approach to LZ Ross; not a wise approach. In a combat situation, helicopter pilots would make a 'corkscrew' descent over an LZ, keeping the helicopter in a safe air space during the descent. Today they expected to make a low pass and return to home base.

'Operations, One-Four is approaching LZ Ross.'

'Roger, One-Four,' replied Operations.

They descended nonchalantly as they headed toward the abandoned firebase.

Dotson said over the intercom, 'Leff, there are a bunch of peasants on the hill.'

'They are looking for anything of value left behind. They are harmless.'

They descended to about 500ft to get a closer look.

'Leff, I'm not so sure. Some may have weapons.'

Connor reached to his right and grabbed Leffert's M16 hung over the first-aid kit. Lee's M16 had three twenty-round magazines taped together in the shape of a 'Y' so each magazine could be separately inserted into the weapon.

Rounds crackled by Leffert's open window. 'Shit, they are shooting at us.'

Connor pointed Leffert's M16 out the open door to return fire and the weapon fired once and jammed.

He manually ejected a round, and again it only fired once.

'Lee,' Lee screamed, 'we are sitting here holding our dicks with nothing to shoot back with. Get us out of here.' He added, 'Your gun sucks.'

More rounds flew around them.

Lee added when they were safely away, 'They looked like civilians. Civilian clothes, no weapons. It looked like they were cleaning up the hill.'

'Right, but did you see any kids? I didn't. They had their weapons hidden.'

'I don't think we took any hits. Everything feels normal.'

They flew back to Ky Ha Heliport and examined the ship with Maintenance. Sergeant Johnson pointed out a round hole in one of the rotor blades.

'Well,' said Captain Duffy, Div Arty Air's Maintenance Officer, 'Strongest part of the helicopter. If you had to get hit, it was a good place to get it.'

'OK,' said Dotson, 'now let's take that piece of crap gun up to the hootches and see what is wrong with it.'

Back up the hill in the hootches, Dotson and Leffert field-stripped the weapon.

'I am almost afraid to ask. When did you last clean it?' asked Dotson.

'Well, one of our crew chiefs cleaned mine and Darryl's M16 last week. I always clean my sidearm myself.'

'Well, maybe we should have shot our 45s at the VC.'

'OK, knock it off, wise guy. It has always worked. Must be the extractor.'

They could see nothing wrong with Leffert's M16. They reassembled it, took it out to the perimeter and requested permission to test-fire it. It worked perfectly.

'Go figure?' said Dotson.

'Well,' replied Leffert. 'you know there is a small port that allows gas to pass through, providing the gas force energy to fire on full automatic. We saw nothing in it when we just examined it, but even a small piece of debris could have made it malfunction.'

'Luckily, we got our tails out of there in one piece. We should not have gotten in there that close, even if they looked like innocent civilians.'

'Well, it was a mistake.'

'Mistakes can get you killed.'

'Indeed, we were lucky.'

'You, my friend, are buying beers tonight.'

'Go clean your weapon!'

'Go clean yours, you turd!'

Chapter 26

'What Are They Going To Do,
Send Me To Vietnam?'

July 1969

About the time Captain Fuller left for the States, Lieutenant Dave Chambers arrived fresh out of flight school. The unit was without a commander. Captain Mark Birmingham had been acting as the unit boss with Captain James acting as Operations officer. After Chambers reported in, Birmingham introduced him to CW2 Booth and indicated that they would be hootch mates billeting behind Lieutenants James and Leffert. Booth had already moved in. The space was unfinished, but Booth did not seem to mind the spartan existence. It was spacious enough for him to make a big mess out of the space. Captain Birmingham was a neat, organized person and wanted the space made neat and livable. He did not want Chambers being forced to billet in Booth's messy living space. Birmingham arranged for some plywood from the Navy CBs with a promise of future Chinook transport support. He made a gift of a three-quarter-ton truckload of plywood to Chambers and Booth.

'Dave,' he said, 'look what James and Leffert did to their room. They nailed up the plywood and burned the surface of the plywood walls with a blowtorch, making a nice knotty pine motif right out of *Homes and Gardens*. Once you nail these plywood walls up, and the crew chiefs promise to help, you and Booth could make some nice digs.'

Booth had a sour look on his face, 'You got to be kidding.'

'Don't mind him, Dave, he is always in a seemingly bad mood, but not really; that's just how he rolls.'

Dave, a quiet, conservative person from the farmlands of Oregon, did not know what to make of the banter that was commonplace at Div Arty Air. He looked at the next-door billets belonging to James and Leffert and said, 'Sure, we can do that.'

Booth groaned.

'Good, you and Booth can have the next few days off from flying to get this done.'

Leffert walked in and said, 'We can help. We will get you fixed up in no time, Dave.'

Later that afternoon, Birmingham had all the pilots meet in Operations.

'Guys,' he said, 'I just got word that Division is sending down Major Billings to be our temporary chief until they find a rated major to lead us.'

That message was followed by a bunch of groans and sour looks.

Booth said, 'That red-headed, pencil-dicked, straight-laced West Point puke is in need of, I don't know, something, he needs to be far and away from us. Why send us someone who can't even fly? Whose bright-eyed idea was that? We are doing fine without him, Birm.'

'Don't get your bowels in an uproar, Tim. Our station is not to question why, but to do.'

Later that afternoon, Major Billings had everyone gather in the Operations room. 'Guys,' he said, 'you are doing what I hear to be a pretty good job providing support to Division Artillery. No complaints in that department; however, there have been complaints that discipline in this unit has been lax. You pilots have been seen drinking beer and socializing with the enlisted men on more than one occasion. Gentlemen,' he paused for effect and looked everyone in the eyes, 'we cannot have officers fraternizing with the enlisted men.'

After a tense pause, Birmingham broke the silence. 'Major, if I may offer, these enlisted men are the crew chiefs and mechanics who keep our ships flying safely. They keep us alive. They are like family to us. We are in combat, after all; shouldn't some relaxation be warranted in military protocol?'

'Not on my watch, Captain Birmingham. I understand you are leaving for the States soon. I want Captain James, who is the next senior officer, to take over as Operations officer.'

'Captain James is already acting as Operations officer.'

'Well,' said the major, a bit flustered, 'good, he is now officially the Operations officer.'

Captain James was studying the cracks in the floor tiles, thinking 'What a bunch of bullshit.' He finally looked up, catching the red-haired major squarely in the eye. The major looked around the room, returned his stare to James and said, 'And as far as mustaches go, use me as an example. I want clean shaves. No facial hair; I hate mustaches.'

James thought to himself, '*That red-haired pussy couldn't grow one if he tried.*'

Mustaches were a rite of passage for chopper pilots in Vietnam. Virtually every helicopter pilot had one. Chopper pilots didn't fly high enough to use oxygen masks like the fixed-wing pilots so it became a rite in Vietnam, as if to say this is our mark for being here; this mustache emulates the wings on my chest.

The major stormed out of the room. Everyone looked at Birmingham and then at James. James had one of the bushiest mustaches in the unit. James stroked his mustache. He looked around at the gaggle of mustache-adorned chopper-drivers. He paused and then quipped, 'What are they going to do, send us to Vietnam?'

Everyone laughed.

Booth said, 'Screw him, I'm not shaving mine off, we'd be the laughing stock of our fellow aviators.'

'OK, guys,' Captain Birmingham said, changing the subject. 'On a brighter note, Sergeant Jenkins got hold of a case of steaks for us tonight. Party time?'

Everyone suddenly became excited.

'Connor,' he continued, 'is, as always, in charge of the grilling.'

'OK Birm, sounds like a winner,' Connor said, 'I'll check with the O Club and see what I can scrounge in the way of vegetables.'

Later That Evening

An impromptu party occasionally busted out at Div Arty Air, and tonight this was the case. Connor scrounged corn on the cob and potatoes. Word got around. People started coming to Div Arty Air.

While Connor was grilling, Steve Lincoln walked up with the ever-present can of beer in his hand. Connor greeted him with, 'What's a Dust-off puke doing here with the lowly Loach drivers?'

'Thought I'd come back to see my buddies at Div Arty. What's for dinner?'

'So, you decided to invite yourself?'

'Sure,' he chuckled, as he shook Connor's hand.

The patio area and recreation room were filling up with folks. A couple of field grades conveniently invited themselves, smelling the meat. They wandered down from Silk Stocking Row on the hill above Div Arty Air's hootches. One major said, 'Smells like a cook-out. Mind if we join you?'

'Sure,' replied Birmingham.

'Heard there's a poker game tonight too,' one of the majors said.

'Yep,' replied Captain Duffy. 'I'm in need of some of your cash,' he chuckled.

'Well, I heard that the MPC is only play money anyway,' one replied.

'Yeah, yeah, but I want it,' added Duffy.

Everyone was eating and drinking beer out by the grill. Notably absent was Major Billings. When it turned dark, the party wandered inside away from the ever-present mosquitoes. Loud music filtered in from Captain Birmingham's stereo in his room near the recreation room. The latter was becoming thick with cigar smoke as the Moody Blues' *Nights in White Satin* filled the room. CW2 Booth came in with a large bottle of Galliano liqueur, which he graciously shared with the gaggle of pilots. James, Leffert and one of the majors were getting more than their share of the golden sweet nectar. The tall, slender bottle yielded a perfectly balanced blend of Mediterranean exotic herbs and plants, all sourced and blended in their natural form. The resulting taste was rounded with a powerful aromatic top note that softened to a mellow deep taste. They were enjoying it all too much.

At 2000 hours, the party was in high gear. Duffy, as usual, was taking everyone's money at the card table. Chambers and Broderick sat in the Philippine wicker chairs deep in discussion. Connor had on a silly hat with a big fat cigar, telling Duffy that he belonged in Vegas. 'The zoo,' he said, spilling his beer on the card table, 'not the casinos.'

'Go sit somewhere else,' Duffy ordered.

Birmingham and Lincoln were discussing if Three Dog Night or Credence Clearwater Revival was best. Pops Baker was holding court with a couple of AOs. James and Leffert were dancing with glasses of Galliano in their hands to the beat of *I've Been Lonely Too Long* by the Young Rascals.

The party died along with the bottle of Galliano at about 2200 hours. Everyone had to work the next day; many had to get up early to fly. The alcohol consumption would not be helpful. The Div Arty gaggle crawled into their beds.

The Next Day
0200 hrs

Chambers awoke in his newly-appointed room to a loud siren. He yelled, 'Booth, what is that?'

'It's a rocket or a mortar attack, Dave. We need to get to the bunker.'

James woke slowly to the loud siren and tried to crawl under his rack. It had too little clearance. He instead turned the entire lightweight single metal-frame bed and mattress over on top of him, as if that would provide protection.

Leffert rushed over. 'What the hell, Darryl? Get out from under there.'

'Lee, if a rocket hits, this might protect me. Besides, we live on the east side of the ridge. The rockets have a flat trajectory. Probably miss us anyway. If not, what the hell, I might as well die here. I feel like shit.'

As he pulled him out, Leffert said, 'Me too, my head hurts. Get your ass moving.'

The two rushed out of the hootch. James, barefoot, landed hard on a steel grate under the steps to their hootch, nearly falling. Lee grabbed him and helped him into the bunker. They waited with their M16s in their laps.

'Shit, Lee,' said James. 'I hurt my heel as I jumped out the door on the darn grating. I will be limping around tomorrow.'

'Shut up! What do you want, a Purple Heart?'

The bunker was a steel container set into the hillside covered with sandbags near the entrance.

They heard several loud explosions vibrating the ground, but none was very near. Then, KABOOM! One hit close, vibrating the walls and ceiling of the bunker and sending dust and debris down on them.

'That was close,' said Broderick.

Thirty minutes later, they heard the 'all-clear'. Later they would learn that the near impact was close, but not as close as it seemed that night. It hit the motor pool a few hundred yards north of them, injuring two soldiers.

That Morning
0800 hrs

After a sparse breakfast of toast and coffee, Captains Leffert and James walked silently through the recreation room. The room was a mess. James looked at Leffert, about to say 'Must have been a hell of a party', but turned back instead, saying nothing. They walked in front of the infamous Div Arty Air Section policy sign, which boldly proclaimed: 'DIV ARTY AIR PILOTS CANNOT UNDER ANY CIRCUMSTANCES HAVE AN ALCOHOLIC BEVERAGE WITHIN 12 HOURS PRIOR TO ANY FLIGHT MISSION. THE NEXT FLIGHT MISSION OUR PILOTS CAN MAKE IS 4 JUNE 1979.'

James thought, 'Well, we can be ready to fly again in eleven years.'

They struggled down the hill, through Operations and on to the flight line. Neither mentioned the tomfoolery of the previous night's wild soirée. None the worse for wear, they put on their flight helmets over their mustaches, climbed into their respective choppers and fastened their harnesses.

It was great to be young!

Chapter 27

The Final Mission

Americal Div Arty Air Operations
1900 hrs, 2 September 1969

The Operations radio chattered away. Everyone was either on the ground or on the way home.

'It's been a good day,' thought Captain James. No screw-ups. Sergeant Jenkins had all the battalions' Hook and Slick support running smoothly. Not a whine or complaint. Sighing with pleasure, he thought, 'Just six days and a "wake-up", then home!'

James looked up as Jenkins walked in. The Ops NCO said, 'No mail today, Sir.'

'OK, well, maybe tomorrow,' replied the disappointed captain, 'I'm overdue for a letter, that's for damn sure.'

Buck Sergeant Jenkins ran the day-to-day activities in Operations. The sharp young college graduate made the job easy for James. All the Ops officer had to do was to schedule the pilot's missions and sign his name here and there. Jenkins loved to fly and had some 'boot-leg' chopper time. Most crew chiefs, however, preferred to ride in back as gunner with an M60. Door-gunners were used on convoy cover and scouting missions as well as covert insertions and pick-ups for LRRPs.

The door opened and CW2 Tim Booth, the last Loach[1] pilot in, entered, all sweaty and dirty.

'Booth, you stink.' The weary pilot gave a dirty look to the Ops officer in clean fatigues and let out a string of expletives. The 19-year-old could cuss like a seasoned sailor.

James sat heavily on the uncomfortable folding chair and began his paperwork. It was getting dark. He was hurrying to catch up with the gaggle of Loach drivers gathering at the Officers' Club. Finishing up, he and Jenkins were about to leave. As Jenkins flipped off the lights, a door flew open and their boss rushed in. The major shouted, 'JAMES! I just got the word: the 73rd needs a FADAC[2] computer out to LZ[3] Stinson, like right now.'

The major was Div Arty Air's new section leader. He was a bit of a mystery. Although he had been their boss for a month, he had not flown any combat missions and kept himself aloof.

'Major, it's nearly dark,' replied the captain. 'We don't fly night tactical missions unless a formal "TAC-E"[4] is declared. Sir, we can take out the computer first thing in the morning. This happens all the time. They usually wait.'

James thought to himself, 'In an emergency they can use those little circle slide rules to shoot those 105mm howitzers. They'll wait!'

James had only forty-four night-flying hours in Vietnam. Generally, most night missions were Admin flights such as taking some colonel home after dark. Night-flying in Vietnam was inherently dangerous. The mountainous terrain and the dark waters of the South China Sea did not provide a visible horizon for the nighttime pilot, causing many to be disoriented and sometimes crash. Because of this danger, Div Arty Air always used two pilots at night. Two pairs of eyes were safer.

James thought back to a dark, cloudy night when Captain Dotson and Captain Fuller, their most experienced pilots, were caught in the nighttime clouds over the Chu Lai airfield. They were taking a lieutenant colonel home to Duc Pho and planning to fly VFR on top of cloud cover. When they climbed in the dark clouds, they got vertigo, lost control and nearly crashed into the sea. Each had a grip on the controls when they recovered from a death spiral. Seeing the welcome lights of the airfield, they decided to abort and return to Ky Ha Heliport. Neither could remember who actually made that decision, or who made the landing. They staggered in visibly shaken, and their passenger had a distinct green complexion to complement his brown pants. The colonel was more than happy to spend another night in Chu Lai.

The captain's thoughts were interrupted as the major barked, 'Then I'll declare a TAC-E.'

'You can't do that, Sir. Only the colonel or the XO can do that.'

The major snarled and grabbed the phone, and the captain began to worry. James turned toward Jenkins and said, 'Sarge, send a runner up the hill and see if you can find someone who's, ah, not drunk...ah, I mean available.'

'Yes Sir.'

Ten minutes later, James learned that all the Loach drivers were at the club playing liar's dice to see who would buy the next round of drinks.

The phone rang. The major snatched it and said, 'Yes Sir.' He looked at the captain with a half-smile and said, 'You got your TAC-E, James. Division is sending over a FADAC. NOW GET SOMEONE TO TAKE IT OUT TO LZ STINSON.'

'Yes Sir, but it looks like you and I will have to fly this mission. Everyone is at the Club.'

'WHAT!' he shouted. 'Why isn't someone available? Shouldn't we have someone on standby? Surely this isn't how you run things around here, Captain James?'

'Sir, this TAC-E is unusual. Sir, this is only the fifth or sixth TAC-E since I've been here. It's rare for us to fly anything other than a scheduled Admin mission at night.'

'Well,' replied the major, sitting down and composing himself, 'get someone else to fly with you. I'll need to stay here and man the radios.'

'This is getting worse by the minute,' thought James.

The door opened and an out-of-breath Spec 4 said, 'I have a FADAC for a Major…'

'OK,' said Sergeant Jenkins. 'Ah, I, I guess you better send it down to the flight line.'

The captain turned back toward the major and said, 'Sir, Sergeant Jenkins can work the radios. Two pilots are needed for safety at night. It's our SOP.[5] In addition, under our policy, with only a week to go, I'm considered "too short" to fly a combat mission. During their last week, a short-timer is restricted to flying only admin, avoiding combat missions. Since no one is available, I'll have to go. I'll do the flying, but I need you to sit in the left seat. Two pairs of eyes…'

'No,' interrupted the major, 'I need to stay here to manage things.' He looked up and said sharply, 'Captain, if all your buddies are ah, inebriated, then do it yourself. It's your deal, get it done.'

'That was uncalled-for,' thought the captain. 'They're not drunk, just having drinks before dinner. Maybe this newbie can't fly well. Maybe he is scared. Either way, I don't think I want him flying with me tonight.' James looked at Jenkins, who stared without expression at the wall. 'Would you like to go, Sergeant?'

Jenkins looked back at the captain and smiled, 'Sir, I would love to.'

They grabbed their chicken-plates, M16s, sidearms and survival gear and walked down to the flight line, leaving the major to operate the radios. At the flight line Wally, one of the crew chiefs, motioned for them to take his Loach. As usual, he wanted to go along.

'Sir,' said Wally, 'I can mount that M60 in the back in two minutes flat.'

'Not this time, Whale, sorry. We won't need it.'

'Sir, you never know what you will run into.'

'Sorry, Whale.'

As mentioned before, Wally's Loach, ship 425, had a bright blue whale painted on the transmission cowling. Wally's nickname was 'Whale' and he decided to brand his aircraft with his handle. Wally was on the chubby side and not particularly fond of his nickname, but he knew there was nothing he could do about it. The nickname stuck. He had become Div Arty Air's 'Whale'. If he complained, the guys would call him that to tease him. By not complaining, everyone thought he liked it. He'd be 'Whale' in either case. It was just one of many examples of 'Catch-22', Div Arty Air-style.

Wally helped Sergeant Jenkins and Captain James pre-flight. This was his baby. He was proud of her and wanted to see that everything would check out perfectly. It did. After pre-flighting, the three watched the Division technicians strap down a large aluminum suitcase (the FADAC computer) in back. They treated it as if it was a case of precious gems.

As Wally helped the captain strap into the right seat, the 'short-timer' thought, 'Don't sweat it, Amigo. Jenkins can fly this Loach a bit, at least straight and level. He can help watch the instruments, and work the radios. Everything's cool.'

James hit the starter button and waited for the compressor gauge to stabilize at 15 percent. Then he slowly cracked the throttle, spraying jet fuel into the engine. The Loach engine temperature had a tendency to spike during rapid starts, causing potential damage. Starting slowly mitigated the spiking tendency. James set the radios, called Ky Ha tower, received permission to taxi and depart. The Loach climbed to the east over the foamy surf of the South China Sea and immediately turned left toward Chu Lai Bay. He leveled off at the required 200ft to stay below the fast-movers' airspace. James was surprised when Ky Ha immediately gave clearance to turn south and continue climbing. 'No jets tonight?' he thought.

It was a clear, beautiful night. Americal Division was spread out before them like a sprawling, sparkling city. The huge Chu Lai airbase off to their left side was lit up like JFK Airport in New York City.

The two heard no radio traffic. They seemed uncomfortably alone as they climbed south along the sanctuary of Highway One. They leveled off at 3,000ft and flew south as the darkness closed around them. Twenty minutes later, they came to a position where they had to turn inland away from the safety of Highway One.

As they turned west, James thought he could hear his butt cheeks pucker as he stared into the horizonless pitch-black masking the mountains he knew were ahead. The captain dimmed the instrument panel lights in a feeble attempt to see the horizon. The foreboding darkness in front seemed like a black hole ready to devour them. The pilot turned off the running lights to hide in the darkness. As he did this, he hit the intercom switch on the cyclic and said, 'They have us on radar with flight following, Sarge. I'm more worried about Charlie seeing us than running into another airplane.'

'Right, Sir,' replied Jenkins. 'It sure is dark ahead.'

'You got that right.'

Every now and then, they saw small dull specks of light and the faint glow of campfires. Their eyes picked up lines of pink tracer flashes. Friendlies, they hoped. They saw none of the green tracer flashes from the ammunition the VC preferred. Each in their minds could visualize lines of green tracers reaching up to devour them. Things seemed quiet below them. Suddenly the darkness ahead was broken by a series of bright white flashes from the 105mm howitzer battery on Stinson. The sight was spectacular.

'Now how can they do that without their little ol' FADAC?' The pilot chuckled sardonically to himself. 'Must be using those cute little circular slide rules.'

'Looks like a firework show at Disneyland, Sir,' Jenkins said over the intercom.

'Big fireworks,' the captain replied. 'Well, we certainly can't miss the hill now. Right?'

'Yes Sir. Just as long as they stop shooting when we get there.'

'They will.'

As they got closer, James forced himself to keep his eyes inside the cockpit. Staring at the artillery flashes would ruin his night vision and he would need sharp eyes to land on the dark hill.

The radio crackled, 'Phoenix One-Three, this is Salvation, over.'

'Salvation, One-Three.'

'One-Three, you will have a check-fire to land at Stinson in zero-five, they recommend you approach directly from the east.'

'Wilco, Salvation, Phoenix One-Three, out.'

James slowed to 60 knots and began descending over the hill in a left corkscrew pattern. Jenkins chatted on the FM with battery operations and confirmed their check-fire. James closed his eyes to retain his night vision and flashed the landing lights twice to allow the battery to see their Loach descending without running lights. The pilot could now make out the gun emplacements and hootches below. Everything appeared quiet. A quarter-ton truck's headlights blinked and then stayed on, lighting up a sandbag landing-pad. The Loach descended toward the pad, turning tightly to stay over the relative safety of the hill.

'This is turning out to be a piece of cake,' thought the pilot.

They settled in softly on the pad. James kept the Loach light on the skids, ready to depart as soon as the FADAC was offloaded. Soldiers grabbed the metal suitcase and threw on an identical case. A Spec 4 came up to the pilot's open door and shouted, 'SIR, CAN I GET A RIDE BACK TO CHU LAI? I AM ABOUT TO DEROS.'

'SURE,' James yelled over the rotor noise, 'JUMP IN; I AM GOING TO GO HOME SOON, TOO.' The soldier climbed in back. James pulled pitch. The Loach leaped into the air, turned left and climbed in a tight spiral over the hill.

At about 200ft they were baptized in intense white light as all six 105mm howitzers fired directly below them. The bright flash blinded the Loach's occupants. A deafening boom immediately followed that penetrated the soundproof helmets worn by James and Jenkins. The passenger's unprotected ears were less fortunate. He covered them and screamed.

The pilot yelled in the intercom, 'HOLY SHIT, I CAN'T SEE!'

The aircraft bucked in the air. James instinctively jerked up on the collective, causing the Loach to climb dangerously straight up. The aircraft hovered high over the hill, then began drifting in dangerous low-speed flight.

Time seemed to stand still. The pilot prayed, 'God, please let me see and keep this thing flying.' It seemed like an eternity but, in reality, the pilot began to regain his vision in twenty or thirty seconds. James scanned the instruments with burning eyes and saw they were at 700ft, 35 knots airspeed and climbing with the power in the red zone. He nudged the nose over slightly, lowered the collective into the green range and stabilized the aircraft in a normal 60-knot climb. The pilot took a deep breath and thought to himself, 'Everything's OK. I can see.

We are still in one piece and flying. We are OK unless our own guys shoot us out of the air.'

Sergeant Jenkins found himself panting. He clicked the button on his cyclic and gasped for breath. 'Ah, ah,' he stuttered, then screamed into the FM radio, 'CEASE FIRE, CEASE FIRE.'

'Ah, Roger One-Three, ah, standby one,' came back the emotionless reply.

The battery's Operations people knew Jenkins. They called him daily for Hook and Slick support. Jenkins willed himself to relax as he thought, 'Those bastards will find themselves dealing with one really pissed-off Ops NCO tomorrow. They will be hard-pressed, getting any extra perks from us for a while.'

Just then, green tracers cut through the night past the pilot's right shoulder. James turned sharply left away from the tracers and climbed hard. His eye caught the transmission torque meter that showed that he was again pulling too much torque. James eased the collective down to bring the needle back into normal operating range and willed his scout helicopter to disappear into the night. 'I should have brought "Whale" along with his M60. Wally will not be happy. His Loach will have its transmission inspected by maintenance for pulling too much torque.'

The Loach headed away from the hill, swallowed by the darkness. The Spec 4 in back, traumatized by the light and noise, sat in a stupor holding his ringing ears. Up front, James barked at Salvation Control on the UHF radio and then switched frequencies to complain to Div Arty Air Ops. The major said he would call Battery Ops on LZ Stinson and personally chew them out.

'You do that,' thought the shaken aviator.

All the way home, folks on the radios said something like, 'Oops, sorry, you were definitely under a "check-fire". That was a screw-up, a big "Charlie Foxtrot".[6] Sorry about that. Anything we can do? Are you OK?'

James and Jenkins ignored the attempts at consolation as they flew home to Ky Ha. They landed and hovered into a revetment. The passenger and the defective FADAC were met on the line by a quarter-ton truck. The passenger looked back at the pilot as he got into the jeep and said shakily, 'Thanks for the ride, Sir.' The captain noticed he didn't kiss the ground.

James and Jenkins found a group of Loach drivers and crew chiefs waiting for them in the Operations hootch. They wanted to hear all the details. The major was noticeably absent.

I did not know it at the time, but that 'hairy' night mission was my last time to fly in Vietnam.

Chapter 28

A Bittersweet Homecoming

0630 hrs, the Morning Following the Last Mission
Div Arty Hootch City

'What a night!' thought James, lying in his bunk. 'Hey, it's eight days and a wake-up; so short I won't have to bend to tie my boots today. OH, LORDY, AM I A SHORTY?'

James dressed, had breakfast and walked down to Operations. No one discussed the previous night's harrowing night-time mission. Several pilots came through and headed to the flight line. Two pilots, CW2 Booth and Captain Lee Leffert, James's hootch-mate, held up their thumb and first finger to the short-timer in the sign for a small amount. Then, as if on cue, they changed their fingers into another universal sign sometimes called 'THE TALL BOY'.

'Ha,' thought James, 'the pukes are just jealous.'

'Hey guys,' he said, 'don't get lost out there today. And Mr Booth, please don't crash again. I hate filling out all those forms.'

Their only acknowledgment was another TALL BOY. This one was emphasized with a sharp upward moving motion.

'Guys,' said James, 'please, show a little respect.'

He looked up from his paperwork and checked the time, admiring his new Seiko watch. It was a beauty: gold and stainless steel. Two days earlier, Lieutenant William ('Gil') Gilyard flew a lieutenant colonel up to Da Nang. James asked if he would stop by the Korean PX in Da Nang and buy a watch for him.

'Get something suitable for this short-timer to go home with. Make it a real nice one, Gil.'

'No problem, Darryl!'

Gil was a buff, mild-mannered Afro-American chopper-driver in Div Arty Air. He was a quiet, reserved pilot that was liked by all. He was raised in a proud religious family and ignored the typical rough language pervasive in Vietnam. He did not curse or have a bad word to say about anyone.

He had arrived in Div Arty a month earlier and had a story to tell. At first, he kept his story to himself. He waited until he was comfortable at Div Arty Air.

Gil told of being initially assigned to a transport company within the 123rd Aviation Battalion flying UH-1Ds (Hueys). The company commander in this unit immediately made it known that 'his kind' was not welcome there and that he may think it wise to find a job somewhere else; a blatant prejudice leftover from another time. It did not belong anywhere and especially not in a combat Army unit.

Gil did not make a fuss; he quietly asked for reassignment, came over to Div Arty Air and found a home.

At Div Arty Air, he was welcomed for his character, flying ability and personality, not for the color of his skin.

Div Arty Air Operations
0900 hrs

Sergeant Jenkins got up and headed for the door. 'I'm off for the mail, Sir.'

'OK,' said James, without looking up from his paperwork. Several minutes later, Jenkins came back with the mail. 'Letter from your wife, Sir.'

'Great, thanks.'

The pilot hesitated as he thought, 'Haven't had one in six or maybe eight weeks.' He tore it open. It began, metaphorically, with 'DEAR JOHN…'

James turned pale. The major and the sergeant looked over curiously. 'Something's wrong,' thought Sergeant Jenkins, 'bad news? Did someone die?'

A tense, quiet pause filled the room. Jenkins thought he could hear everyone breathing. Reluctantly, the Ops sergeant said, 'Sir, ah, is anything wrong?'

James didn't reply. He sat, staring at the wall. Finally, he said weakly, 'Ah, something's happened. Ah, ah, ah, she wants a divorce.'

A heavy silence filled the room. Sergeant Jenkins got up, took the shaken captain's cup and said, 'Let me fill this for you, Sir.'

He went outside and sent a runner up the hill. Several minutes later Captain Leffert came down from their quarters to sit with their shaken Ops officer.

The door burst open. Everyone but James looked up as Captain Duffy, the maintenance officer, burst in. He grabbed James's shoulder and said, 'Darryl, you are one of us. When you hurt, we all hurt. Shit, you were going home in a week or so anyway. What the hell kind of homecoming is she planning? Shoot, Murkowski is already home at Dix. I can call him and get him to…'

'Easy, John,' said Leffert. 'Down, boy.'

'OK, OK. Now, what the heck can I do? Where's the major?'

'He disappeared,' said Leffert.

'Isn't that just great? OK, OK. Johnson, go find the Doc and Father O'Leary; maybe they have some ideas.'

Sergeant Johnson rushed out the door.

The rest of the day was a blur for the hurting officer. Word of the 'Dear John' letter made its way around the Division Artillery and the 123rd Aviation Battalion. Many people called and offered consolation. Father O'Leary authorized a priority satellite phone call to the States through the Red Cross. His call went through at 0400 hrs, New York time. Sadly, he learned that only his mother-in-law and sleeping daughter were at home.

His mother-in-law said, 'Sorry, Darryl, she doesn't want you anymore; it's been hard for her…'

'Huh? What, hard on her? I am the one OVER HERE.'

The captain learned more. Unfortunately, it was what he feared the most: there was someone else. The Loach driver returned to the Div Arty Air recreation room. As he dragged himself into a chair, he thought, 'Maybe this is my home now. Why should I even leave?'

The news spread. The Old Man sent word that he wanted to see James. The captain reported to Div Arty Headquarters. The clerk immediately showed him into Colonel Jones's office. The XO, Lieutenant Colonel Carlton and Doc Cruz were seated in padded leather chairs. The colonel said, 'Darryl, come in here and join us.'

'JOHN,' he yelled outside to his orderly. 'Double Scotch and waters all around.'

'Yes Sir,' said the orderly standing in the doorway with the tray, anticipating the request.

'Carlton,' said the colonel, 'can we get him home tomorrow?'

'Sir, I think we can,' answered the XO. 'If he's grounded, Sir, he's no use to us.'

The colonel looked at the short, boyish-faced flight surgeon and said, 'Doc, ground him; the lad's going home asap.'

Lieutenant Colonel Carlton excused himself, walked into the orderly's office and called Division to have orders cut. He returned, sat down, sipped his double Scotch and said, 'Everything looks good, Colonel. I am worried, though, about the connections Darryl will need to get out of here.' He turned toward James and said, 'Captain, your orders are being prepared, but you need to out-process at Division asap and depart for Cam Rahn, this afternoon if possible.'

The orderly returned and told them there was a problem. The last two Air Force C-130s to Cam Rahn Bay were full. The XO grabbed the colonel's phone and called the captain's temporary replacement. 'Captain Leffert, this is Colonel Carlton. Lee, find James a ride to Cam Rahn, tonight.' The XO hung up and sat down again.

'Darryl,' said the CO, 'your people have done a good job. Remember one thing, son. You have lots of friends here. Some of these men will be your friends for life. They are here for you, me too. You look me up back in the world. I want to know how you are doing.'

'Yes Sir.'

Div Arty Operations
A Few Minutes Later

All the Div Arty Air Loaches were flying. Leffert worked the telephone, trying to find James a ride. Duffy chewed on someone on the other phone. 'Listen,' said the maintenance officer, 'you get that damn helicopter ready or your ass is going to be farting in two places.'

Exasperated, he slammed the phone down and said, 'No dice, Lee.'

Leffert received calls from sister aviation units offering rides late that evening or first thing in the morning. That would be too late. The Rattlers' outfit offered to take him to Cam Rahn in a gunship late that evening. That might work, but it would be close. Leffert was ready to accept their offer when he finally got lucky. Their wayward Otter pilot, Captain Harding, reported in on the UHF radio. Harding was always loaned out to some other unit and gone much of the time. The Otter driver took the news from Leffert and replied, 'Lee, have One-Three meet me at the airbase at 1610 hrs. Get him packed; I'll take him to Cam Rahn late this afternoon.'

'Roger Ops, out.'

Division Out-Processing

James stood in line, getting paperwork prepared and picking up his files. He asked the clerk to expedite the effort. The captain told him he had a personal emergency and had to be in Cam Rahn that night. The specialist went back through the door in the back. A few minutes later, James heard some officer say, 'Tell him he has to wait in line like everyone else. No exceptions.' The clerk came out and said, 'Sorry Sir, the Admin Officer said that you will have to wait in line.'

'May I use your phone, Specialist?'

'Sure, Sir.' James picked up the phone and dialed two, two, zero.

'Div Arty, Commanding Officer's Office, please, Captain James calling.'

'One moment, Sir.'

'Div Arty, CO's Office, Sergeant Ratcliff speaking.'

'Colonel Carlton, please. This is Captain James.' A moment later, he heard Lieutenant Carlton's voice. 'Yes, Darryl.'

'Colonel, I am having problems getting my paperwork finished up this afternoon. They have put me in a rather long queue with the people leaving the Division in the next few days and...'

The colonel interrupted him. 'Darryl, I will take care of this.'

The pilot hung up. Moments later a phone rang in the back office. The captain heard a commotion and then another door burst open. Two minutes later, a fat, somewhat effeminate captain rushed out with his hands full of papers. The Admin officer was breathing heavily as he said, 'Is there a Captain James here?'

'Yes, I am Darryl James.'

'Come with me, Captain. We need to get you taken care of right away. I understand you are going home tomorrow. How fortunate.'

'Yeah, right.'

Div Arty Air Hootches

Sergeant Jenkins came through the door of the pilots' recreation room. He found Captain Duffy, Captain James and three of the crew chiefs drinking a Coors with the departing pilot. One suitcase and James's acoustic guitar stood by the door. CW2 Booth came in all sweaty from a flight and offered to ride with them to Cam Rahn in the Otter. This was a nice gesture because Booth had to fly in the morning. He knew the tired Otter pilot would not like to fly home alone in the dark.

'Booth, you stink,' said Duffy.

Booth ignored Duffy and gave James a huge bear hug. He said, 'We have to boogie, Captain.'

James looked around and said, 'Say goodbye to everyone for me, guys.'

'We will,' the group echoed.

Duffy said, 'Now Darryl, don't think you are getting out of a DEROS party. You, Amigo, are just postponing it until we can get together in the world.'

'OK, that's a date, Duff.'

'COME ON, D', said Booth, 'Quit pussyfooting around. We have a date with an Otter.'

Fifteen minutes later, James and Booth watched as the large single-engine tail-dragger taxied over and shut down. A fuel truck pulled up. A tall, lean pilot came out, stretched and shook hands with James and Booth. The three climbed in the passenger door and walked up the steep cabin floor to the cockpit.

James strapped into the right co-pilot's seat. Captain Jack Harding strapped into the left seat and Booth climbed in the seat behind James. Jack cranked up and departed Chu Lai to the north. At 600ft, they turned steeply toward the south.

James thought to himself as he peered out for his last look at Chu Lai below, 'Is it because of what awaits me in New York, or is it something else that gives me these mixed feelings about leaving? I will miss my friends here and I might even miss this damn place.'

No one said a word on the intercom. Finally, Jack broke the silence and said, 'I am really sorry, Darryl.'

'Thanks, Jack, I appreciate that, and I especially appreciate you and Tim flying me down here tonight. I know you both are tired and will be really beat coming back tonight.'

'No sweat; it's the least we could do for you.'

Booth came on the intercom and said, 'D?'

'Yeah, Tim.'

'GIVE 'EM HELL.'

Hoping that no one could tell in the dim red glow of the lights from the instrument panel, James quietly choked a muffled sob. An hour later, Jack called ahead to have them meet them in Cam Rahn. They landed and deplaned. Tim carried Captain James's bag and guitar and set them in the jeep that had driven out to meet them. The three pilots embraced. As James turned to leave, Booth called out, 'ONE-THREE.'

James turned to him, 'Yeah?'

'You know I don't give a rat's ass for commissioned officers, and I never salute one under the rank of colonel unless some tight-ass makes me?'

James did not respond. After a pause, Warrant Officer Booth cracked off one of the sharpest salutes James had seen since his ROTC days. Captain Harding then joined in with one of his own.

0630 hrs, Later That Evening
Cam Rahn Bay, South Vietnam

James got another dose of paperwork, and then there was nothing to do until the morning. He made his way to the Officers' Club bar. It was crowded and noisy. James ordered a beer and noticed a bunch of rowdy First Cav guys toasting each other. As was customary, they wore their Cav hats inside the club. What was rude to anyone else was just ol' Cav stuff.

A short, drunk warrant officer stood up and proposed a toast, 'Will all Loach drivers stand up?'

Captain James stood and raised his glass of beer along with a lot of other guys.

'You Loach drivers are all a bunch of crazy-ass fuckers,' said the warrant officer. Everyone laughed and drank up.

Next Morning
The captain's American Airlines DC-8 left for Japan at 0900 hours. A collective cheer erupted as the plane left the runway. They deplaned in Tokyo and James wandered the terminal for an hour until they called the flight to board. Depressed and lonely, he climbed back on the plane. When they departed, James took two mild sleeping pills that Doc Cruz had given him. James slept soundly all the way to SeaTac (Seattle-Tacoma) Airport, Washington. The stewardess tried to wake him up for each of the two in-flight meals. He barely stirred. She thought him to be ill.

0630 hrs, 3 September 1969
SeaTac Airport, Seattle, Washington

After clearing Military Customs, the captain called his wife. He learned that she didn't want him to come directly to upstate New York. 'Come tomorrow or the next day; then we'll talk,' she said.

He hung up and thought, 'The hell with her; I am going home tonight if I can.' James called his folks in New Jersey. They didn't know he was coming today. They were initially happy, then sad when they learned the reason for the early homecoming. They would meet him late that evening in Newark. He caught a flight to Chicago, and then made a frantic connection to Newark. The stewardesses invited him up to the first-class section on the half-empty airplane and supplied him with beer throughout the flight. Two of the flight attendants came up to personally welcome home the tired, sweaty, rumpled Army captain. None knew of the dreaded homecoming he was expecting.

2200 hrs That Evening
Newark Airport

A large circle of family met him at the terminal. The group included his mother, three brothers, sister and a brand-new sister-in-law he hadn't met before. Hugs went around to all. At his boyhood home, they ate, drank and talked into the morning. After a little sleep, the captain called to upstate New York and drove three hours to get to his wife's apartment. All the way on the New York thruway, he wondered what to expect.

1100 hrs, 4 September 1969
Canajoharie, New York

The homecoming was tense but subdued; an uncomfortable and miserable experience for all. James sensed the unexpressed heavy veil of guilt coming from his wife and mother-in-law. The meeting turned to demands. His wife wanted an immediate divorce, child support and division of property. He agreed to allow her to keep the car, furniture and wedding presents. The captain kept their small savings and investments. An additional kick came to his already bruised ego when he discovered she had lost his irreplaceable college graduation ring. Probably sold it, he thought.

James played with his 16-month-old daughter until it was time to leave. One insult remained. He walked out the front door and saw an attractive young woman on the sidewalk dressed in a business suit. She smiled and said, 'Are you Arthur Darryl James?'

'Yes,' he replied.

She thrust legal papers into his hand and briskly walked away. Surprised and confused, he looked at the papers. 'Hell,' he thought, 'they're legal papers. I have been served!'

The next day he drove to Fort Monmouth, New Jersey to see an Army attorney. The attorney changed the aviator's will and advised him to ignore the legal papers.

He asked the captain to take a seat in his office while the attorney called his wife's lawyer in Albany, New York. James listened in to one side of the conversation, which quickly grew heated.

'You can't do that,' barked the Army attorney. 'He's an officer in the United States Army for gosh sakes, and I am telling you again YOU CAN'T DO THAT. Ah, ah, no sir…ah, ah, yes sir, that's correct. Listen, no, it is YOU THAT IS NOT LISTENING, he's not going to do that…and no, YOU CANNOT GARNISH HIS WAGES, CAPTAIN JAMES IS AN OFFICER.' There was a long pause while the Army attorney listened on the phone. 'Listen, Sir, NO YOU LISTEN, this is what he will do. He will report to Fort Wolters, Texas and will ignore these papers, Sir, he will pay child support while they are separated…ah, and ah…OK, you just go on and do that…' The attorney hung up.

He looked at James and said, 'What a jerk. Forget about him; he doesn't know anything about military law. I don't think he could find his butt in the closet with two hands and a flashlight. Now, Captain, here's what you need to do. Continue to pay child support; ignore these flipping papers. No, on second thoughts let me keep them for you. My advice to you is go have a drink, spend time with your family, meet some women, keep involved in your daughter's life and, when you are good and ready, give your estranged wife the divorce. This divorce should be at your convenience, not hers. You haven't been home one week yet. Make her wait.'

He did. James made her wait five months.

The captain spent some time visiting friends. Slowly, things began to loosen up for him. His spirit was on the mend. Some time just needed to pass. One morning in the middle of his month-long leave, he thought, 'I need to get on with my life. I want to go home now.'

Two Days Later
Love Field, Dallas, Texas

Captain James flew to Love Field in Dallas and was met by two very familiar faces: Captains Connor Dotson and Mark Birmingham. They had a couple of drinks and drove to Mineral Wells. His friends' wives had prepared a dinner in his honor. It was another homecoming; a nice one among two of his closest friends and their families. The men drove James onto the Post that night at 2350 hours to officially report in. He signed his name and said, 'I'm home. Today, the rest of my life now begins.'

Indeed it did. Although, the 'Dear John' got me home from Vietnam in less than forty-eight hours to a world of hurt, I have since been blessed with a wonderful wife of forty-one years, an awesome family, wonderful friends and a successful career as a geologist in the oil industry. It has been a great life.

God has been in control.

Chapter 29

Epilogue: About the
Americal Div Arty Pilots

Al ('Pops') Baker retired from the Army as a lieutenant colonel with Master Aviator wings. He subsequently worked as a financial planner and as an adjunct professor teaching Personal Finance. He and his wife Janice live in Williamsburg, Virginia, spending time visiting twelve grandchildren and four great-grandchildren.

Mark Birmingham retired from Hewlett-Packard as a sales executive. He loves woodworking; he has made memento Vietnam pens for his band of flying brothers. Mark and his wife Maria live in Round Rock, Texas.

Tim Booth left the Army and continued flying helicopters for the Forest Service and private companies.

Bill Broderick is a retired home-builder. He and his wife Debbie live in Colorado Springs, Colorado.

Dave Chambers taught Vietnamese to fly at Fort Wolters after Vietnam, then returned to Oregon and worked on the family farm. He and his wife Darlene spend as much time as possible at their ocean-side home.

Connor Dotson retired from the Army as a lieutenant colonel. Subsequently, he joined Continental Airlines and retired as an airline captain. He and his wife Vergie live in Huntsville, Texas. They are seasoned world travelers.

John Duffy left a career in securities and real estate, returned to college and received advanced degrees in Psychology. He worked at the US Department of Veterans Affairs, as a Behavioral Therapist at Native American Connections and an associate at Corazon Health. He and his wife Kathie live in Mesa, Arizona.

Warren Fuller served an additional tour in Vietnam flying fixed-wing. He and his wife Jane retired from the NSA. They now reside in Rehoboth Beach, Delaware, where they have become entrepreneurs in the kite-surfing sport industry.

William ('Gil') Gilyard III became a broker/realtor after the Army. He practices under Gilyard & Company. He and his wife Dianne live in Atlanta, Georgia.

Darryl James left the Army in 1970 and enjoyed a long career in the oil and gas industry as a petroleum geologist and oil executive. He lives with his wife Lynn of forty-one years in Midland, Texas. They love spending time with friends in their vacation home in Ruidoso, New Mexico.

Robert ('Lee') Leffert retired from the Forest Service as a hydrologist and Army National Guard. He and his wife Linda of more than forty-five years live in Colorado Springs, Colorado. They love to travel.

Stephen Lincoln retired after a long flying career in the Army. He and his wife Kim reside in Olympia, Washington.

Jim Minter left Army active duty in 1971 and returned to work for them as a DAC in 1979, ran the SFTS at Fort Benning, flew for Picatinny Arsenal for nine years and for OSACOM out of Fort Monroe. He joined the FAA as an Ops Inspector. He and his wife Barbara live in Keller, Texas.

The Div Arty Air pilots all made it safely home and had successful lives afterwards. They typically meet as a group annually with their wives. They also often get together at the Vietnam Helicopter Pilots Association (VHPA) Annual Reunion.

Appendix 1

Some Statistics from the Combat Area Casualty File (CACF) as of November 1993

The CACF is the basis for the Vietnam Veterans Memorial (The Wall):

- 2.5 million served between 1 January 1965 and 28 March 1973
- 58,202 died
- 25 percent were officers
- 25 percent of the officers were helicopter pilots
- The average age of 58,148 killed in Vietnam was 23.11 years
- 304M wounded (153M hospitalized + 153M injured but not requiring hospitalization)
- Peak strength on 30 April 1969 was 543,482 American soldiers
- (Although 58,169 names are in the November 1993 database, only 58,148 have both event date and birth date. Event date is used instead of declared dead date for some of those who were listed as missing in action) [CACF].

Deaths	Average Age
Total 58,148	23.11 years
Enlisted 50,274	22.37 years
Officers 6,598	28.43 years
Warrants 1,276	24.73 years

- Five men killed in Vietnam were only 16 years old [CACF]
- The oldest man killed was 62 years old [CACF]
- 11,465 KIAs were less than 20 years old [CACF].

Myth: The average age of an infantryman fighting in Vietnam was 19
Assuming KIAs accurately represented age groups serving in Vietnam, the average age of an infantryman (MOS 11B) serving in Vietnam being 19 years old is a myth, it is actually 22. None of the enlisted grades has an average age of less than 20 [CACF]. The average person who fought in the Second World War was 26 years of age [Westmoreland].

Myth: The fighting in Vietnam was not as intense as in the Second World War

The average infantryman in the South Pacific during the Second World War saw about forty days of combat in four years. The average infantryman in Vietnam saw about 240 days of combat in one year, thanks to the mobility of the helicopter.

One out of every ten Americans who served in Vietnam was a casualty: 58,169 were killed and 304,000 were wounded out of the 2.59 million who served. Although the percentage that died is similar to other wars, amputations or crippling wounds were 300 percent higher than in the Second World War. Some 75,000 Vietnam veterans are severely disabled [McCaffrey].

MEDEVAC helicopters flew approximately 500,000 missions with 900,000 patients airlifted. The time lapse between wounding and hospitalization was less than one hour. As a result, less than 1 percent of all Americans wounded who survived the first twenty-four hours died [VHPA 1993]. The helicopter provided unprecedented mobility. Without the helicopter it would have taken three times as many troops to secure the 800-mile border with Cambodia and Laos (the politicians thought the Geneva Conventions of 1954 and the Geneva Accords of 1962 would secure the border) [Westmoreland].

More helicopter facts

During the height of the war, the US Army had the largest air force in the world. Approximately 12,000 helicopters saw action in Vietnam (all services); Army UH-1s totaled 7,531,955 flight hours in Vietnam between October 1966 and the end of 1975. Army AH-1Gs totaled 1,038,969 flight hours in Vietnam [Vietnam Helicopter Pilots Association (VHPA) databases].

Endnotes

Author's Foreword

1. The Americal Division (23rd Infantry Division) was originally formed in the early phase of the Second World War following Pearl Harbor. It was formed in response to a potential invasion by Japan into New Caledonia. The name 'Americal' came from American, New Caledonian Division. At the end of the Second World War, the Division was disbanded in December 1945, only to be re-activated in Vietnam in September 1967 using personnel and assets from other units already in-country. The Aviation Regiment consisted of an Assault Helicopter Battalion (123rd), an Assault Support Helicopter Battalion (the 14th), and a Calvary Troop (F of the 8th). Directly supporting each of the artillery battalions was an aviation section assigned to support the needs of the Division Artillery (Div Arty) Commander and his Battalion Commanders.

Chapter 2

1. Reserve Officers Training Corps.
2. Private First Class.
3. An OH-13 is a small two-place helicopter with a bubble cockpit and erector set-looking tail.
4. A Bird Dog is a two-place, high-wing, single-engine observation plane with a tail-dragging third wheel.
5. A Caribou is a large cargo plane with twin jet-engine turboprop engines.
6. Mohawk, OV-1, is an Army twin jet-engine turboprop observation airplane. It is fitted with an oversized bubble cockpit with ejection seats for the pilot and observer.
7. Officers' Efficiency Report.

Chapter 3

1. A large, tactical twin-engine jet fighter-bomber.
2. Rear-echelon motherfucker.
3. The Hercules (C-130) is a large four-engine turboprop Air Force transport airplane.
4. Commonly called 'Spec 4', a specialty rank equivalent to a corporal.
5. Vietcong.
6. A term used in Vietnam for co-pilot.
7. Hueys that carry passengers and cargo.
8. The Bell AH-1A, a two-pilot gunship designated the Cobra by the Army and nicknamed 'the Snake'.

Chapter 4

1. One klick is military slang for one kilometer.
2. The place where the infamous My Lai Massacre took place, just a few months prior to Lieutenant James's arrival in Chu Lai.
3. Viet Cong enemy soldiers.
4. Flight school instructor pilot.
5. A failure slip for the day in flight school.

Chapter 5

1. In the United States Armed Forces, the ranks of warrant officer are rated as officers above the seniormost enlisted ranks, including all candidates and cadets and midshipmen, but subordinate to the officer grade of O-1. Warrant officers are highly-skilled, single-track specialty officers. (https://en.wikipedia.org/wiki/Warrant_officer_(United_States) (4/1/18))

Chapter 6

1. Mounted gun emplacement with four M85 50-caliber machine guns. Originally an anti-aircraft weapon that was used in Vietnam for firebase protection and convoy cover.
2. Instrument flight rules. Under IFR, aircraft are required to fly using instruments under the control of the controlling agency. In combat, the aviator is responsible for keeping his aircraft out of the clouds and flying to the extent possible under VFR (Visual Flight Rules).

Chapter 7

1. The CH-47 was a large twin-rotor helicopter used for heavy cargo transport.
2. Aviation gasoline.
3. Fucking New Guy.
4. Ceramic bulletproof chest protector nicknamed the 'chicken-plate'.
5. AH-1G gunship nicknamed 'the Snake'.
6. Slang for real live officer.

Chapter 9

1. Aerial observers, Artillery officers that ride with the pilots to adjust artillery fire and scout.
2. The controlling stick between the pilot's legs that controls the attitude of the main rotor blades.
3. I.e. within normal operating limits on the engine instruments.

Chapter 10

1. Command and Control aircraft used by the commanding officer and his staff to command a unit while flying above it. The pilots called it a 'Chuck-Chuck'.

2. Bachelor officers' quarters. In this case, BOQ is temporary housing for officers in transit.
3. A large, single-engine propeller airplane used by the South Vietnamese and American Air Force.
4. Olive drab color.
5. Saigon tea is a weak tea served to bar girls at a high price to the American purchasing it.
6. Rest and recuperation vacation. The GIs were provided one week off during their tour for R&R.
7. Vietnam slang for Western girls.
8. Heavy bomber, high-altitude bombing missions.
9. Military ready-to-eat meals in cans.
10. 2.5-ton heavy-duty military trucks.

Chapter 11
1. Nickname for the CH-47 Chinook.
2. OH-23G helicopters.
3. Aerial observers.
4. 'Short' meaning nearly finished with a one-year tour. Div Arty Air's policy was not to assign combat missions to anyone with less than two weeks remaining.
5. Belt-fed machine gun.
6. 'Slick', a Vietnam nickname for the UH1-D helicopter also called a 'Huey'.

Chapter 14
1. https://en.wikipedia.org/wiki/Retreating_blade_stall
2. Supply Staff Officer.
3. VOR: high-frequency radio signals used for navigation.
4. Observation post, usually positioned at a high elevation to spot enemy positions.
5. Velocity never exceed: the maximum safe speed of the helicopter.

Chapter 15
1. Green Beret advisor.
2. South Vietnamese Army soldiers.
3. An elderly Vietnamese/East Asian man.

Chapter 16
1. Fly with 'Visual Flight Rules' on top of the clouds.

Chapter 21
1. An ass-hole.
2. An unarmed Huey helicopter with a red cross on its doors, used for rescue.
3. Passengers.

Chapter 22
1. Noncombatants: rear-echelon mother-fuckers.
2. Long-range reconnaissance patrol.

Chapter 23
1. Non-flying officers.

Chapter 25
1. A Chinook, a large cargo-carrying helicopter with two rotor blades.

Chapter 26
1. DEROS: Date Eligible for Return from Overseas.
2. Everything was picked up.
3. Nickname for the TH-55A trainer helicopter built by Hughes Aircraft.
4. Fucking new guy.
5. 'Guard' is a generic name for preset radio frequencies to be used only for emergencies or to communicate with someone when it is unknown to what frequency their radios are set. 'Guard' is monitored at all times by all aircraft and the pilot only needs to turn a knob on the radio to transmit.
6. Military radio jargon for 'I will comply'.

Chapter 28
1. OH-6 Scout helicopter.
2. A portable computer used to compute artillery data.
3. Landing Zone.
4. Tactical emergency: an emergency with lives at stake.
5. Standard operating procedure.
6. Cluster-fuck.